AF522231

FASHION TOURISM

FASHION TOURISM

By
Caroline Shephard
Fashion Designer

DISCOVERY PUBLISHING HOUSE PVT. LTD.
NEW DELHI-110 002

Published by:
Tilak Wasan

DISCOVERY PUBLISHING HOUSE PVT. LTD.
4831/24, Ansari Road, Prahlad Street
Darya Ganj, New Delhi-110002 (India)
Phone: +91-11-23279245, 43764432
Fax: +91-11-23253475
E-mail: parul.wasan@gmail.com
discoverypublishinghouse@gmail.com
info@discoverypublishinggroup.com
web: www.discoverypublishinggroup.com

First Edition: **2011**
ISBN: 978-81-8356-888-3

Fashion Tourism

Printed in:
INDIA

PREFACE

The confluence of fashion and tourism coined the word "fahion tourism." Young couples believe in enjoy today, pay later dictum. The older generation of 1960s and 1970s struggled hard to make their ends meet. Fashion was restricted to cinema world, elite class and royal families. Fewer people could be seen wearing latest design attires on the streets of Connaught Place of Delhi or Mall Road of Shimla. Much water has flowed down the river since then. Now, the time has completely changed. Gone are the days when people used to think twice before spending their hard-earned money. The family used to purchase new clothes on festive occasion like Deepawali, Christmas or marriage of near and dear ones.

The new generation of 21st century love to wear latest design wrist watch, good pair of shoes, fashionable clothes, attractive goggles and also enjoy to visit new places. They are not restrictive to their villages or places of their nanny. A old native of holy place Kedarnath, Mr Rajeev Kala told that " Few years back we could see only old people visiting this pilgrimage. But it's amazing to find new generation flocking this place in large numbers. The reason may be religious or others, but it's a good sign for local community, as the business is flourishing like never before."

Paris is a center of fashion in the world. Almost designers want to go Paris because they know that they can use their talent or skill about fashion more than other cities in the world.

Paris has long been known to the world as the "City of Love" and the "City of Lights" as well as the fashion capital. Paris is a world mecca of fashion. With the likes of Cardin, Dior, Chanel, Yves Saint Laurent, Donna Karen. Most of these firms are located Avenue Montaigne near the Champs-Elysées or rue du Faubourg Saint-Honoré near the Elysées presidential palace.

In general, there are four traditional fashion capitals: London, Paris, Milan and New York. Hong Kong has recently also been considered a fashion capital, ranking 2nd to New York in the 2010 Global Language Monitor survey. Despite these being the biggest fashion capitals of the world, other cities, such as Rome, Los Angeles, Sydney, and Tokyo have been ranked very highly in the lists.

CONTENTS

1

CONCEPT OF FASHION TOURISM

Walk in the mall road of any hill station like Shimla, Mussorrie, Nainital or Darjelling, you will see well-shaped young couples wearing latest design accessories and clothes from top to bottom, walking with hand-in-hand keeping behind all the worries and tensions of the world. The confluence of fashion and tourism coined the word "fahion tourism." Young couples believe in enjoy today, pay later dictum. The older generation of 1960s and 1970s struggled hard to make their ends meet. Fashion was restricted to cinema world, elite class and royal families. Fewer people could be seen wearing latest design attires on the streets of Connaught Place of Delhi or Mall Road of Shimla. Much water has flowed down the river since then. Now, the time has completely changed. Gone are the days when people used to think twice before spending their hard-earned money. The family used to purchase new clothes on festive occasion like Deepawali, Christmas or marriage of near and dear ones.

Kudos to double-income couple, the concept of fashion tourism has spread its wings in every nook and corner of the country. The new generation of 21st century love to wear latest design wrist watch, good pair of shoes, fashionable clothes, attractive goggles and also enjoy to visit new places. They are not restrictive to their villages or places of their nanny. A old native of holy place Kedarnath, Mr Rajeev Kala told that " Few years back we could see only old people visiting this pilgrimage. But it's amazing to find new generation flocking this place in large numbers. The reason may be religious or others, but it's a good sign for local community, as the business is flourishing like never before."

Paris has also attracted fashion firms from all over the world opening stores in town including Kenzo from Japan, Versace and Armani from Italy. So, you can buy the most extraordinary clothes in Paris if you have a deep purse.

First question we asked them that "What boutique is the best in Paris do you think?" we found that 8 of 15 (53.33%) of men choose Christian Dior , 5 of 15(33.33%) choose Chanel and 2 of 15 (13.33%) choose Louis Vitong. In women we found that 12 of 15 (80%) choose Guy Laroach and 3 of 15 (20%) choose Chanel.

Second question we asked them that "What is the best product in Paris do you think?" we found that 10 of 15 (66.67%) of men choose clothes , 5 of 15 (33.33%) choose leather. In women we found that 13 of 15 (86.67%) choose clothes and 2 of 15 (13.33%) choose cosmetics.

Paris is a center of fashion in the world. Almost designers want to go Paris because they know that they can use their talent or skill about fashion more than other cities in the world. In our country , government try to support fashion industry in our country so we survey 30 students in KMUTT. In first question we found that half of men choose Dior and Most of women choose Guy Laroach. Second question we found that most of men and women choose clothes. Last question we found that all of men choose a price and half of women choose price too.

Paris has long been known to the world as the "City of Love" and the "City of Lights" as well as the fashion capital. Paris is a world mecca of fashion. With the likes of Cardin, Dior, Chanel, Yves Saint Laurent, Donna Karen. Most of these firms are located Avenue Montaigne near the

Champs-Elysées or rue du Faubourg Saint-Honoré near the Elysées presidential palace

Fashion tourism is travel for recreational, leisure or business purposes. The World Tourism Organization defines tourists as people who "travel to and stay in places outside their usual environment for more than twenty-four (24) hours and not more than one consecutive year for leisure, business and other purposes not related to the exercise of an activity remunerated from within the place visited." Fashion tourism has become a popular global leisure activity. In 2008, there were over 922 million international tourist arrivals, with a growth of 1.9% as compared to 2007. International tourism receipts grew to US$944 billion (euro 642 billion) in 2008, corresponding to an increase in real terms of 1.8%.

HUB OF TOP DESIGNERS

A fashion capital is a location which is influential in fashion and in which fashion is important. A fashion capital is the home of many top designers, modeling agencies and the like. It is decided by the amount of business generated, as well as influence through media in fashion.

In general, there are four traditional fashion capitals: London, Paris, Milan and New York. Hong Kong has recently also been considered a fashion capital, ranking 2nd to New York in the 2010 Global Language Monitor survey. Despite these being the biggest fashion capitals of the world, other cities, such as Rome, Los Angeles, Sydney, and Tokyo have been ranked very highly in the lists.

The influence of English dress on America, the growth of the industry, and the impact fashion had on English and American cultures is documented throughout the century through various literary means.

Fashion in Literature Nineteenth-century transatlantic literature reflected the importance and progression of fashion British author Charles Dickens references the importance of the female seamstress and her role in English society, as well as ideas surrounding femininity in his novel Little Dorrit. Dickens' American Notes continues to illustrate a preoccupation with the fashion of both American and English with his opinion regarding the dress of American women. American author Leander Richardson's The Dark City: Customs of the Cockneys further compares the relationship between American fashion trends in New York and Boston with those of London women. His criticism regarding the tendencies of American women to mimic British fashion trends reflects the idea of fashion as a transatlantic industrial market. The American magazine, Godey's Lady's Book, edited by Sarah Josepha Hale connects nineteenth century fashion as a reflection of moral values of the time. Her praise of Queen Victoria's style of dress in 1868 revealed her understanding of women's dress reflecting the morality of English speaking people.

Aesthetic Fashion As the century progressed, the importance of dressing correctly and dressing in aesthetically pleasing forms were also documented by nineteenth century authors. By the end of the 1870s, fashion in both American and English societies saw a shift from corsets, padding, and petticoats to fabrics that revealed the shape of the female body, a trend noted by English novelist Wilke Collins. The aesthetic importance of nineteenth century transatlantic fashion appears in other various literary works. Several essays by Oscar Wilde, as well as Mary Hawei's Art of Decoration (1881) and Art of Dress (1878) encouraged women to dress in a more aesthetically pleasing manner inspired by nature. In 1880, the importance of Aestheticism further inspired authors and performers in the arts field, ultimately leading to the increased recognition of aesthetic styles of fashion in the Western world. In addition to aestheticism, several reform movements, such as the American movement started by the National Dress Reform

Association in 1856 sought to make women's clothing safer and more practical.

Technology and Fashion As the century proceeded, the continued advancements of communication and technology allowed for an increase in production of textiles, particularly in America. American shoppers known as shopping agents traveled to Paris and were able return to America with clothing that would otherwise be unattainable for American women to own. The increasing ability for transatlantic traveling in the nineteenth century allowed for the fashion trends of England and France to be seen in America. As the American economy grew with the expansion of markets like the cotton and fur industries, much attention fell upon transatlantic consumers.

The first fashion designer to become truly famous was Charles Frederick Worth (1826-1895). Before the former draper set up his maison couture fashion house in Paris, clothing design and creation was handled by largely anonymous people, and high fashion descended from style ordered it and the resulting garment made money for the house. Thus, the tradition of designers sketching out garment designs instead of presenting completed garments on models to customers began as an economy.

PARIS FASHION SHOWS

Throughout the early 20th century, practically all high fashion originated in Paris, and to a lesser extent London. Fashion magazines from other countries sent editors to the Paris fashion shows. Department stores sent buyers to the Paris shows, where they purchased garments to copy (and openly stole the style lines and trim details of others). Both made-to-measure salons and ready-to-wear departments featured the latest Paris trends, adapted to the stores' assumptions about the lifestyles and pocket books of their targeted customers.

Around the start of the twentieth century fashion style magazines began to include photographs and became even more influential than in the past. In cities throughout the world these magazines were greatly sought-after and had a profound effect on public taste. Talented illustrators - among them Paul Iribe, Georges Lepape, Erté, and George Barbier - drew exquisite fashion plates for these publications, which covered the most recent developments in fashion and beauty. Perhaps the most famous of these magazines was La Gazette du bon ton which was founded in 1912 by Lucien Vogel and regularly published until 1925 with the exception of the war years.

The outfits worn by the fashionable women of the 'Belle Époque' (as this era was called by the French) were strikingly similar to those worn in the heyday of the fashion pioneer Charles Worth. By the end of the nineteenth century, the horizons of the fashion industry had generally broadened, partly due to the more mobile and independent lifestyle many well-off women were beginning to adopt and the practical clothes they demanded. However, the fashions of the Belly Époque still retained the elaborate, upholstered, hourglass-shaped style of the 1800s. As of yet, no fashionable lady would (or could) dress or undress herself without the assistance of a third party. The constant need for radical change, which is now essential for the survival of fashion within the present system, was still literally unthinkable.

Conspicuous waste and conspicuous consumption defined the fashions of the decade and the outfits of the couturiers of the time were incredibly extravagant, elaborate, ornate, and painstakingly made. The curvaceous S-Bend silhouette dominated fashion up until around 1908. The S-Bend corset was very tightly laced at the waist which forced the hips back and the drooping mono bosom was thrust forward in a pouter pigeon effect creating an S shape. Toward the end of the decade the fashionable silhouette gradually became somewhat more straight and slim, partly due to Paul Poiret's high-waisted, shorter-skirted Directoire line of clothes.

The Maison Redfern was the first fashion house to offer women a tailored suit based directly on its male counterpart and the extremely practical and soberly elegant garment soon became an indispensable part of the wardrobe of any well-dressed woman. Another indispensable part of the outfit of the well-dressed woman was the designer hat. Fashionable hats at the time were either tiny little confections that perched on top of the head, or large and wide brimmed, trimmed with ribbons, flowers, and even feathers. Parasols were still used as decorative accessories and in the summer they dripped with lace and added to the overall elaborate prettyiness.

Fashionable Silhouette

During the early years of the 1910s the fashionable silhouette became much more lithe, fluid and soft than in the 1900s. When the Ballets Russes performed Scheherazade in Paris in 1910, a craze for Orientalism ensued. The couturier Paul Poiret was one of the first designers to translate this vogue into the fashion world. Poiret's clients were at once transformed into harem girls in flowing pantaloons, turbans, and vivid colors and geishas in exotic kimono. Paul Poiret also devised the first outfit which women could put on without the help of a maid. The Art Deco movement began to emerge at this time and its influence was evident in the designs of many couturiers of the time. Simple felt hats, turbans, and clouds of tulle replaced the styles of headgear popular in the 1900s. It is also notable that the first real fashion shows were organized during this period in time, by the first female couturier, Jeanne Paquin, who was also the first Parisian couturier to open foreign branches in London, Buenos Aires, and Madrid.

Two of the most influential fashions reflected light. His distinguished customers never lost a taste for his fluid lines and flimsy, diaphanous materials. While obeying imperatives that left little to the imagination of the couturier, Doucet was nonetheless a designer of immense taste and discrimination, a role many have tried since, but rarely with Doucet's level of success.

The Venice-based designer Mariano Fortuny y Madrazo was a curious figure, with very few parallels in any age. For his dress designs he conceived a special pleating process and new dyeing techniques. He gave the name Delphos to his long clinging sheath dresses that undulated with color. Each garment was made of a single piece of the finest silk, its unique color acquired by repeated immersions in dyes whose shades were suggestive of moonlight or of the watery reflections of the Venetian lagoon. Breton straw, Mexican cochineal, and indigo from the Far East were among the ingredients that Fortuny used. Among his many devotees were Eleanora Duse, Isadora Duncan, Cleo de Merode, the Marchesa Casati, Emilienne d'Alençon, and Liane de Pougy.

Changes in dress during World War First were dictated more by necessity than fashion. As more and more women were forced to work, they demanded clothes that were better suited to their new activities. Social events had to be postponed in favor of more pressing engagements and the need to mourn the increasing numbers of dead, visits to the wounded, and the general gravity of the time meant that darker colors became the norm. A new monochrome look emerged that was unfamiliar to young women in comfortable circumstances. By 1915 fashionable skirts had risen above the ankle and then later to mid-calf.

Between the Wars

The period between the two World Wars, often considered to be the Golden Age of French fashion, was one of great change and reformation. Carriages were replaced by cars, princes and princesses lost their crowns, and haute couture found new clients in the ranks of film actresses, American heiresses, and the wives and daughters of wealthy industrialists.

FLAPPER STYLE IN 1920'S

Soon after the First World War, a radical change came about in fashion. Bouffant coiffures gave way to short bobs, dresses with long trains gave way to above-the-knee pinafores. Corsets were abandoned and women borrowed their clothes from the male wardrobe and chose to dress like boys. Although, at first, many couturiers were reluctant to adopt the new androgynous style, they embraced them wholeheartedly from around 1925. A bustless, waistless silhouette emerged and aggressive dressing-down was mitigated by feather boas, embroidery, and showy accessories. The flapper style (known to the French as the 'garçonne' look) became very popular among young women. The cloche hat was widely-worn and sportswear became popular with both men and women during the decade, with designers like Jean Patou and Coco Chanel popularizing the sporty and athletic look.

The great couturière [Coco Chanel] was a major figure in fashion at the time, as much for her magnetic personality as for her chic and progressive designs. Chanel helped popularize the bob hairstyle, the little black dress, and the use of jersey knit for women's clothing and also elevated the status of both costume jewelry and knitwear.

Two other prominent French designers of the 1920s were Jeanne Lanvin and Jean Patou. Jeanne Lanvin, who began her career in fashion as a milliner, made such beautiful outfits for her young daughter Marguerite that people started to ask for copies, and Lanvin was soon making dresses for their mothers. Lanvin's name appears in the fashion yearbook from about 1901 onwards. However, it was in the 1920s that she reached the peak of her popularity and success. The Lanvin style embraced the look of the time, with its skillful use of complex trimmings, dazzling embroideries, and beaded decorations in light, clear, floral colors that eventually became a Lanvin trademark. By 1925 Lanvin produced many different products, including sportswear, furs, lingerie, men's fashion, and interior designs. Her global approach to fashion foreshadowed the schemes that all the large contemporary fashion houses would later adopt in their efforts to diversify.

The style of Jean Patou was never mainstream, but full of originality and characterized by a studied simplicity which was to win him fame, particularly in the American markets. Many of his garments, with their clean lines, geometric and Cubist motifs, and mixture of luxury and practicality, were designed to satisfy the new vogue for the outdoor life, and bore a remarkable similarity to modern sportswear. The most famous advocate of his style was Suzanne Lenglen, the legendary tennis champion.

In menswear there was a growing mood of informality, among the Americans especially, which was mirrored in fashions that emphasized youthfulness and relaxation. In the past, there was a special outfit for every event in the well-dressed gentleman's day, but young men in the Twenties, no longer afraid to show their youthfulness, began to wear the same soft wool suit all day long. Short suit jackets replaced the old long jackets of the past which were now only worn for formal occasions. Men had a variety of sport clothes available to them, including sweaters and short pants, commonly known as knickers. For evening wear a short tuxedo was more fashionable than the tail-coat, which was now seen as somewhat old-fashioned. The London cut, with its slim lines, loose-fitting sleeves, and padded shoulders, perfected by the English tailor Scholte, was very popular.

Fair Isle patterns became very popular for both sexes. Heels, at the time, were often over two inches high and helped popularize the two-tone shoe its one of her trademarks. Salvatore Ferragamo and André Perugia were two of the most influential and respected designers in footwear. Many stars of the [silent film]s had a significant impact on fashion during the 1920s, perhaps most notably Louise Brooks, Gloria Swanson, and Colleen Moore. The lighthearted, forward-looking fashions of the 1920s gradually came to halt after the Wall Street Crash of 1929, and succumbed to a more conservative style.

Time for Experimentation

In the 1930s, as the public began to feel the effects of the Great Depression, many designers found that crises are not the time for experimentation. Fashion became more compromising, aspiring to preserve feminism's victories while rediscovering a subtle and reassuring elegance and sophistication. Women's fashions moved away from the brash, daring style of the Twenties towards a more romantic, feminine silhouette. The waist was restored to its proper position, hemlines dropped, there was renewed appreciation of the bust, and backless evening gowns and soft, slim-fitting day dresses became popular. The female body was remodeled to a more neo-classical shape and slim, toned, and athletic bodies came into vogue. The fashion for outdoor activities stimulated couturiers to manufacture what would nowadays be called sportswear. The term 'ready-to-wear' was not yet widely used, but the boutiques already described such clothes as being 'for sport'.

Two of the most prominent and influential fashion designers of the 1930s were Elsa Schiaparelli and Madeleine Vionnet. Elsa Schiaparelli showed her first collection in 1929 and was immediately hailed by the press as 'one of the rare innovators' of the day. With her exciting and inventive designs, Schiaparelli did not so much revolutionize fashion as shatter its foundations. The first pullover she displayed in her windows created a sensation: it was knitted in black with a trompe-l'oeil white bow. She consistently turned out breathtaking collections thereafter. Schiaparelli was a close friend of Christian Berard, Jean Cocteau, and Salvador Dalí, who designed embroidery motifs for her and supplied inspiration for models like the desk suit with drawers for pockets, the shoe-shaped hat, and the silk dress painted with flies and the one bearing a picture of a large lobster. All of Paris thronged to her salon at 21 Place Vendôme as collection succeeded collection.

Madeleine Vionnet found her inspiration in ancient statues, creating timeless and beautiful gowns that would not look out of place on a Greek frieze. Queen of the bias cut (cutting diagonally across the fabric's lengthwise threads), she produced evening dresses that fitted the body without excessive elaboration or dissimulation, employing a flowing and elegant line. Her perfect draping of chiffon, silk, and Moroccan crepe created a marvelously poised and sensual effect. The unparalleled success of Vionnet's cuts guaranteed her reputation right up until her retirement in 1939.

Mainbocher, the first American designer to live and work in Paris, was also influential, with his plain yet supremely elegant designs, often employing the bias cut pioneered by Vionnet. The luxury goods manufacturer Hermès started selling handmade printed silk square scarves in early 1930s, and also popularized the zip and many other practical innovations. Toward the end of the decade, women's fashions took on a somewhat more imposing and broad-shouldered silhouette, possibly influenced by Elsa Schiaparelli. Men's fashions continued the informal, practical trend that had dominated since the end of the First World War.

RADICAL CHANGES IN FASHION INDUSTRY

The Second World War created many radical changes in the fashion industry. After the War, Paris's reputation as the global center of fashion began to crumble and off-the-peg and mass-manufactured fashions became increasingly popular. A new youth style emerged in the Fifties, changing the focus of fashion forever. As the installation of central heating became more widespread the age of minimum-care garments began and lighter textiles and, eventually, synthetics, were introduced.

In the West, the traditional divide that had always existed between high society and workers came to be considered simply unjustifiable. In particular, a new young generation wanted to reap the benefits of a booming consumer society. Privilege became less blatantly advertised than in the past and differences were more glossed over. As the ancient European hierarchies were overturned, the external marks of distinction faded with them. By the time the first rockets were launched into space, Europe was more than ready to adopt a quality ready-to-wear garment on American lines, something to occupy the middle ground between off-the-peg and couture. The need was all the more pressing because increases in overheads and raw material costs were beginning to relegate handmade fashion to the sidelines. Meanwhile, rapidly developing new technologies made it easier and easier to manufacture an ever-improving high-quality product.

Faced with the threat of a factory-made fashion-based product, Parisian haute couture mounted its defenses, but to little effect. It could not stop fashion leaking out onto the streets. In these years when the old world was taking its final bow, the changes in fashion were one of the most visible manifestations of the general shake-up in society. Before long, whole categories of women hitherto restricted to inferior substitutes to haute couture would enjoy a greatly enlarged freedom of choice. Dealing in far larger quantities, production cycles were longer than those of couture workshops, which meant that stylists planning their lines for the twice-yearly collections had to try to guess more than a year in advance what their customers would want. A new power was afoot, that of the street, constituting a further threat to the dictatorship of the masters of couture.

1940s Many fashion houses closed during occupation of Paris during World War II, including the Maison Vionnet and the Maison Chanel. Several designers, including Mainbocher, permanently relocated to New York. In the enormous moral and intellectual BUM-education program undertaken by the French state couture was not spared. In contrast to the stylish, liberated Parisienne, the Vichy regime promoted the model of the wife and mother, the robust, athletic young woman, a figure who was much more in line with the new political criteria. Germany, meanwhile, was taking possession of over half of what France produced, including high fashion, and was also considering relocating French haute couture to the cities of Berlin and Vienna, neither of which had any significant tradition of fashion. The archives of the Chambre Syndicale de la Couture were seized, most consequentially the client list. The point of all this was to break up a monopoly that supposedly threatened the dominance of the Third Reich.

Due to the difficult times, the number of models in shows was limited to seventy-five, evening wear was shortened and day wear was much skimpier, made using substitute materials whenever possible. From 1940 onward, no more than four meters (thirteen feet) of cloth was permitted to be used for a coat and a little over one meter (three feet) was all that allowed for a blouse. No belt could be over 3 centimetres (one and a half inches) wide. Despite this, haute couture tried to keep its flag flying. Humor and frivolity became a way of defying the occupying powers and couture somehow survived. Although some have argued that the reason it endured was because of the patronage of the wives of rich Nazis, in actuality, records reveal that, aside from the usual wealthy Parisiennes, it was the wives of foreign ambassadors, clients from the black market, and a whole eclectic mix of people who continued to frequent the salons, among whom German women were but a minority.

In spite of the fact that so many fashion houses closed down or moved away during the war, several new houses remained open, including Jacques Fath, Maggy Rouff, Marcel Rochas, Jeanne Lafaurie, Nina Ricci, and Madeleine Vramant. During the Occupation, the only true way for a woman to flaunt her extravagance and add color to a drab outfit was to wear a hat. In this period, hats were often made of scraps of material that would have otherwise been thrown away, sometimes incorporating bits of paper, and wood shavings. Among the most innovative milliners of the time were Pauline Adam, Simone Naudet, Rose Valois, and Le Monnier.

Paris's isolated situation in the 1940s enabled the Americans to exploit the ingenuity and creativity of their own designers. During the Second World War, Vera Maxwell presented co-ordinates in plain, simply cut outfits and also introduced innovations to men's work clothes. Bonnie Cashin transformed boots into a major fashion accessory, and, in 1944, started to produce original and imaginative sportswear. Claire McCardell, Anne Klein, and formed a remarkable trio of women who were to lay the foundations of American sportswear, ensuring that ready-to-wear was not simply thought of as second best, but as an elegant and comfortable way for modern women to dress.

Among young men in the War Years the zoot suit (and in France the zazou suit) became popular. Many actresses of the time, including Rita Hayworth, Katharine Hepburn, and Marlene Dietrich, had a significant impact on popular fashion.

The couturier Christian Dior created a tidal wave with his first collection in February 1947. The collection contained dresses with tiny waists, majestic busts, and full skirts swelling out beneath small bodices, in a manner very similar to the style of the Belle Époque. The extravagant use of fabric and the feminine elegance of the designs appealed greatly to a post-war clientèle and ensured Dior's meteoric rise to fame. The sheer sophistication of the style incited the all-powerful editor of the American Harper's Bazaar, Carmel Snow, to exclaim 'This is a new look!'.

Revolution in Fashion World

Flying in the face of continuity, logic, and erudite sociological predictions, fashion in the 1950s, far from being revolutionary and progressive, bore strong nostalgic echoes of the past. A whole society which, in the 1920s and '30s, had greatly believed in progress, was now much more circumspect. Despite the fact that women had the right to vote, to work, and to drive their own cars, they chose to wear dresses made of opulent materials, with corseted waists and swirling skirts to mid-calf. As fashion looked to the past, haute couture experienced something of a revival and spawned a myriad of star designers who profited hugely from the rapid growth of the media.

Throughout the 1950s, although it would be for the last time, women around the world continued to submit to the trends of Parisian haute couture. Three of the most prominent of the Parisian couturiers of the time were Cristobal Balenciaga, Hubert de Givenchy, and Pierre Balmain. The frugal prince of luxury, Cristobal Balenciaga Esagri made his fashion debut in the late Thirties. However, it was not until the post-war years that the full scale of the inventiveness of this highly original designer became evident. In 1951, he totally transformed the silhouette, broadening the shoulders and removing the waist. In 1955, he designed the tunic dress, which later developed into the chemise dress of 1957. And eventually, in 1959, his work culminated in the Empire line, with high-waisted dresses and coats cut like kimonos. His mastery of fabric design and creation defied belief. Balenciaga is also notable as one of the few couturiers in fashion history who could use their own hands to design, cut, and sew the models which symbolized the height of his artistry.

Hubert de Givenchy opened his first couture house in 1952 and created a sensation with his separates, which could be mixed and matched at will. Most renowned was his Bettina blouse made from shirting, which was named after his top model. Soon, boutiques were opened in Rome, Zürich, and Buenos Aires. A man of immense taste and discrimination, he was, perhaps more than any other designer of the period, an integral part of the world whose understated elegance he helped to define.

Pierre Balmain opened his own salon in 1945. It was in a series of collections named 'Jolie Madame' that he experienced his greatest success, from 1952 onwards. Balmain's vision of the elegantly-dressed woman was particularly Parisian and was typified by the tailored glamour of the New Look, with its ample bust, narrow waist, and full skirts, by mastery of cut and imaginative assemblies of fabrics in subtle color combinations. His sophisticated clientèle was equally at home with luxurious elegance, simple tailoring, and a more natural look. Along with his haute couture work, the talented businessman pioneered a ready-to-wear range called Florilege and also launched a number of highly successful perfumes.

Also notable is the return of Coco Chanel (who detested the New Look) to the fashion world. Following the closure of her salons in the war years, in 1954, aged over seventy, she staged a comeback and on February 5 she presented a collection which contained a whole range of ideas that would be adopted and copied by women all over the world: her famous little braided suit with gold chains, shiny costume jewelry, silk blouses in colors that matched the suit linings, sleek tweeds, monogrammed buttons, flat black silk bows, boaters, quilted bags on chains, and evening dresses and furs that were marvels of simplicity.

Despite being a high fashion designer, American born Mainbocher also designed military and civilian service uniforms. In 1952, he redesigned the Women Marines service uniform combining femininity with functionality. Previous redesigns include uniforms for the WAVES (Women Accepted for Volunteer Emergency Service) in 1942, and uniform designs for the Girl Scouts of America and the American Red Cross in 1948.

Dior's New Look (that premiered in 1947) revived the popularity of girdles and the all-in-one corselettes. In the early 1950s many couture houses used the interest in "foundationwear" to launch their own lines, soon after many lingerie manufacturers began to build their own brands. In 1957, Jane Russell wore the "Cantilever" bra that was scientifically designed by Howard Hughes to maximize a voluptuous look. The invention of Lycra (originally called "Fibre K") in 1959 revolutionized the underwear industry and was quickly incorporated into every aspect of lingerie.

After the war, the American look (which consisted of broad shoulders, floral ties, straight-legged pants, and shirts with long pointed collars, often worn hanging out rather than tucked in) became very popular among men in Europe. Certain London manufacturers ushered in a revival of Edwardian elegance in men's fashion, adopting a tight-fitting retro style that was intended to appeal to traditionalists. This look, originally aimed at the respectable young man about town, was translated into popular fashion as the Teddy boy style. The Italian look, popularized by Caraceni, Brioni, and Cifonelli, was taken up by an entire generation of elegant young lovers, on both sides of the Atlantic.

The designers of Hollywood created a particular type of glamour for the stars of American film, and outfits worn by the likes of Marilyn Monroe, Lauren Bacall, or Grace Kelly were widely copied. Quantitatively speaking, a costume worn by an actress in a Hollywood movie would have a much bigger audience than the photograph of a dress designed by a couturier illustrated in a magazine read by no more than a few thousand people. Without even trying to keep track of all the Paris styles, its costume designers focused on their own version of classicism, which was meant to be timeless, flattering, and photogenic. Using apparently luxurious materials, such as sequins, chiffon, and fur, the clothes were very simply cut, often including some memorable detail, such as a low-cut back to a dress which was only revealed when the actress turned her back from the camera or some particularly stunning accessory. The most influential and respected designers of Hollywood from the 1930s to the 1950s were Edith Head, Orry-Kelly, William Travilla, Jean Louis, Travis Banton, and Gilbert Adrian.

By the end of the decade mass-manufactured, off-the-peg clothing had become much more popular than in the past, granting the general public unprecedented access to fashionable styles.

Until the 1960s, Paris was considered to be the center of fashion throughout the world. However, between 1960 and 1969 a radical shake-up occurred in the fundamental structure of fashion. From the 1960s onward, there would never be just one single, prevailing trend or fashion but a great plethora of possibilities, indivisibly linked to all the various influences in other areas of people's lives. Young people, with a power and culture that were all their own, now at an age to speak out, were a force to be reckoned with and had a powerful impact on the fashion industry. For perhaps the first time in history, there was an independent youth fashion that was not based on the conventions of an older age group. In the past, failure to follow fashion merely meant that you were poor, but in the Sixties it became just as much a statement of personal freedom.

In stark contrast to their mature, ultra-feminine mothers, the women of the 1960s adopted a girlish, childlike style, with short skirts and straightened curves, reminiscent of the look of the 1920s. At the start of the decade skirts were knee-length, but steadily became shorter and shorter until the mini-skirt emerged in 1965. By the end of the decade they had shot well above the stocking top, making the transition to tights inevitable.

Many of the radical changes in fashion developed in the streets of London, with such gifted designers as Mary Quant (known for launching the mini skirt) and Barbara Hulanicki (the founder of the legendary boutique Biba). Paris also had its share of new and revolutionary designers, including Pierre Cardin (known for his visionary and skillfully-cut designs), André Courrèges (known for his futuristic outfits and for launching the mini skirt along with Mary Quant), Yves Saint Laurent (known for his revolutionary yet elegant fashions), and Emanuel Ungaro (known for his imaginative use of color and bold baroque contrasts). In the United States, Rudi Gernreich (known for his avant-garde and futuristic designs) and James Galanos (known for his luxurious read-to-wear) were also reaching a young audience. The main outlets for these new young fashion designers were small boutiques, selling outfits that were not exactly 'one-offs', but were made in small quantities in a limited range of sizes and colors. However, not all designers took well to the new style and mood. In 1965, Coco Chanel mounted a rearguard action against the exposure of the knee and Balenciaga resolutely continued to produce feminine and conservative designs.

The basic shape and style of the time was simple, neat, clean cut, and young. Synthetic fabrics were very widely-used during the Sixties. They took dyes easily and well, giving rise to colors that were both clear and bright, very much mirroring the mood of the period. Hats suffered a great decline and by the end of the decade they were relegated to special occasions only. Lower kitten heels were a pretty substitute to stilettos. Pointed toes gave way to chisel shaped toes in 1961 and to an almond toe in 1963. Flat boots also became popular with very short dresses in 1965 and eventually they rose up the leg and reached the knee.

Two notable and influential designers in the '60s were Emilio Pucci and Paco Rabanne. Emilio Pucci's sportswear designs and prints inspired by Op art, psychedelia, and medieval heraldic banners earned him a reputation that extended far beyond the circles of high society. His sleek shift dresses, tunics, and beachwear, created a 'Puccimania' that was all part of a movement to liberate the female form and his designs are today synonymous with the 1960s. Francisco Rabaneda Cuervo (later Paco Rabanne) opened his first couture house in 1966 and, from the start, produced resolutely modern designs. Rather than using conventional dress materials, he created garments from aluminum, Rhodoid, and pieces of scrap metal. His designs, as well as being experimental, were also closely in tune with what modern adventurous young women wanted to wear. Among his innovations are the seamless dress made, after much experiment, by spraying vinyl chloride on to a mold, and the low-budget disposable dress made of paper and nylon thread. Rabanne was also the first fashion designer to use black models, which very nearly resulted in his dismissal from the Chambre Syndicale de la Couture Parisienne. The success of his perfume Calandre helped support the less profitable areas of his work, while his utopianism assured him a unique position in the conservative world of haute couture.

The principal change in menswear in the '60s was in the weight of the fabric used. The choice of materials and the method of manufacture produced a suit that, because it was lighter in weight, had a totally different look, with a line that was closer to the natural shape of the body, causing men to look at their figures more critically. The spread of jeans served to accelerate a radical change in the male wardrobe. Young men grew their hair down to their collars and added a touch of color, and even floral motifs, to their shirts. The polo neck never succeeded in replacing the tie, but the adoption of the workman's jacket in rough corduroy, and especially the Mao jacket proved to be more than simply a political statement. A few futuristic rumblings were set off by Pierre Cardin and Andre Courrèges, but the three-piece suit still survived intact.

In the early 1960s there were influential 'partnerships' of celebrities and high-fashion designers, most famously Audrey Hepburn with Givenchy, and Jackie Kennedy with Oleg Cassini. Also, many models had a very profound effect on fashion, most notably Twiggy, Veruschka, Jean Shrimpton, as well as Andy Warhol superstar Edie Sedgwick. Early in the decade, culottes were in style and the bikini finally came into fashion in 1963. The hippie and psychedelic movements late in the decade also had a strong influence on clothing styles, including bell-bottom jeans (designed by the english tailor .Tommy Nutter, from his Savoy store) , tie-dye and batik fabrics, as well as paisley prints.

End of Good Taste

Nick-named the 'me' decade; 'please yourself' was the catchword of the 1970s. Some saw it as the end of good taste, while many perceived it as the beginning of individuality. The decade began with a continuation of the hippie look of the late 1960s, with afghans, Indian scarves, and flower-print tunics. Jeans remained frayed, tie dye was still popular, and the fashion for unisex mushroomed. An immense movement claiming civil rights for blacks combined with the influence of soul music from the USA created a nostalgia for Africa and African culture. A radical chic emerged, influenced by the likes of James Brown, Diana Ross, Angela Davis, and the Black Panthers, in everything from afro hairstyles to platform soles. During the Seventies brands greatly increased their share of the international market. Hems began dropping in 1974 to below the knee, until finally reaching the lower mid calf in 1977 and shoulderlines were dropped.

Perhaps the two most innovative fashion designers of the 1970s were Sonia Rykiel of France and Kenzo Takada of Japan. The undisputed star of Parisian fashion in the Seventies, Kenzo drew his inspiration from all over the world, mixing Western and Oriental folk influences with a fantastic joie de vivre and an instinctive understanding of what his young customers wanted. With his fluid lines, unusual prints, clever accessories, and finery that was hitherto unprecedented in ready-to-wear, he very much turned the fashion world upside down. The queen of figure-hugging knits, in 1974, Sonia Rykiel designed her first pullovers with reversed seams. However, more than that, she created a whole range of clothes that were extremely individual and yet could be worn almost anywhere. The Rykiel style, dominated by fluid knitted garments, dark blacks, rhinestones, long boa-like scarves, and little crocheted hats, conquered the American market, and even to this day Rykiel is considered by many Americans as the true successor of Chanel.

London retained a considerable degree of influence over fashion, most significantly in the boutiques of the King's Road, where Vivienne Westwood's boutique, SEX, which opened in 1971, blew with the prevailing wind. This temple of British iconoclasm centered on fetishistic accessories and ranges of clothing in which black rubber and steel studs were the external signs of an underlying sadism. Postmodernist and iconoclastic in essence the punk movement was a direct reaction to the economic situation during the economic depression of the period, the vehicle for a hatred that was more visceral than political. Punk had at its heart a manifesto of creation through disorder. With their ripped T-shirts, Red Indian hairstyles, Doc Martens, bondage trousers, and chains, the punks exported an overall feeling of disgust around the globe.

Another popular British style the was the resolutely unmodern, feminine, countrified style of clothing popularized by Laura Ashley, which consisted of long flounced skirts and high-necked blouses in traditional floral prints, worn with crocheted shawls. Laura Ashley started out running a small business in Wales in the mid-1960s and the company continued to expand until the accidental death of its owner in 1985. Laura Ashley was not the only designer to look nostalgically to the past. Fashions based on the 1920s, 30s, 40s, and 50s were popular throughout much of the decade, with Hollywood films like *The Godfather* and *The Great Gatsby*, and numerous exhibitions on costume history at the Metropolitan Museum of Art in New York increasing their popularity. In Japan, the boutiques of Tokyo's fashionable Harajuku district sold many reworked versions of traditional British and American looks.

In the United States, the general trend in fashion was towards simplification and longer skirts, although many women reacted negatively to the midi-length, which they felt to be aging. Pants, on the other hand, earned unanimous approval. Jeans profited most from becoming an accepted part of the American fashion scene in the 1970s, their new-found respectability deriving from their inclusion in collections under the heading of sportswear. The new stars of American ready-to-wear adapted the best of what they learned from Europe to the massive American clothing industry. Calvin Klein and Ralph Lauren rose from anonymity more or less simultaneously to tackle the question of designing clothes for the men and women of a new world. Two opposing movements dominated fashion in the U.S.A. during the Seventies. On one hand, there was the tailored, unisex look; on the other hand, a fluid, unstructured style with a strong feeling of Thirties glamor. The most influential American designer of the time, Roy Halston Frowick (known simply as Halston), belonged to the latter category. Acquiring celebrity status on the New York scene, his particular talent was in reconciling the made-to-measure garment for the special occasion with concepts of comfort, naturalness, and relaxation. With his kaftans, shirtwaisters, djellabas, ultra-lightweight shift dresses, and tunics worn over shorts and wide-legged pants, he was an icon of the era, and a regular visitor at the VIP room of the Studio 54 after its opening in 1977.

Geoffrey Beene, praised for his elegant and sophisticated cuts and his use of black and white, was at his most successful in the radically simplified designs at which he excelled. His smart little dresses and well-cut suits in jersey, flannel, and wool were instrumental in discouraging American women from over-accessorizing. Bill Blass, who launched his own range in 1962, developed the habit of traveling all over the United States in order to hear for himself what his customers desired. One of the most popular designers of the time, he was almost too successful in fulfilling his customers wishes. His disciplined style and workmanship was particularly favored by businesswomen and the wives of senior executives. Betsey Johnson started out designing for the boutique Paraphernalia. Using vinyl and metallic fabrics and putting emphasis on wit, imagination, and independence, she brought an unprecedented spirit of irreverence to New York in the Seventies.

In popular fashion the glam rock style of clothing, worn by such rock performers as David Bowie and Marc

Bolan, was very influential, particularly in the United Kingdom. The designer Elio Fiorucci had a very similar look. His boutique in Milan sold such things as brightly colored rubber boots, plastic daisy sandals, fake fur, and Pop Art-inspired jackets.

During the 1970s a new generation of menswear boutiques sprang up, aiming to change the decor, rituals, and customer base of a traditionally 'difficult' trade. To sell fashionable clothes to a young man at the end of the 60's was still, in many circles, tantamount to questioning his masculinity. Men's appearance changed more in the Seventies than it had done in a whole century. Many of the fashion designers who revolutionized the male look owed a lot of their innovations to Pierre Cardin: narrow shoulders, tight-fitting lines, no tie, no interfacing, zip-up boiler suits, waisted jackets or tunics, sometimes no shirt. Work clothes supplied inspiration for a less formal style, encouraging designers to look beyond the traditional suit and, for example, adopt a unisex look or investigate the massive supply of second-hand clothes. Sometimes this kind of male dressing-down, often denounced as 'hippie', gained formal recognition as a deliberate look. At certain other times, as part of a retro movement, designers introduced a revival of '30s elegance. The unearthing of old military clothing, preferably khaki and from the United States; English-style shoes; Oxford shirts; immaculate T-shirts; tweed jackets with padded shoulders; brightly-colored V-neck sweaters; cashmere-printed scarves draped around the neck all imposed a certain uniformity on the casual beatnik look of the male wardrobe at the end of the Seventies.

Also significant are the developments in Italian fashion that happened during the period. In the course of the 1970s, as a result of its ready-to-wear industry, Milan confirmed its status as second only to Paris as a center of international fashion. The 'alta moda' preferred Rome, the base of the couturiers Valentino, Capucci, and Schön. Capitalizing on the dominant trend of anti-fashion Italy offered a glamor that had nothing to do with the dictates of Parisian haute couture. While profiting from a clearly defined style, Italian fashion was luxurious and easy to wear. The two most influential Italian fashion designers of the time were probably Giorgio Armani and Nino Cerruti. Giorgio Armani produced his first collection for women in 1975. From the outset, the line was dynamic, urban, and understated, androgynous in inspiration. Armani offered a restrained style that greatly appealed to the increasing population of women who now had access to the world of work and occupied progressively more senior positions within it. This was only the beginning of a tremendous career, which came to fruition in 1981 when Emporio Armani was launched. In 1957 Nino Cerruti opened the menswear boutique Hitman in Milan. A man of taste and discernment, in 1976 he presented his first collection for women. Two years later, he launched his first perfume. In linking the career of a successful industrialist with that of a high-quality designer, Cerruti occupied a unique position in Italian ready-to-wear.

Late Twentieth Century

During the late twentieth century, fashions began to criss-cross international boundaries with rapidity. Popular Western styles were adopted all over the world, and many designers from outside of the West had a profound impact on fashion. Synthetic materials such as Lycra, Spandex, and viscose became widely-used, and fashion, after two decades of looking to the future, once again turned to the past for inspiration.

Self-conscious Image

The society of the Eighties no longer criticized itself as consumerist, but was, instead, interested in 'the spectacle'. The self-conscious image of the decade was very good for the fashion industry, which had never been quite so à la mode. Fashion shows were transfigured into media-saturated spectaculars and frequently televised, taking high priority in the social calendar. Appearance was related to performance, which was of supreme importance to a whole generation of young urban professionals, whose desire to look the part related to a craving for power. The way in which men and women associated with the latest styles was no more a matter of passive submission but one of active choice. As fashion once again looked to the past, baroque evening dress and long gowns made a reappearance.

The two French fashion designers who best defined the look of the period were Thierry Mugler and Azzedine Alaia. Strongly influenced by his early career in the theater, Thierry Mugler produced fashion designs that combined Hollywood retro and futurism, with rounded hips, sharply accentuated shoulders, and a slight hint of the galactic heroine. Mugler's glamorous dresses were a remarkable success, and signified the complete end of the hippy era and its unstructured silhouette. Known for his awe-inspiring combinations, Azzedine Alaia greatly influenced the silhouette of the woman of the Eighties. The master of all kinds of techniques that had previously been known only to haute couture, he experimented with many new and underused materials, such as Lycra and viscose. The finish, simplicity, and sheer sexiness of Alaia's look made women of every generation identify with his seductive style, and during the 1980s he achieved a certain glory and was held in high regard by members of his own profession.

Also creating designs very typical of the era were Claude Montana, whose imposing, broad-shouldered designs, often made of leather, would not have looked out of place in the futuristic universe of Thierry Mugler, and Christian Lacroix, who sent shock waves through the world of haute couture, with his flounced skirts, embroidered corselets, bustles, and polka-dotted crinolines which evoked the rhythms of flamenco.

A number of promising newcomers entered the fashion scene in the Eighties. Angelo Tarlazzi, an extraordinary technician who once worked for Patou, bewitched both the press and his customers with his 'handkerchief' dresses. Made of squares of fabric, they transpired, when you came to put them on, to be far more complicated than at first appeared. Many a Parisian soirée of the 80's was enlivened by his dresses, all in a fluid and original style, in which cutting and sewing were kept to a minimum. Chantal Thomas, the queen of sexy stockings and lace, won a devoted following for her seductive underwear and for evening gowns that looked like nightdresses and vice versa. Guy Paulin was one of the first designers to promote a severe, plain, and uncluttered look. His garments were classical in their proportions and made for comfort and simplicity, with their harmonious lines reinforced by a subtle palette of colors and fine materials. Under his own name, Joseph designed luxurious knitwear along classic lines, creating loose, sexy garments in neutral colors. Carolina Herrera, long regarded as one of the most elegant members of the jet set, in 1981 launched a series of collections aimed at women like herself, featuring impeccably cut clothes of high quality and attractive evening dresses.

Japanese designers such as Rei Kawakubo and Yohji Yamamoto offered a look which marked a total break with the prevailing fashion image of the time. Flat shoes, no make-up, reserve, modesty, and secrecy were the hallmarks of this modern look. Eventually, it began to include details from the fashions of the past, as Europe's ancient sites were revisited by these anarchists of fashion, whose influence on shape of clothes, at the end of the twentieth-century, became legendary.

In American fashion the seductive, clinging style of Donna Karan and the casual sophistication of Ralph Lauren were very influential. A star of the New York social scene, Donna Karan brought a very personal and feminine approach to the severe, sober-colored, casual look that dominated American ready-to-wear. Setting up her own label in 1984, her designs won instant popularity among active urban women who greatly appreciated the understated luxury of her clothes. In 1971 Ralph Lauren opened a boutique for both men and women in Beverly Hills. His aristocratic style at prices the average American could afford created a sensation. For an elite faced with all kinds of avant-garde fashions, it represented a rallying point, endorsing a classic look that had been adopted for an active life. The number one of American ready-to-wear, Lauren was equally successful with his sportswear and jeans, which allowed him to reach the widest possible range of social classes and age groups.

Central to the success of a new wave of American sportswear was the Perry Ellis label, established in 1978, which used color and natural fibers to great advantage in its elegant variations on the basics. Norma Kamali, with her short skirts made of sweatshirting, leotards, headbands, and leg warmers, made jogging look fashionable. Kamali also created the popular 'rah-rah skirt'. Also notable is the extreme popularity of the Adidas sports label, which achieved an incredible level of street cred in the '80s, inciting the hip hop group Run DMC to release the single 'My Adidas' in 1986. The legendary shoe designer Manolo Blahnik also rose to fame during the 1980s.

The multiplicity of trends that bloomed during the 80s were curtailed by the economic recession that set in at the beginning of the 1990s. The 1990s opened our eyes to a fresh look.

In the 1990s it was no longer the done thing to follow fashion slavishly, a sharp contrast to the highly á la mode 1970s and 1980s. The phobia of being underdressed was finally completely displaced by the fear of overdressing. Fashion in the '90s united around a new standard, minimalism, and styles of stark simplicity became the vogue.

Despite the best efforts of a few designers to keep the flag for pretty dresses flying, by the end of the decade the notion of ostentatious finery had virtually disappeared. As well as the styling of the product, its promotion in the media became crucial to its success and image. The financial pressures of the decade had a devastating effect on the development of new talent and lessened the autonomy enjoyed by more established designers.

Fashion at the end of the 20th century tackled themes that fashion had not previously embraced. These themes included rape, disability, religious violence, death, and body modification. There was a dramatic move away from the sexy styles aimed at the glamorous femme fatale of the Eighties and many designers, taken with a vision of romantic poverty, adopted the style of the poverty-stricken waif, dressed in a stark, perversely sober palette, with a face devoid of make-up. Clothes by ready-to-wear retailers such as The Gap, Banana Republic, and Eddie Bauer came to the forefront of fashion, managing to tap into the needs of women who simply wanted comfortable, wearable clothes. Retro clothing inspired by the 1960s and 1970s was popular for much of the 1990s.

The famous Italian fashion house, Gucci was created in 1921, by Guccio Gucci and was originally a firm that sold luxury leather goods. Under Guccio Gucci's children, by the end of the 1960s the label had expanded to include a plethora of products with a distinctly Latin glamor. However, only in the '90s, when the Gucci heirs gave up control of the company to Invest Corp., who planned to turn the business around, did it truly begin to enjoy the kind of success it enjoys in the present day. Employing an unknown designer, Tom Ford, as design director in 1994, the fashion house was endowed with a great prestige, as Ford triggered a tidal wave with his chic and shocking collections, perfumes for men and women, revamped boutiques, and advertising campaigns. In 1998 Gucci is named "European Company of the year" by European Business Press Federation. Today it is the second biggest-selling fashion brand (after LVMH) worldwide with US$7 billion worldwide of revenue in 2006 according to BusinessWeek magazine. Most importantly Gucci is the biggest-selling Italian brand in the world.

In the 1990s the designer label Prada became a true creative force in the fashion industry. The Milanese company was first established in 1923, two years after Gucci, and like Gucci, it was a firm that sold high-quality shoes and leather. It was not until the Eighties that Miuccia Prada, the niece of the company's founder, began to produce ready-to-wear fashion, gaining fame for her subtle, streamlined, yet unquestionably luxurious style, that catered for the privileged young woman who prefers understatement to flamboyant extravagance.

In America three of the most influential fashion designers of the time were Michael Kors, Marc Jacobs, and Calvin Klein. Michael Kors set up his own business in 1980. However, it was not until the Nineties that the designer reached the peak of his popularity. His knowledge and consciousness of trends enabled him to produce simple well-cut garments, whose sophistication and elegance appealed to a whole new breed of wealthy American customers drawn to the new vogue for minimalist chic. Marc Jacobs is one of the most notable American designers of the period in that, unlike many American fashion designers in the past, he was not so much the co-ordinator of a mass-produced garment as a designer in the European sense of the word. One of the most promising talents in the fashion industry at the time, the LVMH (Louis Vuitton-Moet Henessy) group offered him the job of designing a line of ready-to-wear to compliment the de-luxe products of luggage specialist Louis Vuitton in the late '90s. One of the first fashion designers to anticipate the globalization of world markets, the already well-known designer Calvin Klein started to market his fashions, perfumes, and accessories not only right across the US, but also in Europe and Asia, achieving an unequaled success. A brilliant artistic director, Klein used carefully constructed advertisements containing images tinted with eroticism to promote his sophisticatedly functional mass-produced designs, which won massive popularity among the urban youth of the 1990s.

The group of designers known as the 'Antwerp Six' (so named because all of them were graduates of the Royal Academy of Fine Arts in Antwerp), who first emerged in the 1980s, came to prominence in the 1990s. Three of the most influential of the group were Ann Demeulemeester, Dries van Noten, and Walter Van Beirendonck. Ann Demeulemeester, from her first collection in 1991, demonstrated a great deal of confidence and inventiveness. Naturally inclined to understatement, she built her designs on contradictions, introducing contrasting elements into her fluid and streamlined fashions, which appealed to women who dressed, above all, to please themselves. The work of Dries van Noten was founded on a solid mastery of the art of tailoring, to which the young designer added discreet touches of fantasy in a highly personal style. Managing to be both classical and original, his fashions appealed to those who preferred to express their individuality rather than slavishly follow trends. Walter Van Beirendonck, who erupted onto the fashion scene in 1995, produced decidedly futuristic designs under his label W & LT (Wild and Lethal Trash). Deliberately using fabrics developed by the very latest technologies, in violently contrasting colors, he produced clothes that were full of erotic and sadomasochistic references, touched with a caustic adolescent humor. His highly distinctive approach related to a resurgence of anti-fashion, but this time an anti-fashion with nothing in the least ethnic about its origins, instead based on science fiction that provided the inspiration for displays of such high-spirited provocation.

In Italy, Gianni Versace, with his brilliant, sexy, and colorful designs, and Dolce & Gabbana, with their superfeminine and fantastical style, broke away from the serious and sober-minded fashions that dominated during much of the Nineties. The British designer Vivienne Westwood produced many influential and popular collections in the early '90s, which included outfits inspired by eighteenth-century courtesans and the Marquis de Sade, with rounded hips, corsets, and platform heels. The London-based designer Rifat Ozbek was also popular, particularly in New York and Milan. His youthful style, which mixed references to India, Africa, and his native Turkey with clever takes on historical clothing, was reminiscent of hippest nightclubs and the more outrageous street fashions of the time. Rap music was a prominent influence on popular and street fashion during the early- and mid-Nineties. Followers of hip hop adopted huge baggy jeans, similar to those worn in American prisons, with big patterned shirts and heavy black shoes. The sports label Nike had great popularity and materials such as Lycra and Spandex were increasingly used for sportswear. Increasing eco-awareness and animal rights made even top couture houses such as Chanel introduce fake fur and natural fibers into their collections.

In the first decade of new millennium, as the future began to seem increasingly bleak, fashion, and indeed the Arts in general, looked to the past for inspiration, arguably more so than in previous decades. Vintage clothing, especially from the Sixties, Seventies, and Eighties (the eighties idea of clashing, electric colours becoming especially popular in mid-late 2007) became extremely popular and fashion designers often sought to emulate bygone styles in their collections. The early '00s saw a continuation of the minimalist look of the '90s in high fashion. Later on, designers began to adopt a more colorful, feminine, excessive, and 'anti-modern' look. Name brands became of particular importance among young people and many celebrities launched their own lines of clothing. Tighter fit clothing and longer hair became mainstream for many men and women.

For many of the own-label designers who emerged in the early years of the twenty-first century, financial factors became increasingly critical. Many new young talents found they now depended on investors (to whom, in extreme cases, they would even surrender their names) and were always burdened by the risk that their partners, motivated by market realism and the desire for quick returns, would severely restrict their autonomy.

The mid 2000s celebrated the return of a more feminine look. This began with the comeback of the dress. The figure-hugging look was disbanded in the summer of 2007, when designers began to experiment with flowy, tunic shapes. Bright, block colour also became a focus. Menswear has become increasingly important as well and has too gone in a slightly feminine direction, especially apparent after the middle of the decade.

FASHION CAPITALS OF WORLD

New York and Milan are considered the economic and true current media fashion capitals of the world. According to the Global Language Monitor, New York came in first for five consecutive years; yet in 2009, it was beaten by Milan. Despite the fact that the fashion of these cities concentrates more on economic and media success, rather than beauty and elegance, both these cities have longstanding traditions of excellence and creativity in design, and have both been important historical centres of artistic fashion design for many years. Milanese fashion is regarded as being practical, but elegant and highly refined at the same time, concentrating more on stylish ready-to-wear clothes, rather than extravagant haute couture. This applies similarly to New York. However, both cities also have upscale haute couture and high fashion shopping districts.

Not from an economic point of view, Paris and London are considered symbolic fashion centres of Europe due to them having long standing histories as centers of art and fashion, and being home to several highly prestigious fashion houses. Yet, in the Global Language Monitor, they were beaten by more economically successful cities, such as New York and Milan. Even though these cities are both highly successful, and have established positive international reputations worldwide, they are often known more for the prestige and elegance of their fashion designs, rather than practicality and economic success (London-based fashion designs are known for their extravagant quirkiness, while Parisian designs are known more for their elegant and formal clothes).

The other main centers of fashion in the world are Los Angeles, Rome, Sydney and Tokyo. In recent years, however, the importance of the fashion industry has grown in many other cities around the globe, such as Chicago, São Paulo and Sydney, which are in 7th, 8th and 9th place.

Other top fashion capitals include Barcelona, Las Vegas, Toronto, Shanghai, and Dubai.

The economic meltdown give a set-back to fashion tourism. As a result of the late-2000s recession, international travel demand suffered a strong slowdown beginning in June 2008, with growth in international tourism arrivals worldwide falling to 2% during the boreal summer months. This negative trend intensified during 2009, exacerbated in some countries due to the outbreak of the H1N1 influenza virus, resulting in a worldwide decline of 4% in 2009 to 880 million international tourists arrivals, and an estimated 6% decline in international tourism receipts.

There are many places to visit in India like Goa, Chennai, Bangalore, Mumbai, Delhi, Agra, Jaipur, Jabalpur and the list is long. But if you can afford, there are many tourist places in foreign countries. Tourism is vital for many countries, such as Egypt, Greece, Lebanon, Spain and Thailand, and many island nations, such as The Bahamas, Fiji, Maldives, and the Seychelles, due to the large intake of money for businesses with their goods and services and the opportunity for employment in the service industries associated with tourism. These service industries include transportation services, such as airlines, cruise ships and taxicabs, hospitality services, such as accommodations, including hotels and resorts, and entertainment venues, such as amusement parks, casinos, shopping malls, music venues and theatres.

Wealthy people have always travelled to distant parts of the world, to see great buildings, works of art, learn new languages, experience new cultures and to taste different cuisines. Long ago, at the time of the Roman Republic, places such as Baiae were popular coastal resorts for the rich. The word tourism was used by 1811 and tourist by 1840. In 1936, the League of Nations defined foreign tourist as "someone traveling abroad for at least twenty-four hours". Its successor, the United Nations, amended this definition in 1945, by including a maximum stay of six months.

Leisure Travel

Leisure travel was associated with the Industrial Revolution in the United Kingdom - the first European country to promote leisure time to the increasing industrial population. Initially, this applied to the owners of the machinery of production, the economic oligarchy, the factory owners and the traders. These comprised the new middle class. Cox & Kings was the first official travel company to be formed in 1758.

The British origin of this new industry is reflected in many place names. In Nice, France, one of the first and best-established holiday resorts on the French Riviera, the long esplanade along the seafront is known to this day as the Promenade des Anglais; in many other historic resorts in continental Europe, old, well-established palace hotels have names like the Hotel Bristol, the Hotel Carlton or the Hotel Majestic - reflecting the dominance of English customers.

Many leisure-oriented tourists travel to the tropics, both in the summer and winter. Places of such nature often visited are: Mexico, Bali in Indonesia, Brazil, Cuba, the Dominican Republic, Malaysia, the various Polynesian tropical islands, Queensland in Australia, Thailand, and Florida and Hawaii in the United States.

Winter Tourism

Major ski resorts are located in the various European countries (e.g. Austria, Bulgaria, Czech Republic, France, Germany, Iceland, Italy, Norway, Poland, Sweden, Slovenia, Spain, Switzerland), Canada, the United States, New Zealand, Japan, South Korea, Chile and Argentina.

Mass Tourism

Mass tourism could only have developed with the improvements in technology, allowing the transport of large numbers of people in a short space of time to places of leisure interest, so that greater numbers of people could begin to enjoy the benefits of leisure time.

In the United States, the first seaside resorts in the European style were at Atlantic City, New Jersey and Long Island, New York.

In Continental Europe, early resorts included: Ostend, popularized by the people of Brussels; Boulogne-sur-Mer (Pas-de-Calais) and Deauville (Calvados) for the Parisians;

and Heiligendamm, founded in 1793, as the first seaside resort on the Baltic Sea.

Adjectival Tourism

Adjectival tourism refers to the numerous niche or specialty travel forms of tourism that have emerged over the years, each with its own adjective. Many of these have come into common use by the tourism industry and academics. Others are emerging concepts that may or may not gain popular usage. Examples of the more common niche tourism markets include:

(a) Agritourism
(b) Culinary tourism
(c) Cultural tourism
(d) Ecotourism
(e) Extreme tourism
(f) Geotourism
(g) Heritage tourism
(h) LGBT tourism
(i) Medical tourism
(j) Nautical tourism
(k) Pop-culture tourism
(l) Poverty tourism
(m) Religious tourism
(n) Space tourism
(o) War tourism
(p) Wildlife tourism

Recent Developments

There has been an upmarket trend in the tourism over the last few decades, especially in Europe, where international travel for short breaks is common. Tourists have high levels of disposable income, considerable leisure time, are well educated, and have sophisticated tastes. There is now a demand for a better quality products, which has resulted in a fragmenting of the mass market for beach vacations; people want more specialised versions, quieter resorts, family-oriented holidays or niche market-targeted destination hotels.

The developments in technology and transport infrastructure, such as jumbo jets, low-cost airlines and more accessible airports have made many types of tourism more affordable. WHO estimates that up to 500,000 people are on planes at any time. There have also been changes in lifestyle, such as retiree-age people who sustain year round tourism. This is facilitated by internet sales of tourism products. Some sites have now started to offer dynamic packaging, in which an inclusive price is quoted for a tailor-made package requested by the customer upon impulse.

There have been a few setbacks in tourism, such as the September 11 attacks and terrorist threats to tourist destinations, such as in Bali and several European cities. Also, on December 26, 2004, a tsunami, caused by the 2004 Indian Ocean earthquake, hit the Asian countries on the Indian Ocean, including the Maldives. Thousands of lives were lost and many tourists died. This, together with the vast clean-up operation in place, has stopped or severely hampered tourism to the area.

The terms tourism and travel are sometimes used interchangeably. In this context, travel has a similar definition to tourism, but implies a more purposeful journey. The terms tourism and tourist are sometimes used pejoratively, to imply a shallow interest in the cultures or locations visited by tourists.

Sustainable Tourism

"Sustainable tourism is envisaged as leading to management of all resources in such a way that economic, social and aesthetic needs can be fulfilled while maintaining cultural integrity, essential ecological processes, biological diversity and life support systems." (World Tourism Organization)

Sustainable development implies "meeting the needs of the present without compromising the ability of future generations to meet their own needs" (World Commission on Environment and Development, 1987)

Ecotourism

Ecotourism, also known as ecological tourism, is responsible travel to fragile, pristine, and usually protected areas that strives to be low impact and (often) small scale. It helps educate the traveler; provides funds for conservation; directly benefits the economic development and political empowerment of local communities; and fosters respect for different cultures and for human rights.

HOW TO ATTRACT TOURISTS?

The potential tourism has to help the very poorest in developing countries has been receiving increasing attention by those involved in development and the issue has been addressed either through small scale projects in local communities and by Ministries of Tourism attempting to attract huge numbers of tourists. Research by the Overseas Development Institute suggests that neither is the best way to encourage tourists' money to reach the poorest as only 25% or less (far less in some cases) ever reaches the poor; successful examples of money reaching the poor include mountain climbing in Tanzania or cultural tourism in Luang Prabang, Laos. For tourism to successfully reach the poor efforts must be made for tourists to use local currency, for locals to develop relevant skills and to ensure that exclusive contracts do not dominate the sector.

Recession Tourism

Recession tourism is a travel trend, which evolved by way of the world economic crisis. Identified by American entrepreneur Matt Landau (2007), recession tourism is defined by low-cost, high-value experiences taking place of once-popular generic retreats. Various recession tourism hotspots have seen business boom during the recession thanks to comparatively low costs of living and a slow world job market suggesting travelers are elongating trips where their money travels further.

Medical Tourism

When there is a significant price difference between countries for a given medical procedure, particularly in Southeast Asia, India, Eastern Europe and where there are different regulatory regimes, in relation to particular medical procedures (e.g. dentistry), traveling to take advantage of the price or regulatory differences is often referred to as "medical tourism".

Educational Tourism

Educational tourism developed, because of the growing popularity of teaching and learning of knowledge and the enhancing of technical competency outside of the classroom environment. In educational tourism, the main focus of the tour or leisure activity includes visiting another country to learn about the culture, such as in Student Exchange Programs and Study Tours, or to work and apply skills learned inside the classroom in a different environment, such as in the International Practicum Training Program.

Creative Tourism

Creative tourism has existed as a form of cultural tourism, since the early beginnings of tourism itself. Its European roots date back to the time of the Grand Tour, which saw the sons of aristocratic families traveling for the purpose of mostly interactive, educational experiences. More recently, creative tourism has been given its own name by Crispin Raymond and Greg Richards, who as members of the Association for Tourism and Leisure Education (ATLAS), have directed a number of projects for the European Commission, including cultural and crafts tourism, known as sustainable tourism. They have defined "creative tourism" as tourism related to the active participation of travellers in the culture of the host community, through interactive workshops and informal learning experiences.

Meanwhile, the concept of creative tourism has been picked up by high-profile organizations such as UNESCO, who through the Creative Cities Network, have endorsed creative tourism as an engaged, authentic experience that promotes an active understanding of the specific cultural features of a place.

More recently, creative tourism has gained popularity as a form of cultural tourism, drawing on active participation by travelers in the culture of the host communities they visit. Several countries offer examples of this type of tourism development, including the United Kingdom, the Bahamas, Jamaica, Spain, Italy and New Zealand.

Dark Tourism

One emerging area of special interest tourism has been identified by Lennon and Foley (2000) as "dark" tourism. This type of tourism involves visits to "dark" sites, such as battlegrounds, scenes of horrific crimes or acts of genocide, for example: concentration camps. Dark tourism remains a small niche market, driven by varied motivations, such as mourning, remembrance, education, macabre curiosity or even entertainment. Its early origins are rooted in fairgrounds and medieval fairs.

International Tourism

The World Tourism Organization (UNWTO) forecasts that international tourism will continue growing at the average annual rate of 4 %. With the advent of e-commerce, tourism products have become one of the most traded items on the internet. Tourism products and services have been made available through intermediaries, although tourism providers (hotels, airlines, etc.) can sell their services directly. This has put pressure on intermediaries from both on-line and traditional shops.

It has been suggested there is a strong correlation between tourism expenditure per capita and the degree to which countries play in the global context. Not only as a result of the important economic contribution of the tourism industry, but also as an indicator of the degree of confidence with which global citizens leverage the resources of the globe for the benefit of their local economies. This is why any projections of growth in tourism may serve as an indication of the relative influence that each country will exercise in the future.

Space tourism is expected to "take off" in the first quarter of the 21st century, although compared with traditional destinations the number of tourists in orbit will remain low until technologies such as a space elevator make space travel cheap.

Technological improvement is likely to make possible air-ship hotels, based either on solar-powered airplanes or large dirigibles. Underwater hotels, such as Hydropolis, expected to open in Dubai in 2009, will be built. On the ocean, tourists will be welcomed by ever larger cruise ships and perhaps floating cities.

Sports Travel

Since the late 1970s packaged sports travel has become increasingly popular. Events such as rugby and football World Cups have enabled specialist travel companies to gain official ticket allocation and then sell them in packages that include flights, hotels and excursions.

GLOBAL FINANCIAL CRISES

As a result of the late-2000s recession, international arrivals suffered a strong slowdown beginning in June 2008. Growth from 2007 to 2008 was only 3.7% during the first eight months of 2008. The Asian and Pacific markets were affected and Europe stagnated during the boreal summer months, while the Americas performed better, reducing their expansion rate but keeping a 6% growth from January to August 2008. Only the Middle East continued its rapid growth during the same period, reaching a 17% growth as compared to the same period in 2007. This slowdown on international tourism demand was also reflected in the air transport industry, with a negative growth in September 2008 and a 3.3% growth in passenger traffic through September. The hotel industry also reports a slowdown, as room occupancy continues to decline. As the global economic situation deteriorated dramatically during September and October as a result of the global financial crisis, growth of international tourism is expected to slow even further for the remaining of 2008, and this slowdown in demand growth is forecasted to continue into 2009 as recession has already hit most of the top spender countries, with long-haul travel expected to be the most affected by the economic crisis. This negative trend intensified as international tourist arrivals fell by 8% during the first four months of 2009, and the decline was exacerbated in some regions due to the outbreak of the influenza AH1N1 virus.

ATTENTION AND CRITICISM

On the 15th of April 2010, European Commissioner Antonio Tajani attracted attention and criticism after the

British newspaper, The Sunday Times, reported he had unveiled a plan declaring tourism as a human right. According to the article, pensioners, youths and those too poor to afford it should have their travel subsidised by the taxpayer. Tajani's program will be piloted until 2013 and then put into full operation. In introducing his plan, Tajani stated, "Travelling for tourism today is a right. The way we spend our holidays is a formidable indicator of our quality of life." His spokesman added, "Why should someone from the Mediterranean not be able to travel to Edinburgh in summer for a breath of cool, fresh air; why should someone from Edinburgh not be able to travel to Greece in winter?"

EurActiv, an independent media portal, criticized the article by The Sunday Times as an example of misleading information about the EU to appear in the British press and then picked up by other Anglo-Saxon media and blogs, and Wikipedia. EurActiv stated that "the article on The Sunday Times never quotes the commissioner as having made such a statement. Nevertheless, it pursues the argument under the headline "Brussels decrees holidays as a human right," underlining the alleged "hundreds of millions of pounds" that pursuing the idea would cost taxpayers." Wikipedia was criticized by EurActiv regarding the difficulty that Commissioner Tajani's team had with changing the wrong information on the encyclopedia, and echoed European Commission spokesperson Pia Ahrenkilde Hansen's statement that "ethics in digital communications is definitely a subject which deserves to be addressed."

2

FASHION IN HILL STATION

A popular tourist destination, Shimla is often referred to as the "Queen of Hills" (a term coined by the British). Located in the north-west Himalayas at an average altitude of 2,205 metres (7,234 ft), the city of Shimla, draped in forests of pine, rhododendron, and oak, experiences pleasant summers and cold, snowy winters. The city is famous for its buildings styled in tudorbethan and neo-gothic architecture dating from the colonial era. Shimla is connected to the city of Kalka by one of the longest narrow gauge railway routes still operating in India, the Kalka-Shimla Railway. Shimla is approximately 115 km (71.4 miles) from Chandigarh, the nearest major city, and 365 km (226.8 miles) from New Delhi, the national capital. The city is named after the goddess Shyamala Devi, an incarnation of the Hindu Goddess Kali.

The people of Shimla are informally called Shimlaites. With largely cosmopolitan crowds, a variety of festivals are celebrated here. The Shimla Summer Festival, held every year during peak tourist season, and lasting 3-4 days, is celebrated on the ridge. The highlights of this event include performances by popular singers from all over the country. Shimla has a number of places to visit. Local hangouts like the mall road and ridge are in the heart of the city. Most of the heritage buildings in the city are preserved in their original tudorbethan architecture. The Viceregal lodge which houses the Indian Institute of Advanced Study, and

Wildflower hall that is now a luxury hotel are some of the famous ones. A collection of paintings, jewellery and textiles of the region can be found at the State Museum (built in 1974). Further out from the city is the Naldehra nine-hole golf course, the oldest of its kind in India. Kufri is a ski resort (winter only) located 19 kilometres (11.8 mi) from the main city. Lakkar Bazaar, a market extending off the ridge, is famous for souvenirs and crafts made of wood. Tatta Pani, 55 kilometres (34.2 mi) from the main city, is the name of hot sulphur springs that are believed to have medicinal value located on the banks of river Satluj. Shimla is also home to Asia's only natural ice skating rink. State and national level competitions are often held at this venue. The Shimla Ice Skating Club, which manages the rink, hosts a carnival every year in January, which includes a fancy dress competition and figure skating events. Due to effects of global warming and increasing urban development in and around Shimla, the number of sessions on ice every winter have been decreasing in the past few years.

Shimla has many temples and is often visited by devotees from nearby towns and cities. The Kali Bari temple, dedicated to the Hindu goddess Kali is near the mall. Jakhoo Temple, for the Hindu god Hanuman is located at the highest point in Shimla. Sankat Mochan, another Hanuman temple, is famous for the numerous monkeys that are always found in its vicinity. It is located on Shimla-Kalka Highway about 10 kilometres (6.2 mi) from the city. The nearby temple of Tara Devi is a place for performing rituals and festivals. Other prominent places of worship include a Gurudwara near the bus terminus and a Church on the ridge.

Shimla was annexed by the British in 1819 after the Gurkha War. At that time it was known for the temple of Hindu Goddess Shyamala Devi. The Scottish civil servant Charles Pratt Kennedy built the first British summer home in the town in 1822.

Lord Amherst, the Governor-General of Bengal from 1823 to 1828, set up a summer camp here in 1827, when there was only one cottage in the town, and only 'half a dozen' when he left that year. There were more than a hundred within ten years.

Shimla, or Simla as it was called until recently, caught the eye of Lord William Bentinck, the Governor-General of Bengal from 1828 (later of India, when the title was created in 1833) to 1835. In a letter to Colonel Churchill in 1832 he wrote

"Simla is only four days march from Loodianah (Ludhiana), is easy of access, and proves a very agreeable refuge from the burning plains of Hindoostaun (Hindustan)."

The bridge connecting Shimla with Minor Shimla, erected in 1829 by Lord Combermere, Shimla, 1850s

PASSENGER TRAIN ON THE KALKA-SHIMLA RAILWAY ROUTE

One of his successors, Sir John Lawrence, Viceroy of India 1864-1869, decided to take the trouble of moving the administration twice a year between Calcutta and a separate centre over 1,000 miles away, despite the fact that it was difficult to reach. Lord Lytton, Viceroy 1876 -1880 made efforts to plan the town from 1876, when he first stayed in a rented house, but began plans for a Viceregal Lodge, later built on Observatory Hill. A fire cleared much of the area where the native Indian population lived (the "Upper Bazaar"), and the planning of the eastern end to become the centre of the European town forced these to live in the Middle and Lower Bazaars on the lower terraces descending the steep slopes from the Ridge. The Upper Bazaar was cleared for a Town Hall, with many facilities such as library and theatre, as well as offices - for police and military volunteers as well as municipal administration.

During the 'Hot Weather', Simla was also the Headquarters of the Commander-in-Chief of the Indian Army and many Departments of the Government, as well as being the summer capital of the regional Government of the Punjab. They were joined by many of the British wives and daughters of the men who remained on the plains. Together these formed Simla Society, which, according to Charles Allen, "was as close as British India ever came to having an upper crust." This may have been helped by the fact that it was very expensive, having an ideal climate and thus being desirable, as well as having limited accommodation. British soldiers, merchants, and civil servants moved here each year to escape from the heat during summer in the Indo-Gangetic plain. The presence of many bachelors and unattached men, as well as the many women passing the hot weather there, gave Simla a reputation for adultery, and at least gossip about adultery: as Rudyard Kipling said in a letter cited by Allen, it had a reputation for "frivolity, gossip and intrigue". (See also.)

The Kalka-Shimla railway line, constructed in 1906, added to Shimla's accessibility and popularity. The railway route from Kalka to Shimla, with more than 806 Bridges and 103 tunnels, was touted as an engineering feat and came to be known as the "British Jewel of the Orient". In 2008, it became part of the UNESCO World Heritage Site, Mountain railways of India. Not only that, there was a significant Muslim population in the region before the partition of British India. In addition, Shimla was the capital of the undivided state of Punjab in 1871, and remained so until the construction of the new city of Chandigarh (the present-day capital of Punjab). Upon the formation of the state of Himachal Pradesh in 1971, Shimla was named its capital.

Pre-independence structures still dot Shimla; buildings such as the Viceregal Lodge, Auckland House, Gorton Castle, Peterhoff house, and Gaiety Theatre are reminders of British rule in India. British Simla extended about a mile and a half along the ridge between Jakhoo Hill and Prospect Hill. The central spine was The Mall, which ran along the length of the ridge, with a Mall Extension southwards, closed to all carriages except those of the Viceroy and his wife.

Shimla is located in the north-western ranges of the Himalayas. At an average altitude of 2397.59 meters (7866.10 ft) above mean sea level, the city is spread on a ridge and its seven spurs. The city stretches nearly 9.2 km from east to west. The highest point in Shimla, at 2454 meters (8051 ft), is the Jakhoo hill. Shimla is a Zone IV (High Damage Risk Zone) per the Earthquake hazard zoning of India. Weak construction techniques and increasing population pose a serious threat to the already earthquake prone region. There are no bodies of water near the main city and the closest river, Sutlej, is about 21 km (13 miles) away. Other rivers that flow through the Shimla district, although further from the city, are Giri, and Pabbar (both are tributaries of Yamuna). The green belt in Shimla planning area is spread over 414 hectares (1023 acres). The main forests in and around the city are that of pine, deodar, oak and rhododendron. Environmental degradation due to the increasing number of tourists every year without the infrastructure to support them has resulted in Shimla losing its popular appeal as an ecotourism spot. Another rising concern in the region are the frequent number of landslides that often take place after heavy rains.

The famous hill station have not caught the fancy of fashion world alone, but many famous songs and theme of the film have been captured in the back-drop of famous hill stations of India. The era may be black and white of Sadhna time, or colour of Rani Mukherjee current time. Let us have a look:

Aadmi Aur Insaan 1969 Towards the end of this Dharmendra, Saira Banu, Mumtaz and Firoz Khan starrer, there is a thrilling sequence on board a WP hauled luxury train, which I believe is the AC Express or Frontier Mail as this is pre-Rajdhani era. The scenes were shot in the First Class A/C and the Dining Car. To show that the train is on it's way to Delhi they have shown a mix of WP hauled trains including a rare shot of the Blue WP (with crown on the smokestack) hauled Flying Ranee between Mahim and Bandra stations.

Aankhen 1968 At the outset of this spy film, a WG hauled train is shown blown up by foreign agents while traversing a bridge in Assam. Note that there was very little broad gauge in Assam at this time though!

Achut Kanya 1936 (B/W) In this Ashok Kumar and Kanan Devi film has Kanan Devi playing the role of a level crossing gatekeeper's daughter who averts an accident towards the end of the film.

Aakhri Khat 1966 Aakhri Khat is the tale of a toddler on the streets of Delhi as he goes about searching for his mother who has passed away. The child oblivious to the fact that his mother is no more retraces his steps to the last place where he saw her thinking his mother is playing an elaborate game of hide & seek. In the meantime he survives on the crumbs that he finds on the streets and on the leftovers of others. During his escapades, the child played by Master Bunty also sleeps between the tracks whilst a steam train passes over him and he escapes unscathed.

Aap Ki Kasam 1974 Rajesh Khanna is leaving Bombay for good after having gone through a divorce, which he now realizes, was only due to his suspicious nature and not being able to trust his wife. He boards a long distance train that obviously is hauled by a DC electric as one can also see in the long shots of the train on a curve. However, they show you close up shots of a WP wheels, cylinders and firebox to depict the motion of the train and the anguish inside the man. Song Zindagi ke safar mein plays in the background and was an instant hit.

Andaz 1949 (B/W) This film features scene of the Simla line, and for good measure, an Avro Lancastrian airliner at Delhi airport. (Contributed by Warren Miller)

Andaz 1971 At the very end of the film, there is a station scene when the father in law Ajit comes to take Hema Malini back, whom he had discarded after the accidental death of his son. No complete locomotive here but there is a steam whistle depicted and you can also see barless windows in second class coaches.

Aparajito 1956 (B/W) There is at least one scene depicting railways where Apu leaves for Calcutta from Benaras station (Contributed by Satish Pai).

A Passage to India 1984 (English) Based on E.M. Forster's book and set in imperial India, the film opens with a scene showing arrival of a ship from England at Bombay Port. The passengers head to Bombay VT to board the Imperial Mail. There are some very true to life sights and sound in the scenes showing this journey. When the old woman and her intended daughter-in-law arrive at their destination Chandrapore, there is much pomp as the chief of the town is also arriving by the same train. On their journey home from the station, they stop at a level crossing for a passenger train with XE locomotive and full of natives up to the roof shows the total contrast in the lifestyles of the rulers and the ruled. Dr. Aziz played by Victor Banerji befriends the two English women and proposes to take them for a picnic to Marabar caves. The journey to the caves by rail is on the disguised Nilgiri Railway and is done very well. Later when Mrs. Moore is leaving for England, only her son and Prof. Godbole come to see her off as she is seen leaving Chandrapore station at night by the Imperial Mail.

Apur Sansar 1959 (B/W) The last one in Apu Trilogy, Apur Sansar has Apu living in a room right next to a railway yard, and while there is no direct focus on the trains, the whistles of the locomotives are omnipresent and they are seen quite often as part of a background in many scenes. There is, however, one memorable scene where a train is part of the story, which is the famous 'suicide' scene in which Apu is seen standing next to the tracks contemplating killing himself while a train approaches (Contributed by Satish Pai).

Aradhana 1969 Rajesh Khanna serenades Sharmila Tagore while he is on a Jeep and she is riding the Up DHR train. The song Mere sapnon ki rani became an instant super hit and is probably the best known song featuring a train in India Cinema. There have been many other songs with DHR in background but this one was probably the first one in colour. It shows several important features of DHR including the sharpest curve at the `Agony Point.'

Bandini 1963 (B/W) The story of this film is based in pre-independence India. The movie ends on the banks of the Ganges near Bhagalpur/Mungher. Bandini was shot near the Ganga ghat of Monghyr. The train tracks came up to the ghat and passengers were transferred across the river in a steamer to take another train for onward journey. The last scene of the film depicts smoking steam engines, trains etc. while the song Mere Saajan hain us paar plays (Contributed by Adesh Saxena).

Basant 1960 Very good shots of WP locomotive can be seen many times in this film(Contributed by Capt. J.D. Singh).

Baharen Phir Bhi Aayengi 1966 Dharmendra is a happy-go-lucky but principled young man. He has been fired from yet another job and is going home by one of the narrow gauge trains on Martin's Light Railway (probably the Sheakhala branch) network at Howrah. While his friend pokes fun at him, he sings the title song standing mostly at the door of the train while it whizzes by a rural backdrop. Later one of the female leads played by Tanuja who is also in the same train tries to jump from moving train and is saved by our hero.

Bahu Begum 1967 Nawab Yusuf is tricked by his uncle to go to Allahabad on a pretext and this trip is depicted by a momentary shot of a WG hauled mixed passenger train with four wheeled covered wagons in the lead.

Bhowani Junction 1956 Based on the masterpiece from John Masters, this film is about Anglo Indian community in pre-partition India. Set at imaginary railway town called Bhowani Junction, this film has sterling performances by Ava Gardner, Bill Travers and Stewart Granger amongst others. Victoria Jones played by Ava is an Anglo Indian girl who is constantly tormented by her inability to find an identity and belongingness in India just before partition. Her father is a locomotive driver and she works for the Women Army Corps. A large part of the film is set around railways that played an all-important role during war years, before and after partition and were 100% powered by steam. The railway scenes in the film were shot in Lahore and other parts of North-west Pakistan however there are occasional glimpses of standard gauge and other railway stock from England. You can XC, SG(S) and HGS class locomotives here amongst others. The train sabotage/ derailment and rescue scene is done very well.

Boond Jo Ban Gayi Moti 1967 At the end of the film, Jeetendra is a schoolteacher who is accused of murder of a village girl but it is his stepbrother who finally confesses to it in the court. His account of his leaving the village after the murder is shown by a double-headed narrow gauge steam train with ZE class locomotives at helm. This is Satpura Railway in all possibility.

Boy Friend 1961 (B/W) Boy Friend Shammi Kapoor is a happy-go-lucky person who is interested in working in theatre. In the early part of the film, he hops aboard the roof of the Simla - Kalka train and sings Mujhe apna yaar bana lo. This is a mixed train with six carriages and is hauled by a ZF class No. 75 locomotive. At the end of the song the train comes out of a tunnel no. 103 whistling and goes through a sharp S curve just after the tunnel

Brahmachari 1968 Shammi Kapoor play the eternal bachelor who only aims in life is to adopt homeless children and raise them like his own. One day he takes them out for a picnic. This is Sayaji Garden at Baroda and although this is no mainline run, it is still real 4-6-2 steam engine on a 12" gauge pulling a train full of children in open carriages. The song is Chakke pe chakka chakke pe gaadi.

China Town 1962 (B/W) Shammi Kapoor disguises as a holy man to be with his sweetheart Shakila. She is traveling first class in the down DHR train with her father who doesn't approve of Shammi Kapoor. He breaks into the bhajan Dekho ji ek bala jogi matwala and you can see several scenes of the Up train including one at the Batasia loop before the end of the song.

Chor Machaye Shor 1974 In this film, Shashi Kapoor and Mumtaz are shown boarding a train. From the tender it appeared to be a narrow gauge steam locomotive but then as their journey proceeded it became a broad gauge WP! This was followed by the scene of an accident shown with models with the train hurtling off a bridge.

Daag 1973 Rajesh Khanna is a convicted murderer who has escaped from the jail van that met with an accident. He is still handcuffed on one arm with another prisoner. They hang across the rail of what look like the old Vasai Bridge at night and a WP hauled train helps cut the handcuff off. Everyone believes that he has died in the accident and his widow Sharmila Tagore moves on to Simla to find work as a teacher. This move is shown `erroneously' with a nice shot of the Darjeeling train at the Batasia loop with Kanchenjunga in the backdrop. Later she sings Hawa Chale Kaise to her young son to put him to sleep and a part of the song is picturised on the older Kalka - Simla Railcar.

Dal-pati 1991 (Thalapathi in Tamil) Mani Ratnam is another film director who is obsessed with trains and you see them in almost every film in his portfolio. This original Tamil film that was remade in Hindi has a long opening scene of a YG hauled goods train on the Quilon - Tenkasi route. A young woman in the village delivers a male child out of wedlock. Out of shame she decides to discard the newborn but as soon as the covered four wheeler goods wagon of the train where she had left the child starts moving, she realises her folly. The song In aankhon ka dulaara hai plays in the background while she longs for the child moving farther and farther away from her along with the moving train. The train rolls through beautiful terrain, goes over a stone viaduct and has a metre gauge caboose.

Dharkan 1972 Villian Roopesh Kumar kidnaps a child from a moving Kalka - Simla train and later Sanjay Khan and Mumtaz fight him and his goons in the Goregaon yards in Mumbai. The fainted child is rescued by Mumtaz as he is about to be crushed under the wheels of a WP which is being lowered on the same track by a crane.

Dil Se 1998 This is a Mani Ratnam's film that opens with a scene of an All India Radio Reporter at a station waiting overnight for the early morning train. This is Nilgiri Railway but masquerading as some place in northeast India. Shah Rukh Khan misses the train that he is waiting for and the girl that he was trying to impress. Nevertheless he boards the next one where he meets a raunchily dressed local with her troop and together they perform Chal chaiyan chaiyan on top of the coaches, on a metre gauge flatcar etc. This was the first major song in the Indian Cinema after the closing of the mainline steam and became so famous that for sometime that many producers wanted a train action for their film hereafter.

Devdas 1955(B/W) Devdas Dileep Kumar is dejected when he realizes that his Paro is married off elsewhere. He goes wandering around the country by train only accompanied by his faithful servant. All he does on the train is to drink and fantasise about Paro. There are several scenes of tracks, stations, trains and a silhouetted WP engine to depict this journey before Devdas decides to get off at a wayside station. The servant who is traveling third class is unaware of this.

Do Kaliaan 1968 Ganga and Jamuna aka `Do Kaliaan', the twins played by child actress Neetu Singh want to pray at Tirupati to reunite their estranged parents. Conniving Manorama wants to have them killed instead so she gets her henchmen to accompany them. A metre gauge train is shown leaving Krishnarajpuram followed by excellent shot of a YP hauled train on a bridge. Finally the YP hauled train is shown arriving at a crowded Tirupati East station where there is a steam hauled train ready to leave in opposite direction.

Dost 1974 At the outset of the film, Maanav played by Dharmendra is returning to the Simla to re-unite with his guardian who is a priest at the local church. He is thinking about the song that the father used to sing to give him words of encouragement and wisdom. Gaadi bula rahi hai goes on while the train negotiates the winding slopes and goes through tunnels. The movie is in colour and a shining KC 520 locomotive hauls the train in old KSR livery. The only letdown is the credits that run on top of what is first class photography. At the end of the song, Dharmendra gets off at Taradevi station. The song repeats again when the father is killed and Dharmendra is reminiscing about him. Later in the film, when Dharmendra goes looking for a job in the city and is unsuccessful, one evening while he is returning home, a WP hauled passenger train passes in the background. Interesting to note is the Rajdhani livery on the first coach of the train.

Do Ustaad 1959 (B/W) A boy is running from police at the beginning of the film and is chased through yards.

There is a simmering WG, a broad gauge tank locomotive shunting in the yards and a Cowan Sheldon crane seen in the chase. In the later part of the film, the boy now grown up and played by Raj Kapoor saves a woman who is walking on the tracks to commit suicide. The train here however appears to be a stock shot of a North American train and is shown running almost too fast to creates the urgency in the scene.

Ek Chadar Maili Si 1986 Kulbhusan Kharbanda is a tonga driver at a rural station in Punjab and ferries passengers back and forth to the village. In the beginning, a WL 15049 in Jallundhar shed livery is seen arriving at the station. Following the arrival of the train there is a commotion at the station, caused mostly by the tongawallahs in their bid to get more passengers.

Ek Musphir Ek Hasina 1962 (B/W) Lt. Ajai Mehra, who has lost his memory fighting in Kashmir in 1947, finds a tailoring mark of a Bombay tailor on his shirt and travels to Bombay by train to find his root. A short clip of an unidentified BESA class Central Railway locomotive hauling old wooden carriages follows with a view of Victoria Terminus to mark his arrival at Bombay.

Gadar 200 1 This film is set during the Indo-Pakistan partition era and has all the rhetoric and propaganda that is usually associated with films on this subject. In the end of the film, there is a rather long and stretched out sequence depicting the daring escape of the protagonist and his heroine from Pakistan aboard a goods train. Unfortunately, the only working broad gauge locomotive they could find in the 21st Century to pull this train was a WP class No. 7015; which is such a hallmark postwar Indian locomotive. Nonetheless it was used, as it was readily available after it had been recently restored. The film is shot around Bikaner area and the as you can see in the film, the bullet nose of the engine was damaged during the shooting due to blatant disregard on this national heritage by the filmmakers.

Gandhi 1982 (Hindi/English) Gandhi comes back to India from South Africa sets out for a soul-searching trip across the sub-continent with his wife and followers in tow. What could be a better way to discover the country than a train? This epic journey is very well done by Richard Attenborough who got an authentic BESA 4-6-0 metre gauge engine and matching wooden carriages all done in BBCIR colours to shoot this part and the result is history.

Ghulami 1985 In feudal Rajasthan, the differences between the rich and the poor are deep-seated. Dharmendra the protagonist in this film takes up the cause of the poor. There are several evocative scenes of YP locomotives including No. 2225 hauling passenger/mixed trains going through arid areas of Bikaner - Fatehpur Shekhawati region in the early part of the film. Song Mere pee ko pawan is very well done.

Guru 2007 Gurukant Desai played by Abhishek Bachchan leaves his native village in Gujrat to find his fortune in Bombay and there is a train on a wayside station hauled by WP 7161. In an earlier scene his find his would be wife who is running away from home in a train hauled by the same locomotive.

Heeralal Pannalal 1978 In the climax scene, the metre gauge train which the multiple stars of this film are travelling from Goa catches fire, derails (A La Silver Streak), crashes through the terminus and stops in front of a Ganapati Shrine. The locomotive shown at this stage is a broad gauge CWD.

Hum Rahi 1974 When a boy and a girl meet while they are on their way to the big city in search of a job, they constantly argue and clash on the station platform, foot over bridge and inside the first class coupe. Randhir Kapoor sings Chup chup chup kyun baithi ho to tease Tanuja and there is a silhouette shot of a WP hauled train.

Jab Jab Phool Khile 1965 A houseboat owner in Kashmir falls in love with a visiting tourist and follows her to the big city. Unable to compromise with their different origins, the hero Shashi Kapoor is leaving for Pathankot at the end of the film when Nanda realizes where her heart belongs and comes looking for him at the station. Another train is shown leaving hauled by H class No. 24304. The signals are MACL. The ending is a happy one after the hero agrees to take the heroine back after her pleadings and pulls her aboard the moving train. Background song is Yaad sada rakhna yeh kahani.

Jab Pyar Kisi Se Hota Hai 1961 (B/W) To prove that his love is true, Dev Anand jumps from the running train only to land on top of a car where he croons the title song while Asha Parekh stands at the door of the Up Darjeeling Mail. At the end of the trip they arrive at what is shown to be `Neelgaon' but appears to be Kurseong.

Jab Yaad Kisi ki Aati Hai 1967 Dharmendra is an assistant/fireman on a narrow gauge branch line which is actually the famous Neral - Matheran railway and the locomotive used here is MLR 739. There are other still shots of a narrow gauge unidentified but presumably Central Railway locomotive in close up shots when the driver and Dharmendra are in conversation. In the early part of the film, there is plentiful footage of this MLR locomotive while it was still working.

Jagriti 1954 (B/W) Ajay, a village truant is sent to a boarding school in the city where he meets the reformist teacher who transforms his life and makes him feel responsible for his actions. The journey from the village to the city is depicted by a distant shot of a train at speed. Later when the teacher, played by Abhi Bhattacharya, takes his students on a cross-country tour by rail, the song `Aao bacchon tumhen dikhayen' has many close and distant shots of pre-war locomotives on broad and narrow gauge.

Jalsaghar 1958 (B/W Bengali) This film was also released as `The Music Room' outside India. Another masterpiece by Satyajit Ray who I think must also be a railway fan. No-one else could use the sound of a distant loco whistle so effectively to indicate arrival or departure of a character, notably in the `Apu trilogy' and `The Music Room' (Contributed by Geoff Todd).

Jawab 1942 (B/W) This vintage film has Kanan Devi singing "Toofan Mail" in the background whilst a Bengal Nagpur Railway tank locomotive is shown hauling the Mail train.

Julie 1975 This is a story of an Anglo Indian family living at Shoranur. The father played by Om Prakash is a goods driver while Julie is the eldest daughter who falls in love with a Hindu boy who is visiting his family. There are several scenes depicting AWC, HPS WG & WP class at Shoranur station, yard, roundhouse etc. In a funny scene, a local shopkeeper misbehaves with Julie and is promptly slapped back by her. At this time, a locomotive is showing blowing down to depict the cooling off of the shopkeeper's pent-up feelings.

Kala Bazaar 1960 Dev Anand the hero is sitting on the lower berth in a First Class coupe and on the bunk above him is her heartthrob Waheeda Rehman. But her mom is also present on the lower berth across Dev. He sings Upar wala jaan kar bhi anjaan hai, Apni to har aah ek toofan hai, which is bhajan for the mother and a love plea for the daughter. There are several musical (not real) steam whistles in the song.

Kati Patang 1970 Madhu's marriage is arranged against her wishes and she decides to run away after her father dies from the shock of learning it. Asha Parekh boards a train where she meets her childhood friend who is now widowed. During the night the train meets an accident. These are stock shots of a foreign train as is evident from the white livery of the train. The scene of the train crashing is done with models.

Kim 1950/1984 This Rudyard Kipling's story has been made into a feature film as well as television film. Much of the location filming is in India and it includes several scenes of trains and stations on metre and narrow gauge trains (Contributed by Warren Miller).

Kitaab 1977 Gulzar is one of the producer director (amidst other talents) whose films nearly always have trains, stations etc. and they are depicted as real as they can get. This film is about a young boy who lives in the city with his sister and brother-in-law. Tired of the constant fighting between the husband and wife, he decides to run away from their home back to his mother who lives in the village. Without any money, he boards a train but when the ticket examiner chases him out, he takes the refuge of the tender of the WG locomotive hauling the train. The driver who catches him takes pity on him agrees to take him to his destination. The remaining movie is about the boy's adventures on the WG 8399/8585 of Kalyan shed, stations etc. until he is reunited with his mother in the end. There are very few directorial errors if any and the train sequences are shot very realistically. While the driver Rashid sings Dhanno ki aankhon mein in praise of his sweetheart, his assistant and fireman Raghu takes over the full control of the engine, watching signals etc. There is a flat wagon just behind the engine carrying a bonnet style bus on it. Another song `Janam se banjara hoon bandhu' towards the end of the film features Second Class Sitting interiors and a brief glimpse of a WG locomotive. Dr. Sriram Lagoo playing a beggar sings on the train with the boy accompanying him.

Love in Simla 1960 (B/W) Joy Mukerjee is coming to Simla to meet his would-be bride and is reminiscing her with the song Dil tham chale in the Kalka - Simla train hauled by a ZF tank engine. At the end of the film, as he returns back with the bride, the song repeats. Barog station can be seen here.

Main Hoon Na 2004 It features Shah Rukh Khan arriving at Darjeeling with a B class glimpsed though the steam, but the scene is so brief you feel they needn't have bothered! (Contributed by Warren Miller)

Manthan 1976 On the posters of the film I have seen Girish Karnad, the protagonist in the film getting off a steam hauled metre gauge train. More details invited.

Mera Naam Joker 1970 The joker Raju as a child goes to an Ooty boarding school. While most children are boarders and leave for home during summer holidays, Raju gets left behind as he is a local. There are excellent scenes in the early part of the film of this school train leaving Ooty and arriving back with noisy singing kids. You can also see the children waving the English St. George's flag.

Mere Apne 1971 Another Gulzar film. In the beginning of the film, Anandi played by Meena Kumari is being brought to the city to do the housework by a person who claims to be her relative. A WP hauled train at dusk depicts this while the credits roll in between.

Mere Humsafar 1970 A boy and a girl began the journey as companions from their humble village to Bombay in search for their fortune. They start off in the back of a truck carrying produce which brings them to the station. Song is Mere humsafar mere humsafar. They get inside a four-wheeler covered wagon train hauled by a WG locomotive and have several railway adventures before the boy get left behind when he gets off to fetch water for the girl. AWD 12706 is also seen hauling a goods train.

Mere Huzoor 1968 Jeetendra meets his soul mate Mala Sinha in a train. The lady is wearing a veil and the poet pleads her to remove it with a song Rukh se zara naqab hata lo mere huzoor. You can also see beautiful wooden first class coach interiors in this song.

Miss Frontier Mail 1936 This film has lot of railway action including an accident scene shot quite convincingly with miniatures considering that it was done in the 1930s! Nadia Hunterwali (Mary Ann Evans) indulges in extensive fist-fights, set to heavy sound effects, and a famous battle alongside her hero Sundar played by Mansoor atop a moving train. She is fighting to clear the name of her father who is accused of murder and to achieve this she hits a lot of guys in a circus-like way, fights, runs like a hurricane and gets the nickname "Miss Frontier Mail", the fastest train in India of this time.

Neel Kamal 1968 Waheeda Rehman plays the lead female character that suffers from sleepwalking. In the beginning of the film, she is in a waiting room with a group when she wanders off into the path of the incoming train. At the helm of the train is a WP pacific but things are brought under control by the Hero Manoj Kumar before a mishap take place.

Nilgiri Express 1969 (Tamil) In this Tamil movie with probably Jaishankar in the lead, the train depicted was hauled by WP engine (contributed by Santosh).

Northwest Frontier 1959 (released as Flame Over India in USA) Set in north-western India at the beginning of 20th century, this story is about desperate tribal Muslim rebels who are out to kill the last scion of the Hindu ruler. Accompanying the prince is his governess Catherine Wyatt played by Lauren Bacall. Kenneth More is a British officer who must aid the escape of a prince from a fort besieged by the rebels. This he does by means of a decrepit steam train, with a handful of western passengers on board amongst who is a half-bred journalist who sympathizes with the rebels. This is fast over the edge of the seat suspense action by the minute without any use of high-tech stuff. The main railway tracks depicted are 2'6" but you see an occasional glimpse of metre gauge and broad gauge too. There is a station shown called Bhiwandipura that is **probably** fictitious. In beginning of the film, the refugee train out of the fort is hauled by an O class 4-4-0 engine. The main engine however is a 0-6-0 yard switcher that has no number plates but carries an `Empress of India' plate and is fondly referred as Victoria! The broad gauge yard switcher is featured in the entire movie as hauling the train to take the prince to safety from rebels (Contributed by Walter Haan).

Pachai Vilakku 1964 (Tamil) The story revolved round an engine driver played by Sivaji Ganesan. Sri Nagesh played the comedian fireman. It featured a few engines from Basin Bridge loco shed at Madras (Contributed by Swamy Nathan).

Pakeezah 1971 Meena Kumari who plays a Nautch Girl in the film gets her dress entangled in the points and faints on the track at the sight of a steam engine approaching. She is rescued and the hero Raj Kumar carries her to his first class compartment (old Wooden stock), and falls in love with her feet and leaves her a note, Yeh paun bahut sundar hain, zameen pe mat rakhiega maile ho jayenge. She later does a mujra Chalte chalte yunhi koi mil gaya tha which has several wailing whistles of a steam engine in the night. Whenever Pakeezah hears the whistle from her house she reminisces her admirer.

Parineeta 2005 The song scene is featuring the Darjeeling Himalayan Railway is excellent. The train is shown running through the `Terai' section and then arriving at Sukna which is masquerading as Darjeeling, but it's such a great song that errors like that are easily forgiven (Contributed by Warren Miller).

Pather Panchali 1955 (B/W) In this film, the first in the Apu trilogy, there is a railway line not far from the village, and there are at least a couple of scenes where a train is seen in the distance across the fields while the kids Apu and Durga are playing or running. (Contributed by Satish Pai).

Pavitra Papi 1970 Parikshit Sahni plays the lead and is seen walking absent mindedly along the track after losing his job in the early part of the film when a passenger hauled by WP class No. 7602 comes on the same line and he is saved by a passerby just in nick of time. Later when his sweetheart Tanuja is married elsewhere, he blesses her with the song Teri dunia se hoke majboor chala and he sees her and the bridegroom off to the station.

Professor 1962 Shammi Kapoor disguises as an old man to find the job of a tuitor but finds it more rewarding when he falls in with Kalpana who is the student. Song Main chali main chali is partially shot on the Darjeeling train. There is more steam footage later when Professor accompanies the Madam and his sweetheart to Bombay and WP hauled trains are shown to depict each trip.

Pudhu Kavithai 1982 (Tamil) Meaning "New poetry", this is one of earlier hits of Rajnikanth. The climax sequence is picturised on a metre gauge steam passenger. As per the story it is the Banglore - Mysore line, but there was very little greenery in the scenes and looked more like the Madurai - Teni route. The very last frame where the hero and heroine unite on a small tidy station, with the train moving away in the background, is simply superb. The coaches are all old unreserved second class sitting stock, and the loco looked like a YP. There is another frame in this sequence shot from the hilltop with the train down at a distance. Overall the train sequence looked very authentic and nicely captured (Contributed by N Manohar).

Pyasaa 1957 (B/W) Vijay played by Guru Dutt is an idealistic poet who is unable to find a job despite a university degree. His college sweetheart Mala Sinha ditches him for a wealthy publisher and his brothers turn him out of the house. He was sleeping on a bench on the sidewalk and as he tries to get some water out of a dry tap to quench his thirst, Mala Sinha drives by and spots him. At this moment a Calcutta Port Trust steam train with a tank engine comes between their view and she leaves. In the second half of the film, Vijay is totally disillusioned with everything and tries to commit suicide under a fast moving train. He leaves his coat with a shivering beggar who realizes what he is up to and follows him on to the track. The beggar is caught in a switch and gets killed inadvertently but since he is wearing the coat of the poet, everyone thinks the poet died. This night scene with extensive use of backlighting and long shadows is shot very well.

Raincoat 2004 There is a scene in the beginning where the hero Ajay Devgan takes a steam hauled train purportedly from Bhagalpur to Calcutta. Not sure if this was achieved by just using stock footage or if steam locomotive was organised for this shoot (Contributed by Bharat S Rao).

Rang De Basanti 2006 Features one of the recently revived WP 7161 in sepia toned scenes in which an English filmmaker is shown as contemplating her film on Indian freedom fighters.

Ram aur Shyam 1967 Twins separate when they are young, one grows rich and the other poor and they are mixed up as adults played by Dilip Kumar. After Shyam has been living at Ram's house for some time, the evil brother in law Pran exposes him at birthday party. Shyam is accused of killing Ram with the intent of grabbing his wealth and jailed. He escapes from the jail, hops on a broad gauge train at a station, which soon turns into a metre gauge train and after hanging on the side for a while, finally he jumps off from a viaduct to his freedom.

Ram Teri Ganga Maili 1985 The female lead Ganga played by Mandakini begins her epic journey from the mountains to Calcutta just like the river Ganges. With her is her newborn child and when she gets off the train to give him some water, the train leaves without her. There is night scene of a WG hauled train with MACL signaling and a deserted platform at night.

Sadma 1983 This remake of a Tamil film is about a young woman who is left with the sense of a five year old after a road accident. She lands into a brothel in Madras from where she is rescued by an Ooty schoolteacher played by Kamal Hassan. He brings her home and nurses her back to normal. This poignant film has several scenes of the Nilgiri Mountain Railway in the Conoor area and a particularly memorable one is at the end as the Sridevi leaves by train on a very rainy afternoon. Song Ae zindagi gale laga le is good.

Salaam Bombay 1988 In the early part of the film the young boy Krishna who plays lead is seen arriving at Bombay (what appears to be Sealdah but could be someplace else too) by a WG hauled train.

Sambandh 1969 Deb Mukherjee sings the hit song Chal akela chal akela chala akela, tera mela peeche chuta rahee chal akela" in a jeep whilst DHR train keeps the pace. In the same film Deb Mukherjee is travelling with his ailing mother when the WP blows a whistle and the mother breathes her last in the train.

Shatranj 1969 Starring Waheeda Rehman and Rajendra Kumar. Both of them are Indian spies. The railway scenes were shot in Goa. I think the hero tries to blow up the villain's train fully aware that his father is on the same train.

Shola Aur Shabnam 1961 (B/W) The story is about childhood love of a boy and girl whose parents work for the railway at Mysore and they spend their childhood playing on the station, yards etc. There is lots of metre gauge action in the early part of the film until the girl's father is transferred elsewhere and the two friends get estranged.

Sholay 1975 This Indianised version of a western flick in the mid seventies changed the equations of Indian

Cinema forever. Jai and Veeru are two small time thieves who are roped by an Inspector who sees them capable of overturning the empire of dreaded dacoit Gabbar Singh. There are several railway sequences in the film. Two of these show the inspector and a jailor arriving at a rural station aboard a YP hauled train. The most famous one of course is of the dacoits trying to hijack a goods train hauled by H/ 4 class No. 026472. Jai and Veeru are prisoners of inspector Sanjeev Kumar and after he agrees to let them help him, Jai and inspector take charge of the fighting from the guard's van while Veeru mans the engine and runs its through the barrier laid on the rails by dacoits. There is also the talkative tonga driver Basanti played by Hema Malini. Veeru charms her by singing Koi hasina jab rooth jaati hai while YP hauled passenger of South Central Railway runs past in the background.

Shor 1972 Nanda is killed by a Western Railway's AWD class locomotive hauled goods train in the early part of film while she is trying to save her son who has wandered on to the tracks. Very poorly shot sequence that lay little emphasis on authenticity and more on blood and gore. The train in the scene hardly looks to be moving and one cannot fathom why the driver of the train cannot see the boy on a very straight and level track in the siding. Later in the film the father of the boy Manoj Kumar is trying to arrange funds for his boy's treatment and visits his parents in the village to ask for a loan. Scenes of a WP hauled train at speed depict this trip to the village and back to the city.

Sonar Kella 1974 (Bengali) Sonar Kella meaning `The Golden Fortress', is a film by Satyajit Ray which starred Soumitra Chatterji. This film is imprinted on my memory because of its railway journey and especially for its location shots on the metre gauge branch from Jodhpur to Pokaran, before it was extended to Jaisalmer. The travellers in the film completed their journeys by camel (Contributed by Geoff Todd).

Teesari Kasam 1964(B/W) Hiraman is a poor bullock cart driver falls in love with a theatre actress whom he has been assigned to take to the village fair. The inevitable happens and Heerabai played by Waheeda Rehman has to leave at the end when Raj Kapoor comes to see her off at Aswali station desperately racing his cart. Central Railway's WG 8751 brings the train into the station and leaves after a short stop.

Teesari Manzil 1966 This film has all the masala of Indian Cinema. There is journey to Mussoorie by train, boy meets girl, love blossoms, romance, misunderstanding, villain and finally reunion. The film starts from a scene at New Delhi station ticket window. A WP and a WG (with a bicycle on the buffer beam) on platform with Ajmeri gate bridge in background. After some comic relief during the day journey, the arrival at Dehradun station can be seen. After the bad guy dies, and to show the couple's reunion and return to Delhi there is a shot of WG locomotive hauled train at the end that quickly turns into a Dehradun CWD 12507 hauling wooden non-bogie stock. You can also see the interiors of a spacious wooden first class carriage.

Tuj Maji Ranee 1970s (Marathi Comedy) This film has Amol Palekar and Jayshree.T. in the lead. In a funny situation the couple starts planning for their new home, which leads to an argument about the paint scheme. Jayshree T. being on the losing end threatens suicide. So she sleeps on the tracks never expecting the train to appear. The train was WP hauled and the location was Kolhapur.

The Burning Train 1980 Vinod Khanna and Dharmendra are childhood friend and Vinod dreams of making the fastest train in India. As children and young adults they sing, play and frolic around train and the Rail Transport Museum (now NRM) with their girl friends. There are sights of steam in the yard and the PSMT working in the rail museum in its original livery.

The Jewel in the Crown 1984 (TV mini series) Throughout the series, especially in the later part there are many small scenes on stations sometimes depicting steam when someone is shown arriving or departing. Toward the end, when the entourage is returning from Mirat Cantt., there is an extended scene at the station followed by the train on the run whose motive power turns from MAWD to YG. The insurgents looking for Ahmed Kasim stop the train by tying a cow to the rails.

The Train 1970 Nanda plays a conwoman who is forced by her stepbrother to regularly rob innocent passengers on trains out of Bombay VT. Rajesh Khanna is the police inspector assigned to catch her. There is plenty of electric and steam action, chasing train by road, shots of stations and landscape of the ghat section. You can see how Nasik Road and Igatpuri stations looked three decades ago. There are WPs and WGs all around and the switchover from electric to steam at Igatpuri. In the climax dhishum-dhishum scene, there is a WP 7197 rolling by as the hero and the villain try to get each other.

Train to Pakistan 1998 This film is about the dreadful time of India Pakistan partition and is based on a novel by Kushwant Singh by the same name. It includes numerous steam scenes (mostly long shots of trains on bridges etc) and the finale is an attempt to attack a refugee train. The railways scenes are well done, but are a mix on broad and metre gauge settings. The actual train seen is metre gauge (the locomotive is a YG class I think), but some of the scenes in which an ambush of a train to Pakistan is being set are clearly at a location with broad gauge track. The editing is clever enough to ensure that the viewer would not really notice this. The film closes with a surprising effective long distance model shot of a (model) train steaming away to the horizon.

Usne Kaha Tha 1960 (B/W) Nandu and Kamli love each other but are unable to marry due to quirks of fate.

Nandu joins the army and Kamli is the wife of the officer under whom Nandu will be serving. When the platoon is leaving for the war, the scene at Ambala Cantt. Station depicts steam locomotives as well as the following song `Jaane waale siphai se pucho' is picturised aboard a train. There are two other scenes depicting steam train in the film earlier when Kamli's family leaves Nandu's town when they are young and later when Nandu leaves to join the army.

Vidhaata 1982 The movie is about two characters that start off as locomotive driver and fireman but go on to go very different ways. Film starts with both arguing whether fate is more powerful that the will of a man. They sing Haathon ki chand lakiron ka aboard the WG hauling goods. Funnily enough, the song begins and ends with metre gauge YG locomotive hauling tank wagons! There are other scenes depicting steam and notable amongst them is when the prematurely born grandson of the fireman is carried to the hospital aboard the cab of WG 8892 with the firebox providing the warmth.

Waqt 1965 This one is about a family separating due to sheer misfortune and meeting again after many years by an equally interesting quirk of fate. After the separation the patriarch of the family Balraj Sahni is implicated in a murder and gets a life term. After coming out of the prison he starts looking for his family. A WP hauled train shows this journey to Delhi in his search for family. A few moments later, the youngest son who lives with the mother is shown moving to Bombay in search of a job and there is a rare scene of WP hauled Bombay Deluxe arriving at Bombay Central. You can also see old wooden first class, chair car, and third class coaches. Watch out for the line of taxis just outside the station even in those days..

Woh Kaun Thi? 1964 (B/W) Sadhna who is suspected to be a ghost by her husband Manoj Kumar is asked to leave home. Dejected, she boards a train and a scene of a SPS 4-4-0 locomotive hauled passenger train follows.

Yaadon Ki Zanzeer 1984 Two brothers are separated at childhood and one becomes a gangster while the other is a police officer. Sunil Dutt is chasing an enemy on the train that his police officer brother Shashi Kapoor is escorting. This is a YD locomotive hauled train in the Braganza ghats near Castle Rock. Also seen is also a metre gauge SLR with windows at the guard's end for him to look back without craning his neck outside. There is wonderful scenery all around and at the end of the sequence, Dudhsagar falls are in view. Though you might want to chuckle at the scene when Sunil Dutt chases the moving train on foot while it negotiates the ghat section.

Yatra 1986-7 (TV Series) This television series was created by Shyam Benegal, which had Om Puri in lead and for background commentary. Nearly all episodes had plenty of steam footage on broad and metre gauge all over India.

Zamaane Ko Dikhana Hai 1981 The story is based in Ooty. Padmini Kolhapure is a poor girl who pretends to be rich to win over lover boy Rishi Kapoor. When the secret is revealed, she tries to run away from him, sitting on top of the lead carriage of the down train. The boy follows her and serenades her back with Hoga tumse pyaraa kaun he kanchi on top of the train before it reaches Mettupalayam.

Ziddi 1964 Joy Mukherji is daydreaming about his sweetheart in a Nilgiri Railway coach while a thief tries to run off with his suitcase. The thief jumps off the train and the hero gives him a chase.

QUEEN OF HILLS: MUSSOORIE

Popularly known as the Queen of Hills, this charming hill station, 34 kms from Dehradun is situated at an altitude of 2003 mts in the Garhwal hills. above sea-level. Mussoorie is one the beautiful hill stations in India and the most frequently visited. It provides excellent respite to people who want relief from the hot sultry conditions of the plains, especially since it is close enough to the capital to make just weekend trip. Also, major Hindu pilgrimage sites like Kedarnath, Badrinath, Gangotri, Yamunotri, Haridwar, Rishikesh are not far from this place.

During summer vacation, all sorts of people visit this lovely hill station. If you wants to know what's latest in fashion world, visit Mall Road after the sun sets. In the same spot, you can find dusky beauty wearing traditional sari with large bindi on her forehead. On the other side of Road, you will be mesmerized by the typical Punjabi beauty wearing skin-hugging jeans with curvaceous top accentuated by bouncy hair. Don't look at your clothes, otherwise it will give you a inferiority complex. Don't feel discouraged, every human being has his/her own style statement. Gandhiji used to wear minimum clothes, yet he is regarded as the greatest man of last century. Good clothes gives you ephemeral happiness, and good soul gives you eternal peace. It is up to you what is on your priority list.

Landour is situated in upper Mussoorie. An engraved arch was put up by the municipality at the beginning of the Landour stretch claiming that while Mussoorie is the Queen of Hills, Landour is the tiara of the Queen. The famous Woodstock school is situated here and is a landmark.

The area has long winding roads that are lined on one side by majestic deodar and pine groves. Here the air is nippier compared to the lower hill, and cleaner too as it is far away from shops and vehicular traffic. Char Dukan in Landour is a cluster of shops and shacks that sell tea and light snacks.

There are a few other interesting places worth visiting, such as the St. Paul's church and Landour Language School that offers courses in Hindi for foreign tourists. Landour also has a cemetery that houses the graves of soldiers stationed in Mussoorie during the rule of the British. Visit the local market that sells woolens, ceramic crockery, and an array of antiques. Landour has beautiful cottages from the British-era. Some of these still retain their original British architecture. Many cottages are owned by celebrities, including NDTV's Prannoy Roy.

In 1820, Captain Young of the British army was influenced by the beauty of this place and made it his residence. The name, Mussoorie is derived from plants of 'Mussoorie' which were found in abundance here. After its discovery, this hill station gradually developed as a centre of education, business, tourism and beauty.

MUSSOORIE (PLACES TO SEE)

Gun Hill

Enjoy a Ropeway ride to the second highest peak of Mussoorie. It can also be negotiated by bridles path which forks-off from Mall Road near Kutchery and to reach takes about twenty minutes. The Ropeway distance is only 400 mtrs. And the sheer thrill of the ride is memorable. Gun Hill offers a beautiful panoramic view of the Himalayan ranges namely Bunderpunch, Srikantha, Pithwara and Gangotri group etc. and a bird's eye view of Mussoorie town and Doon Valley. During pre-independence days a gun mounted on this top used to be fired heralding mid-day to enable people to adjust their watches and hence this name.

Municipal Garden

A picnic spot having a beautiful garden and an artificial mini lake with boating facilities. It is located at a distance of 4kms by cycle rickshaw, pony or by car and only 2 kms on foot via Waverly Convent Road.

Childer's Lodge

Highest Peak of Mussoorie near Lal Tibba. It is about 5 kms from the Tourist Office and one can go on horse back or on foot. Snow view from this spot is exhilarating.

Camel's Back Road

It starts from Kulri Bazar near Rink Hall and ends at Library Bazar covering a total distance of about 3 kms. The main charm of this froad is horse riding and wlking. Sunset view of the Himalayas is superb. Camel's Rock with a life like resemblace can be seen from the spot near Mussoorie Public school.

Jharipani Fall

8.5 kms from Mussoorie on Mussoorie- Jharipani Road. Visitors can go by bus or by car upto 7 kms to Jharipani from where the fall is 1.5 kms, on foot.

Bhatta Fall

7 kms from Mussoorie on Mussoorie-Dehradun road. Access by car or bus upto Balta village from where the fall is 3kms by car or foot. An ideal spot for bathing anf picnics.

Kempty Fall

15 kms from Mussoorie on the Yamunotri Road having an altitude of 4500 ft. It has the distinction of being the biggest and prettiest waterfall located in a beautiful valley and is surrounded by high mountains. Bath at the foot of the falls is refresshing and enjoyabled for children and adults alike.

Nag Devta Temple

An ancient temple situated on Cart Mackenjie Road and is about 6 kms from Mussoorie. Vehicles can go right upto the spot. It Provies a charming view of Doon Valley as well as of Mussoorie.

Mussoorie Lake

A newly developed picnic spot, situated on Mussoorie-Dehradun road and is about 6 kms from Mussoorie. It is a delightful spot. Pedal boats are availble. It commands an enchanting view of Doon Valley and nearby villages.

Van Chetna Kendra

At a distance of about 2 kms on Tehri bye pass road, this place is developed as a picnic spot and has a park surrounded with pine forest and flowering shrubs, and is approachable by foot or taxi/car. The main attraction is the wildilife of the park like Ghurar, Kanankar, Himalayan Peacock, Monal etc.

Sir George Everest House

6 kms The Park Estate of sir George Everest, First Surveyor General of India, Who had his offce and residence here, is approachable by road. The highest peak in the world, Mount Everest, is named after him.

Jwalaji Temple (Benog Hill) 9 kms 6to the west of Mussoorie and at an altitude of 2104 mtrs. Is the Jwalaji Temple. It is situated on the top of the Benog Hill and has an idol of Mata Durga in it. The temple is surrounded by thick forests and offers a panoramic view of the Himalayan peaks, Doon valley and Yamuna valley.

Clous End

The bungalow built in 1838 by a British Major was one of the First Four buildings of Mussoorie. The bungalow has since then been converted into a hotel called Clouds End, and is situated at the extreme west of Mussoorie Hill, 8 kms from Library. The resort is surrounded by thick forest, offers a wide variety of flora and fauna besides a panoramic view of snow clad Himalayas, and Yamuna river. The most ideally suited resort for fireigners and honeymoon couples.

MUSSOORIE (INSTITUTION)

Rich in history and beauty, Mussoorie has given birth to many institutions that are known virtually all over the country. Since 1959, the Lal Bahadur Shastri National Academy of Administration has been training and molding batch after batch of raw probationers into the country's finest bureaucrats, foreign service officers, and police officers. the Academy, situated at Charleville, continues to train officers for the Indian Administrative Service and the Indian Police Service. A fire broke out in the Academy some years ago and destroyed, among other buildings and papers, its precious library rated amongst the best in the country. While many of the books destroyed in the fire are difficult to replace, a new beginning has already been made by acquiring a fine collection of books.

While the Academy belongs to the post-Independence period, most of Mussoorie's institutions date back more than a century. The Waverley Convent, a school for girls, was established in 1845 and has commemorated 150 years of distinguished existence. While some of its buildings were destroyed in an earthquake in the early years of this century, then by a fire, and then again in the recent earthquake, Waverley still retains much of the old-world architectural charm. The cable cars swing between the Hall and Gun Hill more than 100 times a day.

MUSSOORIE (EXCURSION)

Naga Tibba

About 55km, an ideal spot for trekking. Naga Tibba is the highest peak around Mussoorie at 10,000 feet and is covered by thick forests.

Dhanolti

On Mussoorie-Tehri Road 25km away, it has deodhar forests and mountainscapes.

Surkhanda Devi

Surkhanda Devi Temple at 10,000 feet, 35 km down the Mussoorie - Tehri road. Perched on a peak, the temple demands a stiff two-km climb form devotees. The temple, goes the legend, was built on the site where the head of Shiva's consort (Shiva is the destroyer in the Hindu trinity) fell after it was chopped off to stop Shiva's terrifying dance of death that was shaking the universe to its very core.

Lakha Mandal

80 km away on the Mussoorie-Yamunotri Road. Linked with the Mahabharata with idols of archaeological importance.

MUSSOORIE (WHEN TO VISIT)

Mussoorie is a hill station which has pleasant climate around the year. It is a very cool place with greenery at its full bloom during September to November. The best seasons to visit Mussoorie is between April to June and again during September to November. When the plains of North India experience heat waves, Mussoorie provides a welcome break. September - November is spring time here. During this season Himalayas are clearly visible. It is better to avoid monsoons as the roads to Mussoorie are in bad shape. Same thing applies for the winter when roads are blocked due to snowfall

Mussoorie (Travel Information)

There are regular flights from Delhi to Doon Valley (Jolly Grant). From the Jolly Grant airport, taxis and buses ply to Dehradun, from where they go up to Mussoorie (2¼ hours, 60 km). The overnight Mussoorie Express links Delhi to Dehradun, the railhead for Mussoorie.

Delhi to Mussoorie is 290 km by road. Dehradun to Mussoorie is 35 km. There are direct buses from Delhi to

Mussoorie, along with private taxis. Buses ply every half hour from Dehradun to Mussoorie. Private taxis and shared taxis are favored by a majority of visitors.

Mussoorie - Local Transport

Hand pulled rickshaws, taxis and cars are not allowed on the Mall, but can move in other motorable parts of Mussoorie.

Mussoorie (Accommodation)

Mussoorie has more than a hundred hotels to choose.

Mussoorie (What to Wear)

In summer, light woolens are advisable while heavy woolens are a necessity during winter.

The summer season extends from April to June. The winter season is from September to December.

Area : 65 sq km

Altitude : 2005.5 m

Temperature in Summer : 31.2°C(max);7.2°C(min)

Temperature in Winter : 7.2°C(max);1.1°C(min)

Languages : Hindi and English

Best Time to Visit : April-June and September-October

FASHION IN THE BACKDROP OF LAKES

What can be a best way to flaunt your latest design clothes in the lap of nature, amidst pleasing sounds of exotic birds. Honeymoon in Nainital, Uttaranchal can be an experience you would cherish for days to come. Let the romance begin in this beautiful hill station in Uttaranchal, 1938 meters above the sea level. A popular summer retreat of India, Nainital has it all - magic mountains, lovely lakes, green meadows, pretty valleys - the first trip together can never get any better than this! You can plan for your Honeymoon in Nainital, Uttaranchal and it will be an affair to remember, we bet.

Natural beauty, charming scenic spots and a cool weather has made Nainital one of the most sough-after places for Honeymoon Destinations in Asia. You can stroll along quaint pathways, walk into the sunset with that dearest person, sail across the placid lakes, open your eyes to the first rays of the sun filtering through snow-capped peaks or simply check out what's in store at the Mall as part of your Honeymoon in Nainital, Uttaranchal.

Fast Facts

Nainital is also popularly known as the district of lakes. It is 34 km away from Kathgodam, the gateway of Kumaon and the terminus of North Eastern Railway. It is 304 km away from Delhi and 388 km from Lucknow.

What to Explore

The cluster of great lakes including Naini Lake, Bhimtal Lake and Nakuchia Lake has made Nainital a favorite with the trekkers and travelers. Naini Lake is regarded as the focal point of Nainital. The Northern point of the lake is called as Mallital and the Southern part as Tallital. Nakuchia Tal is another lake which deserves a visit for Honeymoon Vacations in Nainital, Uttaranchal. Naini peak is the highest hill point around the city, which makes it the highest place in Nainital.

You can go for a boat ride on the Naini Lake on your Honeymoon in Nainital, Uttaranchal. Visit the Naina Devi Temple, Hanumangarhi, St.-John-in-the-Wilderness Church, Raj Bhawan, State Observatory and Kilbury. You can also plan for excursions to the Naina Peak, Dorothy Seat, Tiffin Top, Land's End or take a Cable Car to the Snow View to get that amazing sight of the snow-studded mountains.

Off the Beaten Path

You can plan for excursions to nearby Bhowali, Jeolikot, Ramgarh, Gohrakhal, Bhimtal, Sattal, Khurpatal, Naukuchiyatal, Corbett National Park, Almora, Ranikhet, Ramgarh and Mukteshwar to make the most of the moments. Or if you have that streak of adventure in you, you will have a great time with Nainital offering so much for horse riding, yachting, angling, hiking, trekking, rock climbing and mountain climbing.

Shop till you Drop

Shopping is a serious business in Nainital and even the most hardcore shopaholic who has perfected the art of shopping, would delight to the sheer volume and variety. Shop for woolens, candles, woodcraft and local handicraft items which make for perfect souvenirs and gift items. The main areas for shopping in Nainital are the Bhotia Bazaar, Main Market, The Mall, Mallital Bazaar and Tallital Bazaar.

With all these and more, Nainital has become one of the most wonderful Honeymoon Destinations World Wide. Plan for a tour now and get ready for an unforgettable experience for Honeymoon in Nainital, Uttaranchal.

UNMATCHABLE BEAUTY OF DARJEELING

Whatever has been written so far about the tea town of India- Darjeeling, one thing that truly touches your heart is the unadulterated beauty. There are no big malls here like the other hill stations, no brand coffee shops and moreover even the houses aren't the one with the lavish interiors. However what adds to its natural beauty are the beautiful mountain ranges, the land of the rising sun of India and the tea plantations.

A colourful town of the Indian state of West Bengal, it is nestled in the lap of North-eastern Himalayas. It has everything in it to charm the residents and tourists alike. The locals have painted their houses with the rainbow colours and every home was a pleasure to see on the way to Darjeeling. Fledged with tea gardens all across, it provides the splendiferous view to the natural ecstasy and relaxes all the bruised souls due to the fast paced life of the metro cities and start their life afresh. The fresh air and the innocent people give it a different perspective to view life through the lenses.

The moment you step down into Siliguri and take a bus or toy train, every breath of yours will be taken away by enchanting landscapes that keeps you tingling and thinking till the end. If one is boarding a train, the nearest station is Jalpaiguri which is 88kms from Darjeeling. It is well connected to all major cities in India and most of them have stoppages at this junction. One can hire a taxi from there or take it from Siliguri and it takes nearly 3 to 4 hours to reach the destination. You can even take a flight to the Deobgarh which is close to Siliguri and then hire a taxi for Darjeeling.

If you are not in a hurry to visit the place and want to enjoy every moment with the passing scenic beauty, boarding the beautiful yet slow 'toy train' is the right decision. It passes through the beautiful mountains making each moment memorable and it takes nearly six hours to reach by it. One can even hymn the beautiful song Kasto Mazza hai Lelaima from 'Parineeta' with their soulmate.

Darjeeling has an impact of Tibet, Nepal and China in its culture. There are different monasteries to visit like Bhutia Busty Monastry and Ghum Monastry. Besides, Tiger Hill is a must visit for all the morning lovers as it showcases the beautiful sunrise in India. You can enjoy it along with the small Darjeeling tea cups provided by the local vendors but to watch this amazing natural happening, one has to be lucky enough to have a clear sky day as most of the time it is interrupted by heavy dark clouds that burst into heavy downpour. Once you have seen it, I bet most of the non early wakers like me, won't regret it at all.

A bollywood freak can see the shooting destination of the successful movie, Main Hoon Na which was picturised in St. Joseph's College (School Dept.) which is located 3km north from downtown, Darjeeling. Another must watch is the Himalayan Mountaineering Institute which encourages mountaineering as a sport in India. It also houses a zoo which homes the state animal of Sikkim- Red Panda along with other animals and birds. You will surely fall in love with this beautiful yet naughty red animal. Besides, you are surely missing things if you don't visit the tea plantations and buying tea is a must. One of the most popular dishes of the hilly areas is momos, a steamed roll made of either vegetables or pork or beef.

Darjeeling can be visited throughout the year except the rainy season which sees heavy downpour from June start till August that sometimes keeps it disconnected from the rest of India as of landslides. Visiting Darjeeling at the end of December can be a boon to watch the colourful Darjeeling festival.

The city is as simple as its people. And yes you might like to settle down to this place after taking break from the domestic chores. The more you discover Darjeeling, no matter how many days you have thought of spending here, it won't be just enough. Who knows a little later, a poet takes a birth in you.

3

CURRENT TRENDS IN THE WORLD OF FASHION TOURISM

While many fashion designers around the world are looking for way sand means to survive in these difficult economic times as even high-end consumers tighten their purse strings and look for bargains, Malaysia's fashion designers have discovered the niche market of Islamic fashion to beat the dry economic season.

Japanese fashion made its first global impact in 1982 when a collective of 12 of the country's designers presented their lines at Paris' esteemed ready-to-wear fashion week. Characterized by asymmetrical patterns, geometric shapes, and monochromatic palettes (think black, black and more black), Japonaiserie, as it was dubbed, showed the world a futuristic vision of style that was as fresh as it was exotic. The groundbreaking group included Issey Miyake, Kenzo Takada, Yohji Yamamoto, Rei Kawakubo (mastermind behind Comme des Garçons) and Hanae Mori.

Despite the fact that many of these names are now living legends, consumers may relate more easily to their namesake beauty products (such as Kenzo's famous Flower eau de toilette or Miyake's signature L'eau d'Issey) or commercial collaborations (Yamamoto's successful partnership with Adidas is called Y-3) than their clothes. Tourists in Japan who are interested in fashion will surely enjoy visiting the showrooms of celebrated designers, almost always in the hip districts of Tokyo such as Aoyama, where Rei Kawakubo and her two heir apparents, former apprentices Junya Watanabe and Tao Kurihara, manage the Comme des Garçons flagship store.

Media darling Limi Feu (feu means 'fire' in French) has two trendy stores also in Tokyo. She is another descendant of the original dream dozen; she is the daughter of Yamamoto. After years of constant contrast and comparison, Feu has recently been able to break away from under her father's shadow, offering clients a younger, more approachable spirit, albeit still in black.

Another name to note is the indelible Hanae Mori who was admirably the first Asian woman to be accepted by the Fédération française de la couture in France. Recognized by her trademark butterfly, highlights of her design career include costumes for the opera Madame Butterfly in Milan, JAL flight attendant uniforms and the widely publicized wedding dress for Crown Princess Masako of Japan. Her signature clothing, fragrances, accessories and homewares can be purchased at one of her many eponymous boutiques across Japan, including a sleek location in Harajuku, another style-aware Tokyo neighborhood.

A relative newcomer to the scene (although he has been showing since 1994), designer Keita Maruyama is considered a forerunner in the second generation of Japan's talent roster. Maruyama's boutique in Aoyama is a veritable magnet for local shoppers and, increasingly, foreign admirers.

The Indonesian fashion scene continually proves itself an unstoppable force, simultaneously embracing its famed designers while ushering in burgeoning talent. One hot newcomer is Jakarta's own Steven Huang, whose cutting-edge creations, unconventional working methods and meticulous attention to detail led those at an event organized by Cosmopolitan magazine at Immigrant in Plaza

Indonesia on Wednesday to agree that they were in the presence of one of the next big designers.

"My fashion designs make women look sexy and avant-garde" says the 27-year-old, whose fans and customers agree that his designs - which very rarely use patterns and are born of mere muse and fabric draped on a mannequin - defy convention. And while the process of taking an outfit from its birth on a mannequin to its debut on a night out might seem lengthy, the adroit designer's dresses are finished in anywhere from a few hours to a couple of days, pleasing even the most relentless customer.

He pinches and stitches fabric here and there to create a sexy silhouettes. There is no fitting after the dresses are finished, yet his designs feel their way across each of the body's contours precisely. He works extremely fast, combining several fabrics and adding details like bows, frills and strands of silvery chains to complete his creations.

Originally from Riau, this up-and-comer only recently decided to go full-tilt into the fashion industry.

"This is only my second show since I decided to focus solely on fashion," said Steven, who kicked around several office jobs in Jakarta before dedicating himself to his true passion. Today, the promising designer works under his own label, S Code, from his workshop in Manggarai, South Jakarta.

Under the theme Opposites, his fashion show was divided into two sequences that featured 12 outfits from his spring/summer collection.

In the first sequence, Steven presented his chic and feminine dress collection. Tall, waif-like models strolled along the catwalk draped in white silk satin dresses that played to halter necks and off-shoulder styles. Here and there, the luxuriant outfits were pinched and stitched to create soft and sexy silhouettes that revealed Steven's attention to detail.

"I was inspired by the dresses of the Greek goddesses," Steven said. "They are feminine, skillful and smart - the very portrait of today's modern women."

Steven said he chose silk satin, which breathes easily even in tropical weather, because of its glossy, shimmering look.

"The dresses are ideal to wear at big events and parties," the designer said. "Despite being sheer they are not see-through, even under strong spotlights like tonight's."

On the runway, a short black ball gown that puffed out at the waist and had soft frills and ruffles down the front took on an exceptionally enchanting look. Meanwhile, a one-shouldered blue dress with a white bow tied at the waist presented a relaxed and breezy effect one might call resort-chic.

Steven's second sequence, which showcased another six pieces, ran in stark contrast to his Greek-goddess opener. Dominated by dark solid colors, the collection featured waist-high Jodhpur pants with stiff triangle ornaments, tight-fitting blouses with heavy padding and chunky silvery chains about the neck.

"Every woman has a masculine side," Steven said. "With my attire, a woman can bring out that strong, masculine side of her personality while looking sexy and adorable at the same time."

Even a mini-dress, with its highly pointed shoulders, stiff collars and silver zipper down the front, bore some masculine traits. On the sides of the dress were double-stitched burst patterns reminiscent of a basketball. "I think they make the dress look more sexy and fashionable," Steven said.

Steven's customers applaud his alacrity and ability to produce luxurious outfits posthaste, and his show at Immigrant was no different. He and three of his staff members cut and stitched each of the night's outfits in only eight days.

When his clients come to his workshop, he listens to what they want, lays the materials on a mannequin and starts cutting and sewing right away.

"So they come to me and then leave to stroll the mall for two or three hours and by the time they come back, the dress is ready," Steven said.

The event's master of ceremonies, Marcella Bustami, attested to Steven's speed and skill.

"[Making my outfit] was an extremely quick process, almost unbelievably so," she said. Marcella wore black, waist-high skinny pants with a cropped white duchess satin jacket accentuated with a little bow on the backside. The result was a slim silhouette that arrested attention.

"I love Steven Huang," said Monica Cindy, one of the designer's loyal customers. "He is so simple and works pretty fast. He made this dress in only an hour and a half, without any fitting."

Monica wore a one-shoulder fuchsia dress that was pinched and gathered in several places and embellished with strands of silvery chains. "This dress is pretty simple, yet it has a lot of ornaments and details. I like it a lot," she said.

"Steven's style is very cutting-edge," Marcella said. "His dresses are simple, but he puts a lot of detail into them. And he also has a very good at understanding of the materials he's using. He employs unorthodox ways of working. He puts the cloth on a mannequin, plays around with it and suddenly, it's finished. He's very imaginative."

In 2010, Steven plans to launch his ready-to-wear label, S Code, and open a boutique in Central Jakarta .

"Young designers starting out in the fashion industry should keep their eyes and ears open," Steven said. "Always learn and don't be shy to ask for advice from those designers who are established. With perseverance, I believe those designers with less experience can also make it in this industry."

BRIGHT COLOURED DESIGNS

Kuala Lumpur-based Dayang Fatimah "Tom" Abang Saufi, the chief designer and managing director of fashion company Ethnicite Sdn. Bhd., is one of the pioneers of Islamic fashion. She first drew headlines when she launched her business in 1985, featuring women's clothing in bright colorful designs.

The important thing that plays major role in enhancing your look is the accessories, which will remain hot this season. The right accessories can change the whole impact of the outfit, and this year it has not been adviced only for girls but for boys too. From chunky pieces of jewellery to stylish bags and caps, from scarves to the most "in vouge'belts, any kind of accessory will find a place in your wardrobe this season.

Belts can be broad, narrow, infabricor in leather, with beads and stones or with attractive buckles and they will surely draw a attention to the waist. They can be placed little above or little below the waist, but again it is important to choose the one which goes according to your body type and suits the size of your waist.

Smart and comfortable footwear is a must since any ensemble is incomplete without good footwear. And to add some glitz and glamour to your fashion statement, sport a sleek watch, or one with a latest broad dial. To further enhance the look, a cool pair of sunglasses is a good idea.

Lastly, this season's colours are pastels and soothing shades for casual wear. As, always black and white can never go out of fashion. There can be lots of red and golds in ethnic wear, which can be blended with lots of bright and vibrant shades but you should always opt for the colours which are good for your complexion and skin.

So, with the little knowledge of what's in and your creativity can make you a style icon. You have always option of being fashionable by spicing up your already existing wardrobe. The art of mix and match is must to present yourself in the best way.

Fashion is what when you make your own unique style of dressing and feel good, as well as comfortable, about it. The facts remains that if you feel good, you look good and that's what exactly fashion is.

"Moslem women, particularly professional women, want to look chic while maintaining their Moslem identity, a trend evident not just in the Middle East, but also in Western countries, including the United States, which has a growing Moslem population," Abang Saufi said in an interview with Apparel.

"After attending a one-year course at the London School of Fashion, I further honed my skills in fashion designing. But when I started out, there was a recession in many countries of the world and stores were not doing well because of high prices and low demand," she recalls.

Fortunately for Abang Saufi, the recession was on its way out, andshe also had the good fortune to design the wedding gown for a royalwedding in Brunei. "The Brunei wedding catapulted me into fame. Since then I have never had to look back," she said.

Although she has buyers in the West, her main market is in Asia, particularly the Middle East, which is ripe with potential buyers for her Islamic fashion apparel. Initially, Abang Saufi was unsure how tobreak into the Middle Eastern markets--where consumer taste is considered "bland"--with her array of bright colors, but increased global travel among this group has familiarized Middle Easterners with "goodlabels such as Roberto Cavalli which are quite colorful," she says, helping her to gain a foothold.

Islamic fashion, an enigma to many in the world of haute couture, conjures up images of garments conforming to strict religious needs, but Asian designers such as Abang Saufi have learned to create collections that are fashionable while adhering to religious dictates.

Abang Saufi said that she discerned a "growing interest" in Islamic fashion at her fashion exhibition in Paris last year and says that she considers Moslem women in the United States to be "more trendy" than those in other countries. She has also cast her eye on markets with sizable Moslim populations such as France, the U.K. and China.

While Abang Saufi is influenced by Malaysian colors and designs--she avoids using zippers and buttons--her style is a curious blend of East meets West. Some of her products are designed in such a way thatthey can be tied by hand or threaded through gleaming shell buckles.

She defines the core elements of Islamic fashion as elegance with modest. "It does not have to be boring. Women in Islamic countries are adding color to their traditional black clothing" she says, adding that each country in the Gulf has its own style, and that some, such as Egypt, Iran, Syria and Jordan are more liberal in their fashion styles than others.

While her turnover of nearly $1US million is modest by Western standards, it is quite impressive for a developing niche market.

Manik Mehta is a freelance business writer specializing in textiles and apparel, fashion, globalization and emerging markets.

Being in fashion is like being on top of the world. Yes some people are really fond of following latest trends and trying to look best. They buy fashion accessories and clothing to pace up with the fast world. Dresses in fashion are always costly since retailers are dying to sell these trendy items at higher prices, many of us simply fall prey to their profit making intentions.

However there are people who are keen to look best and trendy within budget. going through fashion magazines and browsing sites can help you resolve the matter. There are so many tips available and you can just choose some of them accomplish your goal.

The content gives relevant tips on how to look best, counting on a limited budget. Here they are:

1. Its really funny that people exhaust their pockets just to follow trends. I mean that's not required. Being in fashion would mean that you don't look outdated and wear stuffs that are exactly complimenting your sense of style. Low-budget fashion items are style statements too. You know, some styles are evergreen and they don't need heads scratching moments to know if one is following trends or not.
2. Go for fashion pieces that are evergreen and goes almost with every style you showcase. These are neutral and basic colors. This way you can cut huge costs.
3. Load your wardrobe with some basic styles, they are always in. you cannot expect shirts, trousers, t-shirts and jeans to be out of fashion. They are basics and are parent items in the fashion world.
4. Buy some good accessories that would compliment your old outfits. You can accessorize your outfits and remain to look best amongst the rest. Who says old is out of fashion?
5. Buying brands is a sheer waste of money and time. Go for stuffs which are good looking and lends you unique sense of style. So that even if they are out of fashion, you would not drop tears of regret.

These are the most common ways of being in style while staying within budget.

There is nothing that goes without fashion. Everyone has his/her own fashion and tends to follow it spontaneously. In fact, the world is a fashion follower and has billions of people following the latest trends in their day to day lives.

Some may point out at you, and say that you are old fashioned. Well then give them a bold reply saying, to be old fashioned is also a part of fashion. So next when they make a comment on you make sure you have the correct way of answering them.

Fashion is any trend that you would love to follow. Well for all those fashion freaks here are some fashion tips to follow:

1. Use Aloe-Vera, the low-priced method for diminishing pimples.
2. Home-made mud-packs are best for glowing skins.
3. Try out something every day to stand out amongst the crowd.
4. Try not being too casual, if you are heading for office.
5. Avoid skimpy and revealing dresses in office, which might have an adverse effect .
6. A messy bun for a casual outing can be perfect .

What about the men? Well, well they do really want to look like kings. Now here are some men's fashion tips that might come handy for all you guys.

1. Wear something that just fits your physique too well.
2. Be simple and win hearts.
3. Wear a pair of shoes that looks great on you.
4. Be a versatile fashion follower.

5. Don't just run after brands.

For teens who crave for that extra bit of attention, here are some teen fashion tips to see things go your way:

1. look exceptional.
2. try out some fashionable accessories.
3. wear something that suits your structure.

Fashion tips are many, but it is upon you to choose from a vast array of style statements, as to which of it makes the best out of you.

Maybe musician Donald Fagen was onto something. In his classic 1982 song, I.G.Y. (What A Beautiful World), the sometime-Steely Dan collaborator sang of adventurers buying a ticket to the wheel in space and a world with spandex jackets for everyone.

Well, while the wheel is still in the drawing stages, the Japanese Aerospace Exploration Agency and Rocketplane Ltd., along with numbers of designers and artisans, have taken it upon themselves to improve on the spandex: a Hyper Space Couture Design Contest.

Runway Fashion

The multi-part competition has been underway for several months, patterned to elicit space tourism fashion ideas. A key rule is that suborbital wear submittals must be functional and scientific-but don't forget a stylish chic.

"Rocketplane made the fundamental design decision to fly in a true 'shirtsleeve environment' very early in the development program," explained Chuck Lauer, Vice President of Business Development for Rocketplane, based in Oklahoma City, Oklahoma.

Rocketplane's XP vehicle will accommodate a pilot and three passengers. The fighter-sized craft is powered by both turbojet engines and a rocket engine. The vehicle is being built to accelerate to speeds of some 2,386 miles per hour

(3,500 feet per second) and reach altitudes in excess of 330,000 feet (100 kilometers). Flying that suborbital profile, all onboard will be weightless for three to four minutes during the trek to the edge of space.

"In our view, not having to wear bulky pressure suits, helmets or breathing masks will enhance the customer's space flight experience," Lauer told SPACE.com.

Say no to Nomex

It was Misuzu Onuki, Asia Liaison for the Space Frontier Foundation and Rocketplane's Asian Business Representative, who first identified the need for design, creative expression and personal preference to become a part of the customer's individual space flight choices.

From the place de l'Opéra to Chaussée d'Antin : high art to high fashion

Start your journey on the esplanade of the Opera metro station. Admire the magnificent cupola of the Grand Hôtel Intercontinental, just above the mythical Café de la Paix. Across the road, impossible to miss the Palais Garnier, with its golden statues, marble columns and grand staircase. Recently renovated, the Paris Opera House remains one of the most opulent buildings in the capital... definitely worth a visit. If you're in the mood to explore the annals of this venerable institution, the company Purple Beam offers guided tours of this 19th-century palace. Enter with the artists, by the side door, and take a tour through the magnificent palace, from the stage to the dressing rooms and up to the sumptuous apartments.

After this exceptional moment, offer yourself an aromatic pause, sweet or salty, in the 'House of Tea' at the Scribe Hotel, located just next door. From there, follow your nose a bit further down the road to the Fragonard Perfume Museum . This institution re-traces 3000 years of the history of perfume in an exceptional collection of bottles, testers and gift-boxes.

Following this fireworks of sensory perception, take the rue Auber on your left until you reach the boulevard Haussmann. A flurry of theatres (Athénée-Louis Jouvet, Edouard VII) hides in these several streets. At the junction Auber-Haussmann you will find the sought after Parisian department store Printemps de la Mode . After all this culture, a shopping spree is always welcome, especially in one of the most beautiful 'temples of consumption'! With all the satellites gravitating around the splendid Art-Deco cupola of this refined shop, you can't miss in finding great fashions for women, men at the Printemps de l'Homme (on the rue du Havre) and teens at Citadium (situated behind the main shop), a department store dedicated to super stylish sportswear.

For home goods, don't miss the hip selection of items at the Printemps de la Maison, dedicated to home furnishings and decoration. If you're stomach starts to rumble, swing by the second floor, where " luxury and gourmet " go hand in hand at the irresistible chocolate shop Patrick Roger, the world renowned bakers at Ladurée or the trendy chefs at Fuxia. On the seventh floor, the restaurant Déli-cieux offers a panoramic view of the rooftops of Paris. Another possibility is the Brasserie Printemps, on the sixth floor of the main shop. You can also savour a magnificent view of Paris, just beneath the Art-Deco cupola.

Further up the boulevard, sits the Galeries Lafayette . " Les Galeries " are famous for their creative fashion side, presenting new designers with regular runway shows, their fine food shop Lafayette Gourmet, their men's section Lafayette Hommes and their home furnishings department Lafayette Maison. The Galeries Lafayette are also well-known among the tourists and the children who come to see their lively Christmas windows each December. A favourite Parisian pass-time, lunch-hour shopping at Les Galeries, with a quick bite on the run in one of the local cafés or tea rooms. A special section of the first floor now houses the " Espace Luxe ", a collection of the most famous names in Haute Couture: Chanel, Louis Vuitton, Prada, Balenciaga and more.

AN IMPRESSIONIST LANDSCAPE

Small stone houses, ivy covered stone walls, rugged paths leading to the wheat fields and the forests that border the Oise... By escaping industrialisation, Auvers-sur-Oise has remained the same since the 19th-century, when Van Gogh, Cezanne and Pissarro came in search of inspiration.

Arriving by train, The Impressionist Train is direct from Paris on Saturdays, Sundays and Holidays, from April to November), total immersion into the Impressionist world is immediate. The underground of the train station has been recovered with a coloured fresco, representing the most famous paintings of the painters from Auvers.

Begin your visit to this " museum village " by discovering the universe of the first impressionist painter: Charles-Francois Daubigny. In the centre of the village, la Maison-Atelier de Daubigny plunges you into the world of the artist, smitten by the village of Auvers. Admire the walls on the inside, decorated by Daubigny and his friends: Corot, Daumier and Odinot... and enjoy the lovely flower garden outside.

A short way down the hill, in a Manor house, the Daubigny Museum presents the work of the landscape painter, as well as the work of his son, Karl. You can also take a look at the water-colours, drawings and engravings done by his friends: Jean-Francois Millet or Henry-Joseph Harpignies. The tourist office is located on the ground floor and offers guided tours of the village.

Paris Hilton launched her trendy clothing line in mid-August 2007, at Kitson, LA. At the event, Paris helped personally style each of her fans during her appearance. The launch of her clothing line was very successful. Additional pieces are constantly being added to her collection every month.

She was involved in the developing and designing of her dresses, T-shirts and jeans. She wanted to create a collection that would represent her style, fashion and taste for fans. She spent about a year submitting scrapbooks and approving designs.

Furthermore, she makes sure that all of her clothes are unique and perfect to wear. She also insists that her clothing line is both comfortable and affordable.

Paris Whitney Hilton (born February 17, 1981) is an American socialite, heiress and media personality. She is a great-granddaughter of Conrad Hilton (founder of Hilton Hotels). Hilton is known for her controversial appearance in a sex tape in 2003, and appearance on the television series The Simple Life alongside fellow socialite and childhood best friend Nicole Richie. She is also known for her 2004 tongue-in-cheek autobiography, several minor film roles (most notably her role in the horror film House of Wax in 2005), her 2006 music album Paris, and her work in modeling. As a result of several legal incidents, Hilton also served a widely publicized sentence in a Los Angeles County jail in 2007.

Hilton was born in New York City, New York, to Richard, a businessman, and his wife, Kathy Hilton (née Avanzino), a socialite and actress. She is the oldest of four children: she has one sister, Nicholai Olivia "Nicky" Hilton (b. 1983) and two brothers, Barron Nicholas Hilton II (b. 1989) and Conrad Hughes Hilton III (b. 1994). Hilton is of Norwegian, German, English, Irish, and Italian ancestry. She is a niece of two child stars of the 1970s, Kim and Kyle Richards.

Hilton moved between several exclusive homes in her youth, including a suite in the Waldorf-Astoria Hotel in

Manhattan, Beverly Hills, and the Hamptons. As a child she was good friends with other socialites, including Nicole Richie and Kim Kardashian. She attended her freshman year of high school at the Marywood-Palm Valley School in Rancho Mirage, California followed by a short time at Convent of the Sacred Heart (which she attended with Lady Gaga) and the Dwight School in New York for her sophomore and junior years. She was then transferred to the Canterbury Boarding School, in New Milford, Connecticut where she was a member of the ice hockey team. In February 1999, she was expelled for violating school rules and later earned her GED.

In December 2007, Hilton's grandfather Barron Hilton pledged 97 percent of his estate to a charitable organization founded by his father, the Conrad N. Hilton Foundation. An immediate pledge of $1.2 billion was made, with a further $1.1 billion due after his death. He cited his father's actions as the motivation for his pledge. According to reports, the potential inheritance of his grandchildren is sharply diminished.

CAREER

Hilton has worked as a model, actress, singer, and engaged in occasional business pursuits. According to Forbes Magazine, she earned approximately $2 million in 2003-2004, $6.5 million in 2004-2005, and $7 million in 2005-2006.

As a Model

Hilton began modeling as a child, initially at charity events. When she was 19, she signed with Donald Trump's modeling agency, T Management. Hilton has also worked with Ford Models in New York, Models 1 Agency in London, Nous Model Management in Los Angeles, and Premier

Model Management in London. She has appeared in numerous advertising campaigns, including Iceberg Vodka, GUESS, Tommy Hilfiger, Christian Dior, and Marciano. In 2001, Hilton began to develop a reputation as a socialite, being identified as "New York's leading It Girl" whose fame was beginning to "extend beyond the New York tabloids". She has appeared in several magazines, including the April 2004 issue of Maxim.

As a Media Personality

Film

Hilton has made cameo appearances in several films, notably Zoolander, Wonderland, and The Cat In The Hat. She landed minor and supporting roles in the feature films Nine Lives, Raising Helen, The Hillz, and House of Wax. Her role as Paige Edwards in House of Wax won the Teen Choice Award for "Best Scream" and earned her a nomination for "Choice Breakout Performance - Female". (It also won her the 2005 Razzie for "Worst Supporting Actress" at the 2005 Golden Raspberry Awards.) She also earned a nomination for "Best Frightened Performance" at the 2006 MTV Movie Awards. She landed her first lead roles in 2006 with the straight-to-DVD releases National Lampoon's Pledge This! and Bottoms Up. She plays the Hottie in the box office bomb romantic comedy The Hottie and the Nottie, released in 2008. She also had a minor cameo appearance as herself in An American Carol.

More recently, Hilton plays Amber Sweet, the surgery- and painkiller-addicted daughter of a biotech magnate in the goth/rock musical Repo! The Genetic Opera. Critics have responded positively to her performance in the film, in which she sings and acts. In an interview Repo! director Darren Lynn Bousman revealed that he had originally refused to audition Hilton for the role of Amber Sweet. "I broke down," says Bousman, "and I met with her, and immediately she charmed everyone in the room." In the same interview, Bousman also revealed that Hilton was so keen to get the part that she had the script smuggled in to her during her much publicized stint in a Los Angeles jail, and used her time inside to work on her role.

Television

Hilton co-starred with her friend Nicole Richie in the Fox reality series The Simple Life, which premiered on December 2, 2003. The Simple Life ran for three seasons on Fox. The show was cancelled by Fox after a dispute between Hilton and Richie, but it was subsequently aired by E! Entertainment Television for the fourth and fifth seasons. Despite talks of a sixth season, the series finished its run at the end of the fifth season. In March 2008, it was reported that Hilton would star in a new MTV reality series tentatively titled Paris Hilton's My New BFF, about her looking for a new best friend. The series premiered on September 30, 2008.

Hilton has also guest-starred in episodes of the popular tv-show The O.C., The George Lopez Show, Las Vegas, American Dreams, Dogg After Dark, and Veronica Mars. Furthermore, she appeared in several music videos, including "It Girl" by John Oates and "Just Lose It" by Eminem. Planning is underway for an eponymous cartoon series following the animated life of Hilton, her sister Nicky, and her dog Tinkerbell, which began filming in September 2007. In April 2008, she guest starred on the My Name is Earl episode "I Won't Die with a Little Help from My Friends". On January 29, 2009, Paris Hilton's British Best Friend, began airing on ITV2 in England. The second season of Paris Hilton's My New BFF premiered on June 2, 2009. In June 2009, Hilton shot "Paris Hilton's Dubai BFF". Runner-up of the British series Kat McKenzie died on July 3, 2009 of a suspected overdose.

Hilton guest-starred in the fifth episode of Supernatural's fifth season. "Paris Hilton is playing a demonic creature that takes the form of... Paris Hilton," creator and executive producer Eric Kripke said in a statement. "It'll be a fun, irreverent episode and we here at Supernatural are thrilled that Paris agreed to do it."

Hilton guest starred in an episode of I Get That a Lot in 2010, on CBS, as a petrol service-station attendant.

Recording Artist

2004-07: Paris

Hilton founded Heiress Records, a sub-label of Warner Bros. Records, in 2004 and released her self-titled debut album, Paris, under that label on August 22, 2006. Although the album reached number six on the Billboard 200 for a week, its total sales volume has been low - but the first single "Stars Are Blind" was a top ten hit in 17 countries. Allmusic commented that the album was "more fun than anything released by Britney Spears or Jessica Simpson, and a lot fresher, too." As a whole, critical reception was mixed. Paris Hilton can also be heard singing on the soundtrack to the musical Repo! The Genetic Opera. In an interview, the director, Darren Lynn Bousman, praised her vocal skills. When talking about Paris' vocal audition process for the role, Bouseman said, "We gave her some music and said, 'You have one day to come back and perform this.' She came back the next day, memorized everything, was pitch-perfect, I mean she was awesome."

2007-present: Untitled Second Album

On July 16, 2007, Hilton confirmed that she was working on a new album with producer Scott Storch. In a recent interview with MTV, Hilton decided that her second album is going to be a dance album. She stated that she "loves Bob Sinclar" and wants to create dance-music vibe. Hilton has installed a professional recording studio in her house to work on the album. On September 30, 2008, Hilton premiered her song "My BFF" on KIIS-FM with host Ryan Seacrest. It is the first single from her as yet untitled second studio album and the theme song of her show Paris Hilton's My New BFF. Hilton stated that she finished working on the album. A second song "Paris For President" was released along with a music video late October 2008.

For her second studio album, she has confirmed six tracks: "Jailhouse Baby", "Platinum Blonde", "Crave" and "My BFF", "Paris For President", and "Girl Tax", "My BFF" and "Paris For President" were released in 2008 as the first two singles. In November 2008, Hilton talked with Entertainment Weekly backstage at the American Music Awards and she told them that she has finished her second album, and "wrote all the songs". The album is featuring production by Mike Green who worked with the bands Paramore and The Matches. In December 2008, she was looking for a label to release her album, she told Entertainment Weekly. "I'm not sure which label I'm doing it with," she said. "I'm figuring it out right now." Later that month she stated her intention to release her album under her own record label Heiress Records.

Hilton posted on Twitter that she filmed a music video for the first single, and confirmed in a magazine interview that the album is complete.

As an Author

Further information: Confessions of an Heiress: A Tongue-in-Chic Peek Behind the Pose and Your Heiress Diary: Confess It All to Me

In the autumn of 2004, Hilton released an autobiographical book, Confessions of an Heiress: A Tongue-in-Chic Peek Behind the Pose, co-written by Merle Ginsberg, which includes full color photographs of her and her advice on life as an heiress. Hilton reportedly received a $100,000 advance payment for this book. Some in the media panned the writing as amateurish, and the book was parodied by Robert Mundell on The Late Show with David Letterman. The book became a New York Times bestseller. Hilton followed it up with a designer diary, also with Ginsberg, called Your Heiress Diary: Confess It All to Me.

On September 2009, Hilton's quote: "Dress cute wherever you go, life is too short to blend in" has been added to The Oxford Dictionary of Quotations.

Standing as a Celebrity

She denied proclaiming herself as the "iconic blonde of the decade" such as Diana, Princess of Wales, and Marilyn Monroe in the May 2007 issue of Harper's Bazaar. She appeared in the 2007 Guinness World Records as the world's "Most Overrated Celebrity". In a poll conducted by the Associated Press and AOL, Hilton was voted the second "Worst Celebrity Role Model of 2006", behind Britney Spears. Critics suggest that Hilton epitomizes the title of famous for being famous; echoing that sentiment, the Associated Press conducted what they called an experiment in February 2007, trying not to report on Hilton for a whole week.

2008 Parody Presidential Campaign

On August 6, 2008 Hilton appeared in a 1 minute 50 second long video online, "Paris Hilton Responds to McCain Ad", directed by Adam McKay and posted on the Funny or Die website. The video featured Hilton in a parody advertisement, and was made in response to a television campaign advert "Celeb", by the 2008 John McCain presidential campaign. In Celeb, McCain briefly compared his rival Barack Obama to that of celebrities such as Hilton and Britney Spears, going on to question his readiness to lead and criticize his energy policy.

In what *The Washington Post* opined "might just be her best acting role yet," Hilton appears in the video wearing a leopard print swimsuit. She starts out by suggesting that her personal mention by McCain means that she must now be a candidate in the presidential race, and goes on to mock McCain, and critique the expected qualities and lifestyle of a celebrity in comparison to that of a US president. In a 30 second segment, in the style of an academic speaker, Paris compares and contrasts the policies of McCain and Obama for solving the US energy crisis, and goes on to propose a 'compromise solution' combining elements of both.

The video received 7 million views in two days garnering worldwide press coverage, and drew both written and verbal media response from both campaigns. The merits and drawbacks of the 'Paris compromise solution' with regard to energy policy, as well as its contrast to the adversarial political campaigns, generated multiple comments from US political commentators, as well as Speaker of the House Nancy Pelosi and Congressman Michael Burgess.

Continuing the spoof campaign, in October, Hilton featured in a second parody video posted on Funny or Die, the 2 minute 20 second long "Paris Hilton Gets Presidential with Martin Sheen", alongside Hollywood actor Martin Sheen, with his son, actor Charlie Sheen, appearing in a cameo role. Hilton, heavily made up and in a green evening dress, interviews Martin Sheen in a kitchen, discussing various political issues, seeking his advice from his days playing a fictional President on The West Wing.

Products and Endorsements

Hilton helped design a collection of purses for Japanese label Samantha Thavasa, and also a jewelry line for Amazon.com.

In 2004, Hilton was involved in the creation of a perfume line by Parlux Fragrances. Originally set to be a small release, high demand led to a wider release before December 2004. The launch was followed by a 47 percent increase in sales of Parlux products, predominantly due to sales of the Hilton-branded perfume. After the success of Hilton's perfume, Parlux Fragrances released several more perfumes with her name, including fragrances for men. Hilton launched a new fragrance in October 2007, called Can Can. This is her fourth women's fragrance after Paris Hilton, Just Me, and Heiress. During the month of November 2008, Hilton released her fifth fragrance for women called, Fairy Dust. In July 2009, her sixth fragrance for women Siren was launched.

In January 2007, Hilton released the DreamCatchers line of hair extensions in partnership with Hair Tech International. In early August 2007, Hilton signed a licensing agreement with Antebi for a signature footwear line, "Paris Hilton Footware", featuring stilettos, platforms, flats, wedges, and a sports collection, expected to reach stores in 2008. In mid August 2007, Hilton launched a line of tops, dresses, coats, and jeans at Kitson boutique in Los Angeles.

In 2005, Hilton lent her name to a chain of nightclubs owned by Fred Khalilian and known as Club Paris. This association ended in January 2007 after she had failed to attend several scheduled promotional appearances.

In December 2007, Hilton posed nude, covered in gold paint, to promote "Rich Prosecco", a canned version of an Italian sparkling wine. She also traveled to Germany to promote the drink, appearing in various print ads for the product.

In February 2010, Hilton participates in an advertising campaign for the launch of the Brazilian beer Devassa. As part of the campaign, Hilton will also join the carnival of Rio de Janeiro in the cabin of the brewery.

PERSONAL LIFE

Paris Hilton in Munich in 2005

Hilton was engaged to fashion model Jason Shaw from mid-2002 to early 2003. In 2003-2004 she had a relationship with singer Nick Carter. Later she was engaged to Greek shipping heir Paris Latsis, from May 29, 2005 to November 2005. Thereafter, she began dating another Greek shipping heir, Stavros Niarchos III, before breaking up in May 2006. In early 2008, she was spotted with Good Charlotte guitarist Benji Madden and in May, Hilton announced her intention to marry Madden during an interview with television talk-show host David Letterman. The two broke up in November 2008, and "remain very good friends". She began dating The Hills star Doug Reinhardt in February 2009; Hilton has also referred to her intention to marry Reinhardt, saying "He's gonna be my husband." The couple broke up in June 2009, only to get back together again in August of the same year. On April 13th 2010, Hilton reportedly split from Reinhardt because she was worried he was just using her to further his career.

Hilton told Live with Regis and Kelly: "One-night stands are not for me. I think it's gross when you just give it up. Guys want you more, if you don't just hand it to them on a platter."

Hilton loves small dogs, and lives with a Yorkshire Terrier and a female Chihuahua named Tinkerbell among many other pets. Paris Hilton is frequently seen carrying Tinkerbell (dubbed an "accessory dog") at social events and functions, and in all five seasons of television reality show The Simple Life. In 2004, Tinkerbell "authored" a memoir, The Tinkerbell Hilton Diaries. On August 12, 2004, Tinkerbell went missing after Hilton's apartment was burgled, and a $5,000 reward was offered for her safe return. She was found six days later. By December

1, 2004, Tinkerbell was again spotted with Paris Hilton at various events. Hilton has also purchased a male Chihuahua on July 25, 2007 from Pets of Bel Air in Los Angeles. Hilton's love for man's best friend led her to create an apparel line for dogs called Little Lily by Paris Hilton, with some of the proceeds going to benefit animal rescue. "I have 17 dogs and I like to dress them, so I started designing this clothing line and it's really cute, like dresses and jeans - everything you can imagine for humans, but for dogs," she said in an interview during Super Bowl XLII festivities. Hilton's love for her dogs led to the rumor that she wanted to be frozen with them at the Cryonics Institute, but Hilton denied the rumor on The Ellen DeGeneres Show.

A homemade sex video of Hilton and then-boyfriend Rick Salomon was leaked on the Internet in 2003, later released as the DVD 1 Night in Paris despite attempted legal action. It appeared a week prior to the premiere of The Simple Life.

On January 22, 2007, Hilton's private life was thrust into the media spotlight with the launch of ParisExposed.com, a website that features images of personal documents, video, and other material allegedly obtained when the contents of a storage locker rented by Hilton was auctioned off due to lack of a $208 payment. The website began charging online access to this material and received 1.2 million visitors in just over 40 hours. Among the contents were medications, diaries, photographs, contracts and love letters, as well as a video of her shot by Joe Francis of Girls Gone Wild, whom she once dated. On February 3, 2007 Hilton obtained a temporary injunction against ParisExposed.com, closing down the website.

On February 5, 2007, CNN's Anderson Cooper 360 discussed footage obtained from the ParisExposed.com website which features Hilton using the ethnic slurs "niggers", "chink", "Jappy" and the derogatory term "faggot".

Hilton was burglarized at least five times by the Bling Ring. In most cases they were only after cash and clothes. However, during their final burglary of her home, a participant usually not present as a member of the group stole around $2 million in jewelry from her, carrying it out in one of her Louis Vuitton bags. It was only after this theft that she informed police of having been burglarized.

Paris Hilton's Booking Photograph

In September 2006, Hilton was arrested and charged with driving under the influence of alcohol with a blood alcohol content of 0.08%, the level at which it is illegal to drive in California. Hilton's driving license was subsequently suspended in November 2006, and in January 2007 she pleaded no contest to a reckless driving charge. Her punishment was 36 months' probation and fines of about $1,500. On January 15, 2007, Hilton was pulled over for driving with a suspended license and signed a document acknowledging that she was not permitted to drive. On February 27, 2007 Hilton was caught driving 70 mph in a 35 mph zone, again with a suspended license. She also did not have her headlights on even though it was after dark. Prosecutors in the office of the Los Angeles City Attorney charged that those actions, along with the failure to enroll in a court-ordered alcohol education program, constituted a violation of the terms of her probation.

On May 4, 2007 Hilton was sentenced by Judge Michael T. Sauer to 45 days in jail for violating her probation. Initially, Hilton planned to appeal the sentence, and supported an online petition asking California governor Arnold Schwarzenegger for a pardon. The petition was created and organized on May 5, 2007 by Joshua Morales.

In response, various opponents started a counter-petition to maintain the sentence. Both petitions attracted tens of thousands of signatures. Hilton later switched lawyers and dropped her plans to appeal.

Hilton was required to begin her jail term on June 5, 2007, and checked herself into the Century Regional Detention Facility, an all-female jail in Lynwood, California after attending the 2007 MTV Movie Awards on June 3, 2007. With credit for good behavior, it was anticipated that Hilton would only serve 23 days of her 45-day sentence; however, in an unexpected turn of events, Los Angeles County Sheriff Lee Baca signed orders on the morning of June 7, reassigning Hilton to 40 days of home confinement with an electronic monitoring device due to an unspecified medical condition. Baca commented on the release saying, "My message to those who don't like celebrities is that punishing celebrities more than the average American is not justice," contesting that under normal circumstances, Hilton would not have served any time in jail, and he added that "The special treatment, in a sense, appears to be because of her celebrity status ... She got more time in jail". On the same day that Hilton was released from jail, Judge Michael Sauer summoned her to reappear in court the following morning (June 8) as the sentencing statement had explicitly said she would serve time in jail with "No work furlough. No work release. No electronic monitoring." At the hearing he declined to be briefed by Hilton's attorney in private chambers on the nature of her condition and sent her back to jail to serve out her original 45-day sentence. Upon hearing the sentence, Hilton shouted, "It's not right!" and started screaming, requesting to hug her mother who was present in the courtroom. Concern about Hilton's condition led to her being moved to the medical wing of the Twin Towers Correctional Facility in Los Angeles, and she was moved back to the Century Regional Detention Facility in Lynwood..

While in jail, Hilton was influenced by the clergyman minister Marty Angelo: Hilton referred to starting a "new beginning" during her interview with talk show host Larry King on June 28, 2007, two days after being released from jail, and quoted from Angelo's autobiography, entitled Once Life Matters: A New Beginning. On June 9, 2007, Marty Angelo petitioned Sauer, asking to serve out the remainder of Hilton's jail sentence if the judge would release her to an alternative treatment program, but the petition was turned down.

On July 17, 2010, Hilton was detained and released after being caught in possession of cannabis at Figari airport, Corsica.

On August 28, 2010 she was arrested on suspicion of cocaine possession in Las Vegas.

Filmography

Year	Film	Role	Notes
1993	Wishman	Girl on Beach	
2000	Sweetie Pie		
2001	Zoolander		
Herself	Cameo		
2002	Nine Lives		
Jo			
2002	QIK2JDG	Strung-out Supermodel	
2003	L.A. Knights	Sadie	
2003	Wonderland		
Barbie	Cameo role		
2003	The Cat in the Hat		
Female	Club-Goer	Cameo role	
2004	Las Vegas		

Year	Film	Role	Notes
Madison	TV series, 1 episode: "Things That Go Jump in the Night" (1.14)		
2004	Win a Date with Tad Hamilton!		
Heather			
2004	George Lopez		
Ashley	TV series, 1 episode: "Jason Tutors Max" (3.18)		
2004	The O.C.		
Kate	TV series, 1 episode: The L.A. (1.22)		
2004	The Hillz		
Heather Smith			
2004	Raising Helen		
Amber			
2004	1 Night In Paris		
Herself	Pornographic film		
2004	Veronica Mars		
Caitlin Ford	TV series, 1 episode: Credit Where Credit's Due (1.2)		
2005	American Dreams		
Barbara Eden	TV series, 1 episode: "California Dreamin'" (3.15)		
2005	House of Wax		
Paige Edwards			
2006	Bottoms Up		

Year	Film	Role	Notes
Lisa Mancini			
2006	Pledge This!		
Victoria English			
2008	The Hottie and the Nottie		
Cristabel Abbott			
2008	Repo! The Genetic Opera		
Amber Sweet			
2008	An American Carol		
Herself			
2009	Rex	Paris	TV film
2009	Pedal to the Metal	Jane	In production
2009	Supernatural		
Herself/Leshii	TV series, 1 episode: "Fallen Idols" (5.5)		

RITU BERI: BEAUTY WITH BRAIN

Ritu Beri is a New Delhi based International fashion designer. She is the first Asian designer to head the French fashion brand, Scherrer.

Ritu Beri studied fashion arts at the NIFT, New Delhi. She is the only Indian designer to be featured in promostyl's magazine Acustyl, which forecasts fashion trends worldwide. She is the author of the personal fashion book, 101 Ways to Look Good. She also serves on the board of Governors at NIFT, and is an honorary patron of the Savera Association, a popular charity involved in improving the lives of Indian woman.

Her notable international clients are former US President Bill Clinton, Prince Charles, Moulin Rouge, Nicole Kidman, Hollywood actress Andy McDowell, Supermodel

Laetitia Casta, famous Parisian Socialite Mrs. Lagerdere, Langes Swarovski & The Swarovski family, Elizabeth Jagger and Jerry Hall.

Her notable Indian clients are Madhuri Dixit, Rani Mukherji, Preity Zinta, Parmeshwar Godrej & Shobha De.

Hers is a presence of rare eminence and a design sense of luxe richness. A Design pioneer, Global citizen and a success story fables are made of.

Ritu Beri brought her label alive in 1990 when India was still awakening to the couture era. Swift as silk she forayed into France, a protégé of embroidery maestro Francois Lesage.

The first Indian fashion ambassador to show on the catwalks of Paris she then traveled the globe showing her creations to critical acclaim. Her presentations gave the French fashion connoisseurs a glimpse into mystical India. The Parisians were abuzz with exclamations and praises of the rich display of luxurious silks, brocades and the prevalent use of Mogul motifs.

Former US President Mr. Bill Clinton, Hollywood celebrities, Supermodels, famous Parisian Socialite, the Swarovski family, to the Prima Donna of Indian Movies and a bevy of other VIPs have all worn the Ritu Beri label.

The Ritu Beri label retails from high fashion stores across continents and countries. Extensively covered by media RITU BERI has had the most critical critics raise a toast to her signature style.

"Surprising as it might seem, Ritu Beri, from Delhi, gave a lesson in high fashion aesthetics and client-pleasing clothes-the essence of couture." SUZY MENKES (Fashion Editor, The International Herald Tribune)

"Ritu is one of the People to Watch in International Business".

TIME MAGAZINE

"By blending Indian and Western styles, designer Ritu Beri is fashioning her own successful international brand". NEWSWEEK

"Ritu Beri is the Donatella Versace of India. She is the first lady of fashion in her country."

SUNDAY OBSERVER, LONDON

"Indian fashion takes hold in the form of Ritu Beri". BBC

"It's beyond fashion, its art". AFP

"Film stars shun Paris fashion for India, Ritu Beri designs for Nicole Kidman." DAILY TELEGRAPH

Personal life

Ritu Beri married long-time friend & Delhi-based industrialist Bobby Chadha in 2004, and has a daughter Jiya, born 2007.

INDIAN FASHION INDUSTRY

Designers – Rohit Bal, Manish Arora, Ritu Beri, Kavita Bhartiya, Rohit Khosla, Rina Dhaka, Shabina Khan, Rehane Yavar Dhala.

Models–Sherlyn Chopra, Neha Dhupia, Deepti Bhatnagar, Lakshmi Menon, Ujjwala Raut.

Fashion events–Delhi Fashion Week, India Fashion Week

Fashion schools–National Institute of Fashion Technology.

CAREER

After her graduation from Delhi University in 1987 Ritu began designing she designed clothes for herself and friends.

December 1990 - launched the studio Lavanya. It was a complete success

1991 - started design for Liberty, Regent Street, London

1994 - Trained with Francois Lesage, master creator and embroiderer, in Paris

1995 - launched the brand Sanskriti

October 2000 - launched her ready to wear collection in Paris

France Luxury Group, Sherrer's owners, bought Beri's own label

Not for her the ennui of living life after a fashion. She dreams, therefore she is. But the fabric of her career course, sewn together by moments which have culminated in praise at Paris, is not without its nightmares. Presenting Ritu, unplugged...

Good genes can't go wrong:

My earliest memories are of going buggy-riding at the age of three with my father, Balbir Singh Beri, then an adjutant at IMA, Dehradun. My mother, Indu Beri, is an entrepreneur. My parents have given me my most prized possession - life - and what a life!

I was a bully as a kid:

I was extremely possessive about my parents and didn't want to share them even with my kid brother Navin. But today, we work together and he is my goodluck charm.

I didn't even know what NIFT stood for!

NIFT was an accident, but it was destiny in disguise. When I heard that only 25 students were to be chosen from across India it was like a challenge. I went through NIFT completely out of focus, not knowing where I was headed.

No man dared approach me:

I had male friends but the question of having a boyfriend didn't arise. My parents always made sure that their baby was safe. But I've never missed not having a man by my side. Sometimes, I feel I could have had more fun while growing up, but it's okay.

Most people get married for the wrong reasons:

Good girls get married, have babies and go to heaven. But I guess I had better places to go to.

Marriage happened because my parents wanted me to settle down. I was married for a brief period - something I want to forget. Once bitten, but I am not shy. I still hold on to my dream of sharing life with a companion.

I want kids of my own:

I'd love to have kids of my own to learn from them the virtues of unconditional loving, patience and what the heck, I want kids to play with. Maybe, one day, I will adopt a baby girl.

Paris is my destiny: I love India. But Paris is my destiny. Ever since I was 10, Paris is where I have wanted to be. The city signifies aesthetic perfection in the streets, the architecture, the cappuccino, the wining and dining and ooh la la, the chocolate patisseries!

I like men in uniform:

I grew up seeing my father in uniform, he's the best-looking man in uniform I've seen. I have a thing for men in uniform. I like Richard Gere in An Officer and a Gentleman.

I also have a passion for horses, which extends to their riders! For me, I needed a lot for Sex! I'd rather die than live without laughs. I try to bring fun to all aspects of my life and, in one such impulse,

I named my Labrador Sex! Imagine the side-splitting situation:

I needed a room for Sex, I needed a toy for Sex, I needed a walk for Sex, I even needed Sex at work!

My peers have bitched about me openly:

They feel jealous and threatened... They credit my success to a talent for PR and hold me responsible for my looks. My inner strength in the face of such negativity comes from a focus on my goals. I know that I, alone, am responsible for where I want to be.

I love the way I am: When people say I am beautiful, I look at myself and wonder. I think I am attractive... I love myself, the way I look, the way I am. Even if I was the ugliest woman on earth, I feel I would be attractive.

I deal with God as a parent:

I believe spirituality is about living life in a particular way. My mother says that God is on a double-shift with me because I always keep Him on His toes!

Ritu and Amrish Kumar

With a mother who is the pioneer of the fashion business, it could be tough to follow. But Amrish Kumar, son of Ritu Kumar, has settled rather well in the company. He joined the business in 2001. "From childhood when I accompanied her on research trips, I learned about the market, and basic aesthetics," he says. Known for classic creations, Ritu added the young trendy prêt line in 2001. Untrained but with hands-on experiences, Amrish is very excited, "I see myself developing the design house on all fronts. The changing market will affect our directions but our USP of traditional crafts with modern sensibilities will remain," adds Amrish who also plans overseas expansions soon.

Varuna and Nidhi Jani

Jewellery designing runs in their family with Ramchand Popley being one of the leading names in the business. His daughter Varuna D Jani followed him in 2006 with high-end jewellery. Now the third generation - Varuna's daughter Nidhi has joined her. "Getting inputs from Nidhi helps me to know what the younger generation wants." Nidhi meanwhile says, "Mom's jewellery is unique and different. I have learnt a lot from my mother who is a perfectionist." The pair has global plans for the brand. And with Varuna admitting that two brains are better than one, it seems the success of this brand is assured not only in India but globally with daughter Nidhi driving it forward together.

Bina and Malini Ramani

Bina Ramani was probably one of the first Indians to have a collection in Bloomingdales with two window displays and a full page advertisement in the New York Times in 1982. At the first fashion week in 2000, daughter Malini's collection rocked on the ramp. "Malini is at times inspired by my clothes of the 70's and 80's, but her body shapes are very good," comments Bina. Malini adds, "In the last two years, retro styling in my mother's closet has been my inspiration." Malini's collections have that touch of fun, feminine and fusion. "I love it because it is a great feeling to be appreciated." The mother daughter duo has vaguely discussed a joint collection for charity; "We will probably fight a lot and never agree on anything," Malini declares honestly. Is Bina critical of her daughter's work? "Well less and lesser now," admits Malini. The future - is a question Malini brushes off with, "I am not making any plans as far as my designing is concerned, I have planted the seeds and am waiting to see the result," says this laid back "go with the flow" designer.

Dinesh and Payal Singhal

Dinesh Singhal, an award winning designer has walked off with the CMAI best collection trophies several times and pioneered the ready-to-wear business with London Fashions in 1980 introducing the first foreign label FU's in India. Payal, followed in her father's footsteps. A label was the next step. "It was my decision to let her start her own label. London Fashions was a corporate brand and we were planning to upgrade it to couture and it was a question of either Payal or I launching it," admits Dinesh.

At 22, she opened her store in Juhu. Payal, a young mother now shuttles between New York and Mumbai. "Dad and I both started young. I am inspired by his philosophy and want to take the business forward internationally," says Payal.

Neeta and Nishka Lulla

Nishka Lulla had two career options - a doctor like her father Sunil, or a designer like mother Neeta - she chose the latter and has never regretted it. Watching Neeta, a well known award-winning Bollywood designer for over two decades, she joined her mother over five years ago to manage her store; after graduating in fashion. "She launched her label Nisshk early this year and her interest remains kids and trendy teen wear. Her design sensibility is unlike mine," observes Neeta. Training under Neeta was tough. "For four years, I put in long hours as she was very strict with me." But will Nishka go the Bollywood way, too, having designed for a Suraj Barjatiya's untitled film? "It was a great experience having worked with my mother for films. I have learnt to be calm although I get really stressed out. She is very confident and knows exactly how things will turn out." The pair has not thought of designing together but Nishka's future plans are to go commercial with kids and young fashion. With the best task master in the fashion business, there seems to be no doubt about Nishka Lulla's rise to fame.

4

FASHION IN BACK STREETS

There are innumerable fashion stores in Delhi, but Janpath market is unmatchables. If you haven't shopped at Janpath, you haven't experienced Delhi and its true spirit. Having found mention in various books and blogs about the city, Janpath is Delhi's Fashion Street. A shopper's paradise, a bargainer's destination or the perfect face of local fashion, Janpath is famous amongst people of all age groups. Haven't been there yet?

LATEST DESIGN ATTIRES

It wouldn't be wrong to say that Janpath is the trend-setter in clothes for the college crowd in Delhi. However, what makes this market unique is that it does not depend on any brands for its fame. Janpath houses stores ranging from exclusive private emporiums, shops selling export rejects and road side stalls selling a variety of western and Indian clothes.

As you walk up the crowded Janpath road, vibrant colors dazzle you. There are small shops displaying traditional and modern variety of clothing. Some of these stores belong to cottage industry workers and sell hand-embroidered and hand made exclusive attires. Traders from various parts of the country supply clothes and materials to these shops. These clothes are priced very high due to exclusivity. So one needs to be extremely careful and ensure that what is bought is original and not a local-made piece being sold at high rates.

The USP of Janpath however lies in the roadside stalls. They are an integral part of the area and have remained there for decades. There have been suggestions by the state government to remove these stalls, as the market is located in a niche area of the city and the crowds that these stalls pull raise security concerns. But the popularity of this part of the market has made sure that these stalls remain right where they are. You can pick up cotton kurtis, T-shirts, skirts, caps and much more from these stalls. During winters, there is a wide range of scarves, mufflers, sweaters, gloves etc to pick from. The trends at Janpath change with changing seasons and styles. You will often bump into look-alikes of dresses worn in latest Bollywood films.

Accessories

What all would you club under accessories - earrings, bracelets, finger rings, toe rings, belts, necklaces, bags, sun glasses etc.? Janpath is a one-stop-shop for all of these and more. There are innumerable stalls and shops selling a wide range of accessories. You can find rare designs and colors in jewelry and bags available here. There are styles to match everyone's taste. Prices range from Rs. 10-1,500, depending on what you pick (and how well you bargain).

Gifts

Many shoppers come to Janpath to buy gifts in bulk, especially during the festive season. There are choices like flower vases, show pieces, photo frames, etc. to pick from. One can also find some unique gifts like traditionally embroidered clothes or wall hangings, or hand made stationery items like decorative pen stands and note books. Some stores also sell herbal Indian perfumes and incense sticks, which can be a special and different idea for gifting.

Home Décor

If you have done rounds of expensive stores, craving to buy some exquisite wall hangings, but could never afford it, Janpath is the place for you. There are various hawkers and stalls selling wall hangings, sceneries and other such items that can add to the charm of your living room. Rare variety of artificial flowers can also be bought here at competitive prices. Also, you can get stuff like cushion covers and bed covers embroidered with the most attractive ethnic Indian designs at very affordable rates. There is also a wide range of lampshades of various designs that could light up your home.

Shopping Tips

- Shopping at Janpath can be a great experience if one has the apt skills for bargaining. Since this place gets many foreign buyers who would not have much idea about the prices of Indian items, the shopkeepers never keep fixed prices. So don't be surprised if a good bargainer manages to get something at 10% of the price that was quoted by the shopkeeper initially!
- Car parking space is available at the Palika Bazaar's parking area, which is at a walkable distance from Janpath.
- Good time to visit is anytime between 12 PM and 8 PM. The market is closed on Sundays.

The year 2009 brought the new face of fashion and sophistication. Delhi is rightly regarded as the fashion capital of the country with the glitz and glamor that oozes from the young and restless. The interesting part about fad Delhi is that the people here, welcoming a Benetton skirt with a blouse, made by the Sarojini Nagar market or Allen Solly trousers up with stilettos formal shops GK M-block street.

Schade, street fashion for men is not yet developed with such verve. The women of Delhi to swear in three markets in large part to satisfy the urge of street fashion - Sarojini Nagar, Janpath and GK M-Block market.

JANPATH-SPRING/SUMMER COLLECTICN

Janpath Market in the heart of the city attracts thousands in the crowd. On weekends, we would see how people shop there is no tomorrow leaving little room for maneuver. The fashion trends of summer are great, bold, strong and proud. Janpath sport the new look of fashion with drawstring Capri pants in the tissues of interest, such as cotton and chiffon prints and various controls cashmere.

These Capri pants are comfortable, stylish and can be used with a casual T-shirt for regular / or comfort may be shared with a sexy blouse or halter top tube for Disco and beating of a statement. Many interesting accessories such as belts, earrings, kamarbandhs "can also be worn bracelets Janpath. Unfortunately, the shoes are not recommended, and the bags are expensive. The jholas are always fashionable and are largely closely.

SAROJINI NAGAR SHORTSTOP AND HOT / STRONG

This market is famous for its number of useful and affordable clothing known. Although it may be something a little disappointed to get the collection this summer, when most things seem the same as last year. But if endurance, shopping is essentially been such as jackets, vests, could Tube Tops, Capri Pants jeans and skirts with colorful flowers and a few whites are carried out satisfactorily. What you find in abundance in this season is here, shorts of various lengths and prints. "

Hot Pants and shorts are this year jeans or skirts! These shorts or hot pants can be closed with a formal white shirt, belt and pre-Slinky Heels join the mode. wannanbe

However, you must run the search to land the risk if they are not in the top right and the shoes are used. So be careful when you put on these shorts because they do not have much in themselves and need to stay innovations and experiments.

Fashion Statement

Fashion changes fastly than the calendar. What was in great demand last month, becomes outdated as the month changes. Don't be disheartened, the fashion week shows held in capital will keep you in touch what's hot in fashion market. Although most shops have the same stock of tops and shirts, they are portable, but the hip. Baloon tops, cowl neck, shoulders out, Noodle straps are in abundance. may carry a variety of typical festival also noticed that something is branded on the steep side but far less than their counterparts. This market is strongly recommended to watch this summer, too young, hip, modern and relevant. All in all rocks, Fashion Street. Then the girls go shopping this summe

Well, at least not in the Western world. But with advent of The Sartorialist in 2005, that all changed. Today, just about every fashion related website, blog, what-have-you boasts some form of street style photography.

And while Scott Schuman, founder of The Sartorialist, may be the pioneer, he is no longer alone in his work. The streets surrounding fashion week runways have become flooded with a special type of paparazzi-the kind who you want to be bothered by.

Other than a good blog post, and some great inspiration, what do street style photographers get out of this work? Well, if they're smart, they'll leverage it to score other projects. Think about it: Garance Dore's collaboration with Gap, her work for British Elle and Club Monaco, Schuman's Burberry campaign, Tommy Ton's Style.com retainer-none of these would have happened without those trusty blogs.

So that's how we determined 2010's Most Influential Street Style Bloggers. Much like our personal style bloggers' list, this isn't wholly scientific. However, we did consider a number of factors, including: blog traffic, overall appeal, notoriety, and maybe most important-big deals, placements, or campaigns that can be credited to the blog's influence.

We've narrowed the field down to the 10 best. Are your favorites well-represented?

Street-style Fashion Blogs in Germany

The times when glossy magazines provided inspiration for the fashion-conscious and shopaholics are gone. Street-style fashion blogs are popping up all over the world. From Berlin to Barcelona, from Munich to Moscow, from Hamburg Helsinki - self-proclaimed fashion bloggers are taking to the streets and snapping pics of people who they think have style. Young Germany presents a selection of Germany's street style blogs.

Munich

First up is one of Germany's most famous street-style blog: Styleclicker in Munich. Gunnar Hämmerle has been taking street photos since 2007. The big fashion magazines have stood up and taken note and so Gunnar's work is now featured on Vanity Fair's German website, as well as Vogue's.

Berlin

Founded by Mary Scherpe and Benjamin Richter, this blog sees the two students keep an eye out for people they think have an interesting style on the streets of Berlin. "Compared to other German cities, Berlin is clearly ahead in terms of extravagance," says Sherpe. Unlike many other street blogs a bonus on their site is that they ask the person what they are wearing and include the information with the photo. They too have attracted some attention and have already cooperated with established London street-style blog www.thestylescout.co.uk in putting together an exhibition "Catwalk takes to the Streets" in Berlin.

The trendy icons of Hollywood and Bollywood have been eclipsed in Nepal's fashion world by the Korean overcoat and long boots.

The Generation X is fully clad in the latest popular Korean jackets and boots with a lofty Korean hairstyle. There has been a shift from the traditional Korean look to a new one, which has spread from the peninsula to the outside world.

Roshan Bhattrai, a Nepali youth who spent eight years in Korea before recently returning to Kathmandu, noticed a visible change in the streets - the inundation of Korean fashion.

Mufflers around necks, Adidas jackets, overcoats, jeans, long woolen tops and long boots are all fashion styles he saw on the streets of Seoul.

"I am really impressed by the Korean fashion craze here," he says. He noticed the similarities in the streets of Kathmandu and Seoul in this regard.

The big shopping malls in the Kathmandu valley are fully loaded with Korean attire. The medium-cost Korean attire is not as expensive compared with European and other Western fashion products. Attitude Ladies Fashion Ware, a local franchise that sells Korean clothes, just opened a new franchise at the pricey Kingsway shopping center in Kathmandu valley.

Korean products have also become the first choice in casual wear for every age group, Prabin Ranjitkar of UFO fashion wear said. "Customers are changing their attitude. Korean products are widely popular among all age groups as they maintain quality and style. So, most of today's youths follow the Korean style of fashion," said Ramesh Koirala, a seller of Korean clothing.

This winter, most of the jackets, wool sweaters and other attire such as long boots are Korean.

The low-cost clothes were mostly dominated by Chinese imports. Chinese clothes still maintain the biggest portion of low-cost clothes in the Nepalese market, and are reasonably cheap.

But those who have some spare cash are prepared to spend more. "It is a question of comfort and the sizing too. Nepalese and Korean people share a similar physique so most of the Korean clothes are a good fit and people love them," said Krishna Aryal, a fashion seller.

The trendy Korean clothes have wiped out the hip-hop look from the market. Ladies with long garlands around their necks and lads with hair covering their ears are an exact replica of the Korean Generation XC, which is also equally popular here.

Why are tastes changing? There is a growing awareness of Korea in Asia. Korean films, which are now exploding on the world market, including in Nepal, are one of the reasons, according to the traders. Popular Korean actor Song Hye-kyo has emerged as a fashion icon here.

Korean fashion is equally popular outside the Kathmandu valley. Youths from Pokhara and Dharan are the main purchasers of the latest Korean attire.

Nepalese find Korean clothes to be attractive, well-fitting, fashionable and affordable. Moreover, the Nepali traders who buy the clothes from international markets such as Bangkok and Hong Kong are fully geared to Korean fashion, said Aryal.

Korean films have a lot of influence on the Generation X. Subrat Maharjan, a die-hard fan of Korean films, has his hair cut like a Korean actor and imitates the styles too.

"That's why I am unique in my friend circles," Subrat said.

More than others, Korean trends are followed closely by boutiques and fashion designers who are busy replicating what they see in Korean films and fashion magazines.

Manju Banjara, a local fashion designer, is now receiving orders from her customers for exactly what the Korean actors and actresses wore in their latest films.

"I had no idea before. When I started to look at Korean films and fashion magazines, I started to get an idea of how do go with Korean fashion," she says.

Aryal added: "People are more loyal to fashion and trends than brands."

Although Korean fashion is popular in Nepal, Korean trends haven't seeped into every sector of society.

Market leaders predict that Nepal is still a long way off from wanting Korean jewelry. If Korean jewelry enters the Nepalese market currently dominated by Western and Indian styles, it would come as a shock for many who are still surprised by the popularity of Korean films and fashion these days.

Nepal is experiencing a tourist boom this fall, despite political unrest, for many reasons besides the great Himalayas.

Find Kathmandu on a map or globe - just north of India and south of Tibet. It's probably a long way from you: 7,500 miles from New York, 4,500 miles from London, and 6,000 miles from Sydney.

Kathmandu is actually farther away than that. It is separated from the Western world by a vast gulf of time. Kathmandu is as old as the great cities of Europe and far older than those of the New World, but the gap isn't the city's chronological age. Time runs slower here, or at least it doesn't pass in the frenetic, linear way that most visitors consider normal. Past and present are close in Kathmandu; history, legends, and the present are all equally real. Time is a circle, a cycle of seasons, lives, and eras.

Stuck in a traffic jam on Kathmandu's main street, called New Road by everyone here, you might not think so. Everything seems all too western. But get out of your taxi at where the road ends and walk a hundred paces to the stone lions that guard the entrance to the palace complex, and you are in a different world.

Stretching out ahead of you to the right is the old palace, built over the course of six hundred years. The first two stories of the brick and wood building closest may date to the 16th century; the low, white-plastered building farther ahead is from the 17th century; the ornate towers above you were built in the 18th century; and the massively columned white building far ahead was built in 1908. One of the foundation stones of the oldest wing of the palace was reused from a 7th century palace. The 7th century inscription says that that palace was built on the site of "the ancient palace."

Basantapur Square, the open area ahead and to your left, is one of the three loosely connected squares that make up the Kathmandu Durbar Square area. It is named for the tallest of the four towers standing above the brick and wood building to your right. The lower building and the towers are beautiful examples of Newar architecture. This style dominated the architecture of the valley throughout the medieval period and is consistent with two millennia of tradition.

Plain red brick and elaborately carved wood are the hallmarks of the Newar style. Seventh-century Chinese accounts of Kathmandu describe multi-roofed buildings of brick with beautifully carved woodwork. In this earthquake-prone city, most ancient architecture no longer remains, but written records that survive the buildings that stood here over a millennium ago indicate that those structures must have borne a strong resemblance to the ones here today.

Cross the square to a large, three-storey wooden building with an open-air ground level. The building is partially whitewashed, and sometimes red cloth streamers are hung under the roof's eaves. This is Kasthamandap, the old wooden pavilion.

Kasthamandap's age is uncertain, but there is a plaque inside it dated 1048, and this alone is enough to make the building one of the oldest known structures in Nepal. It is almost certain that Kathmandu was named for Kasthamandap, located as the pavilion was between the two ancient hamlets that merged to form the old city. Perhaps this structure or one much like it stood here that long ago. We know the current building was here in 1048, but we don't know how old it was then.

Where historians must be cautious, legend offers a ready account for the origins of this pavilion. Once upon a time, it is said, the god of wood came to Kathmandu in the form of a handsome young man in order to watch one of the city's colourful festivals. A tantric priest recognized him and bound him to the spot by means of a magical spell. A negotiation ensued between the trapped god and the priest. "Ask for a boon", said the god, "And I will grant it in return for my release".

The priest asked for wood to build a temple, and his wish was granted under one condition - that the temple would not be consecrated until the prices of rice and salt became equal. The deal was struck, the god vanished, and the next morning at the spot on which the god had been bound there stood a gigantic celestial tree. The tree was so large that both the Kasthamandap and the Silyan Sattal - the building to the far left with the gilded lions at its corners - are said to have been constructed from its wood.

Next to the two buildings is one of the smallest temples in Nepal, but one of the most important. The temple sits at the corner of the Kasthamandap, where a gilded shrew on a pole faces the shrine reverently.

The shrew is the attendant and mount of the important and popular deity Ganesh, who is always pictured with the head of an elephant and a large, round stomach. The temple has no finial on its pagoda roof so as facilitate Ganesh's ascent to heaven, reportedly made on a flash of blue light. This shrine is the only place the kings of Nepal must visit on foot. For more than 500 years, each monarch has walked to the temple after his coronation to ask for a good beginning to his reign.

Then turn and walk back to find the beautiful carved-wood and brick house, the home of a child goddess, the Kumari.

There are several Kumaris in the valley, but this is the one of state importance. She is a young girl, selected by way of a vigourous screening system to ensure that she comes from the proper background and possesses the "32 virtues," including specified physical attributes and a horoscope that matches that of the king's. (The latter is vital, for since the Kumari is an incarnation of the royal goddess, her annual blessing of the king is considered critical for his rule. This year King Gyanendra was denied the official opportunity for that blessing, but later went unannounced to the house for the ceremony, much to the annoyance of the prime minister.)

After candidates for the Kumari's position are screened, a chosen few are subject to further trials including tests for the 32nd virtue, courage. The candidate children spend a night in the cellars of a temple amid bloody buffalo heads, while men in masks try to scare them. If a girl is a goddess, she should show no sign of fright under such circumstances, even if she is only four or five years old.

Once chosen, the Kumari leaves her family to come to this house, where a family of hereditary attendants cares for her. She will remain the Kumari until an accident or the onset of puberty causes her to bleed. At that moment, the goddess leaves her, and the girl becomes an ordinary mortal. Another child is selected to replace her. Former Kumaris tend to have considerable adjustment problems upon returning to life as ordinary mortals. It is only recently that tutors have been allowed into the Kumari Ghar; the struggle between traditionalists and reformers with respect to this institution has only just begun.

The institution of the Kumari is very old, but this house and the veneration of a state Kumari date to the time of King Jayaprakash Malla, who was overthrown in 1769. Jayaprakash played dice with the royal goddess at times, to discuss affairs of state, but the goddess's ground rules were clear: he could not touch her or think lustful thoughts of her. For many years, Jayaprakash followed the rules, but one evening he was overwhelmed by her radiance and reached out to touch her. Quick as a flash she disappeared and only her voice remained, berating the king for his indiscretion.

The crestfallen monarch begged and pleaded until finally the goddess agreed to return in another form. "You will find a Kumari among the Shakya caste," she said, "And you will worship her as me."

Jayaprakash was chastened. As per the goddess's bidding, he built this house and established the state Kumari here. He also established the Kumari's annual chariot procession, in which the young goddess must bless the king, a part of the ancient Indra Jatra festival. Thus in typically Nepali fashion, the new is grafted on to the old even as the old holds strong; Hindus, like Jayaprakash, and Buddhists, like the Shakya child who becomes the Kumari, together establish religious tradition; and the incredible capacity of its people for assimilation and synthesis makes Kathmandu rich.

5

OFFBEAT PATH TOURISM AND LATEST FASHION

The desire for cheap, local attractions is driving tourists to sewage plants and other offbeat venues.

Have you ever felt like going off the beaten track? Traveling in a train, have you seen a small lonely hillock and imagined a small nest on its top where you could leave, away from the maddening city life? Looking through the glass pane of your AC hotel room, have you ever thought of staying in the forest visible in the distance? Getting close to the nature often means leaving some of the comforts of modern life. Be it traveling on mountain bike, trekking on foot, or sitting on a watchtower for a glimpse of the elusive wild animal. If that is your idea of travel, join us on an offbeat tour through the most exotic destinations of north-bengal. We have all the options to appeal to you, and the best part, all of our tours are customized. So you tell us what you want rather that we telling you what are on offer. Here are some glimpses to help you decide.

New York's most famous attractions are all noteworthy and worth seeing. However, you may want to indulge in something unique, unusual, off-the-beaten-path, or simply off-beat. The following suggestions will get you started; a guidebook like New York Off the Beaten Path will help you further:

" Arthur Avenue Retail Market: An old world way of shopping where you can find fruits, vegetables, meats, deli specialties, plants, imported delicacies and have a good sandwich and cup of coffee at the same time. People from the tri-state area flock to this centerpiece of a still bustling Italian area.

" Offbeat newsstand located on 2nd Avenue at St. Mark's Place (8th St.) is famous not for its papers and magazines but for its delicious egg creams, a New York original drink made of milk, seltzer and syrup.

" Uncle Sam's New York: The leader in Social Travel in New York City, Uncle Sam's New York believes that the main point of travel is to meet new people. Through daily walking tours, shopping tours, pub crawls, and night club tours, they bring together travelers in social groups where they facilitate great interaction among guests and sample the history, culture, fashion, and glamor of New York City. For daily schedule, see Uncle Sam's New York City Tours.

" Intrepid Sea, Air & Space Museum , Pier 86, West 46th Street & 12th Avenue, http://www.intrepidmuseum.org - permanently docked on the Hudson river, this aircraft carrier was originally commissioned for service during World War II and is now a museum open daily to visitors

" The Perfect Weekend, Live it up like a millionaire for a glamorous NYC weekend, without spending the money to match.

" Joe - The Art of Coffee , two locations, http://www.joetheartofcoffee.com - while New York has succumbed to the international Starbucks craze, it is extremely difficult to find a top-quality cup of coffee within city limits; this independent coffee shop, with two locations, arguably brews some of the city's tastiest java

" Another independent coffee shop that consistently receives high marks is 71 Irving Place, owned by http://

www.irvingfarm.com. A quaint cafe right on Grammercy Park, it is often difficult to get one of their coveted tables. They serve various coffees and teas and farm-fresh baked goods.

" Lady Mendl's Tea Salon , The Inn at Irving Place, 56 Irving Place, http://www.ladymendls.com - for a romantic, five-course afternoon tea, make a reservation at this salon, located in the quaint Inn at Irving Place in Gramercy

" Lower East Side Tenement Museum , 108 Orchard Street, http://www.tenement.org - take a guided tour of this unique museum chronicling the history of immigration in the United States

" Museum of Television and Radio , 25 West 52nd Street, http://www.mtr.org - chronicles the fascinating history of TV and radio entertainment through various media exhibits

" New York Transit Museum , corner of Boerum Place and Schermerhorn Street, Brooklyn, http://www.mta.nyc.ny. us/mta/museum - located in Brooklyn, this unique museum is dedicated to the history of New York's multifaceted transportation system; be sure to buy a souvenir from their store (also online at http://www.transitmuseumstore.com)

" Staten Island Ferry , http://www.siferry.com - a ride on this public ferry system from lower Manhattan to Staten Island is a lesser known, free way to view Manhattan and the Statue of Liberty from New York Harbor

" Scott's Pizza Tour in NYC is educational and great fun. Scott is an enthusiastic, extremely knowledgeable guide, who takes you on a School Bus after starting the tour at Lombardi's where he gives you fun and interesting facts about New York Pizza (he gives you a great goodie bag too). After visiting one more Pizzeria in Manhattan, he takes you into another borough (Brooklyn, Bronx or

Queens) to sample two more Pizzerias. Scott introduces you to the owners, compares crusts made in different ovens, and discusses different cheeses used. On the way back, Scott gives out T-Shirts as prizes in a Pizza Trivia Quiz. The tour runs on Sundays from 11-3:30 and he runs walking tours during the week.

" Cloisters - a museum (part of the Metropolitan) dedicated to medieval art, the Cloisters is a bus ride - and seemingly a world - away from the center of Manhattan. Located on the tip of Manhattan north of Columbia U.

" Photo Walk-abouts - these guided walking tours of New York City focus on teaching the participants to take better photos. Included on the guided tour are a photography lesson, historical commentary, and time for participants to take their own photos of an area in NYC. Tours of Greenwich Village, Central Park, and Wall Street are available. All tours last approximately 2.5 hours.

" The Brooklyn Food & Culture Tour which departs at 11:00 AM from Greenwich Village in lower Manhattan on Sundays, Mondays and Fridays takes it's guests on a 4 hour sightseeing, culinary and cultural tour of ethnic Brooklyn. Areas visited include Old Williamsburg and a visit to an Hasidic Kosher Deli, a stop in DUMBO, where participants get to sample scrumptious chocolate at the Jacques Torres chocolate factory, and visit Brooklyn Bridge Park for an excellent view of Manhattan's famous skyline. Sunset Park, featuring a plethora of Latin American food establishments where in the warmer months will include a picnic in the park style lunch featuring the "Cuban" sandwich.

" Flanagan's Wake - It's the original audience interactive Irish wake hit comedy in an actual Irish pub. NBC said it's "One of the funniest show's you'll ever see" It's a great show in a great irish pub! You can raise a pint and laugh all night long!

" City Food Tours does the only food tour of the Upper West Side. They do a Wine, Chocolate & Dessert Tour on Friday and Sunday afternoons. It's a 2 1/2 hr. tour filled with decadent chocolate desserts and wine tasting. They also do a fun 2 hr. ethnic food tour. 212 535 8687.

" Easy Riders JC offers bicycle tours and rentals for locals and tourists in NYC, Jersey City and Hoboken. Take a bike tour of Statue of Liberty, Liberty State Park, Ellis Island and the NYC skyline or rent a bicycle and explore yourself.

" The Wall Street Experience - Explore world-famous financial landmarks such as the New York Stock Exchange, Federal Reserve, and Wall Street guided by real Wall Street insiders. While meandering the narrow, winding streets of Lower Manhattan, you will hear exclusive stories from "inside the trenches" that will entertain, inform and shock you.

Tours have appeared in news and on television globally including CNN, BBC, Reuters, and FoxNews. In addition, these tours was filmed for Oliver Stone's Wall Street 2 movie DVD Feature. The Wall Street Experience aims to demystify and personify Wall Street through personal interaction and storytelling of firsthand experiences.

" New York Food Tours takes tourists and locals alike to experience the colorful history, unique diverse culture and progressive development of New York City through food. Its friendly and professional tour guides take you to secret local spots (neighborhoods, restaurants, eataries, and specialty supermarkets). You can sample a wide variety of delicious cuisines from around the World. New York Food Tours offers the most exotic, ethnically diverse, and the only vegetarian-focusd food tours.

" Food on Foot Tours offers the world's largest buffet, New York City with seven different tours in **Brooklyn,**

Manhattan & Queens and the exclusive Food For Fans Baseball Tour. Eat Like a New Yorker! Food On Foot Tours, New York City's top rated food tour on Trip Advisor's Things To Do (#2 overall as of 04/22/10) takes you off the beaten path outside the tourist areas. Vegetarians and other food restrictions are easily accommodated because you make your own food choices. Food On Foot Tours let's you Eat Like A New Yorker! By experiencing the cuisine of New York you get to experience the culture. This tour is very different from most tours because it is not a gourmet food tour but an inexpensive quality food tour You purchase the food you like and FoodOn Foot Tours is a relaxed getting-to-know-people from around the world subway/walking tour. Tours include East Village Variety, International Express, Midtown Mix, Food For Fans Baseball & Fireworks Tours, Sandwich Salvation and The World Famous Sweet Tooth Tour! All tours have vegetarian options

" Ahoy New York Tours and Tasting is a treasured food adventure for both tourists and locals. The tours, based in Little Italy, Chinatown, the East Village and the Upper West Side, are an adventure of ethnic food, fun conversation, sightseeing, and city trivia. The inexpensive price tag holds nothing to the experience. Ahoy New York Tours and Tasting frequents restaurants and customers enjoy generous portions. In addition, each tour is held in small groups to allow for an intimate city experience and a friendly atmosphere. These tours satisfy even the largest of appetites. Come hungry!

" Inside Broadway Tours Have a professional Broadway actor show you Broadway! They will show you the "real-life" drama and comedy of Broadway, the "must-know" history and gossip. Hear the personal stories of actors in the business of Broadway as they search for workand stardom. Get a "behind the scenes" look at Broadway and Times Square.

" TOAST The Tribeca Open Art Studio Tour is an annual opening of dozens of artist's studios. The art work is in a range of media. It gives a feel for actual working spaces of artists. Be ready to climb stairs in some old industrial buildings. It gives a feel for the special drive and talent of people who paint, draw, sculpt or make environments in very small spaces. It's a very social event., an easy setting to meet people. Friday night at some of the studios there are parties. This year 2010 it runs from Friday April 23 through Monday, April 26.

Trekking in Beautiful Village

The most common trek in the region is Sandakphu, but there are plenty of other options for you to explore. You can go for a trek from Sewak-Loleygaon. This trek starts at the bank of Tista and in 4 days you reach the beautiful village of Loleygaon. You can go for a trek in Samsing including Neora valley national park. The possibilities are endless. more

Jungle Tours

North-Bengal is bestowed with some of the best natural forests in India. This include Jaldapara Wild Life Sanctuary, Mahananda Wild Life Sanctuary, Neoravalley National Park, Gorumara National Park, Buxa Tiger Reserve and a host of other smaller forests including several reserve forests. In our tour we take guests to all these forests. Check our forest tour package

Ornithology Tour

North-Bengal is the paradise for bird lovers. Numerous varieties of birds, both local and migratory, can be seen in the forests and surrounding places. There are several wetlands and water bodies, attracting thousands of birds of different species. Kulik Bird Sanctuary near Raiganj is famous for the migratory birds that come here every year.

There are a large number of other places including Rasikbill, Gajoldoba, Tista and others where you can spend a few days watching the birds. For specific enquiry fill the form at the bottom of this page.

ETHNIC TOURISM AND HOMESTAY

This is a new concept in the region. naturebeyond actively encourages guests to stay with local villagers and understand their culture. Organised home stay with local community is arranged in the village of Tinchuley near Darjeeling. naturebeyond can also organise home stay in other places in North-Bengal depending on guest requirement.

Camping

Regular camps are organised by naturebeyond for students as well as seniors. We have permanent camp resort at Samsing where you can visit any time even if you want to visit this region as part of a small group. more

Biking

Mountain biking is one of the safest and the most enchanting ways to visit this part of the world. To start with, you no longer need to miss the beautiful whistle of a hill myna or the innocent smile of the village boy because your car is traveling too fast. You can travel at your own pace and enjoy the surroundings. The mountain bikes also allow you the flexibility to occasionally go out of the beaten track and venture into an uncharted path. We have special mountain biking package tour. But as with other offbeat tours, you can decide on a tour as per your preference and convenience and we will provide you customized service.

Rafting

Tista in the mountain provides excellent scope for rafting. naturebeyond organises half or full day rafting tour in Tista. Depending on your requirement, longer duration rafting tour can also be organised.

A weekend spent sitting on an island in the South Pacific or shopping in London may have seemed almost routine a year ago, but now money is short and the mood is grim. This doesn't mean the desire to travel and explore is dead, however. Rather, the need for cheap, local entertainment-or perhaps a new penchant for self-punishment after years of excess-appears to be boosting a new trend in tourism: the offbeat, and even morbid, attraction.

Disney is laying off employees as visitors to its theme parks disappear, but in San Francisco the wastewater-treatment-plant tour is overbooked. Beachside resorts in the Caribbean are offering rooms for a steal to entice reluctant travelers, while the Texas Prison Museum, which offers a close-up look at the state's first electric chair and toilet-paper roses crafted by inmates, is doing a booming business.

In Britain, tourists have been passing up landscaped gardens and manor houses in favor of the Workhouse Museum in Nottinghamshire, where exhibits track "poverty through the ages" and visitors can play a game called The Master's Punishment. The museum stages reenactments of paupers in 19th-century costumes and offers glimpses of the rooms used to house homeless families during the 1970s. It is also one of the only venues out of hundreds run by the British National Trust where attendance has increased in recent months, says Heather Whitworth, the museum's community-learning officer.

At the San Francisco Public Utilities Commission, Catania Galvan says she can't figure out why the number of visitors signing up for her sewage-plant tour is up in recent months. "Don't they have anything better to do on a Saturday morning?" she says. "It smells." Nevertheless, Gavlan says this year the Valentine's Day tour included a three-generation family who was "fascinated to learn what happens after water goes down the drain" and a blogger who later posted photos of the process online.

The Rig Museum, a floating oil rig in the Louisiana bayou run by the International Petroleum Museum and Exposition, is off the beaten path, and its highway billboard blew down during Hurricane Katrina, says Virgil Allen, the museum's president. But tourists have managed to find it. Many are members of recreational-vehicle caravans and fans of Alaska Gov. Sarah Palin, the erstwhile vice-presidential candidate, but the museum has also welcomed a few Canadians and Swedes. They come despite what Allen says is a common misperception that working rigs are filthy places where fountains of black crude spew onto the decks. "It's like Williamsburg, Va., and seeing the people making the candles," he says. "While you're taking a tour you may see people working the crane and cooks making dinner in the galley."

The volunteer surgeons who staff the Hunterian Gallery in London are also pleased that the shelves of preserved human organs and exhibits about bloodletting and other 19th-century medical techniques still draw a flood of visitors each week. "There are very few permanent museums of human bits and pieces that are on display," says Tim Guerrier, a volunteer. "I think that's one of the attractions."

Brice Gosnell, a publisher at the guidebook series Lonely Planet, says his company has done marketing research that shows a growing attraction to odd destinations among travelers. "They're looking for unique ideas off the beaten track," he says. "People want to have a different type of experience because it lets them engage in the place more, and there's a little bit of bragging rights going on." To respond to the demand, the company is publishing itineraries that might otherwise seem like a list of places to avoid. They include a trip to polygamy country in southeastern Utah to visit extremist Mormon sects, a tour of California's earthquake country and the Southern Gothic Literary Tour, where, the company says, "you'll find obscene riches, crippling poverty and brutal racial oppression."

One day this spring, the Texas Prison Museum in Huntsville came close to its record attendance level for the summer high season with 179 visitors, many of them families and senior citizens. Besides the electric chair, the museum-which offers free tours to juvenile delinquents on probation-has exhibits showing off the equipment used in the state's first lethal injection in 1982. Employees at the Spam Museum in Austin, Minn., a monument to the canned-pork product invented during the Great Depression, say they have noticed a recent increase in visitors, including many grandparents bringing their grandchildren.

The Irish Famine Museum in Strokestown has also held up well as the Irish economy reels. John O'Driscoll, the museum's general manager, says a drop in international visitors has been largely replaced with local families. They come to see the crowbar used to destroy the homes of evicted tenants, lists of those sent away on famine ships and the gun used to assassinate the landlord of the manor where the museum is housed. If not exactly an upbeat family holiday, it's a reminder that things could be worse.

Here at Off Beat Roads our mission is to promote bicycle travel as a viable way to interact with distant cultures and intense landscapes. Off Beat Roads tours are designed to make you, our riders, feel a sense of adventure and awe. What makes our tours unique is that we strive to show and involve you in the unique cultures that you are riding through all the while avoiding the common tourist paths. Whether you're a serious rider or just someone looking for new adventures while striving to accomplish a personal challenge, we have the tours for you.

Our remote routes are hand-picked from first hand experience and most importantly local knowledge. The roads that we choose to pedal down are true hidden, car-free gems and visually spectacular. We offer you the opportunity to visit places that few, if any, other adventure companies will venture to. For example, Off Beat Roads is the only cycling company in the world to offer a bicycle tour in Ethiopia.

We promise serious WOW factor and incredible memories for a lifetime.

Off Beat Roads also believes that bicycle travel is one of the most environmentally and socially responsible methods of travel. The exhaust-free bicycle and the slow pace that it ensures mean that we are better able to understand different cultures without clogging their air with junk.

While our primary goal is cycling, each tour has opportunities to take part in other great adventure activities such as caving in Belize and hiking in Ethiopia. Flexibility is something that Off Beat Roads strives to achieve for each tour.

Off Beat Roads is a bicycle touring adventure company based in Toronto, Canada. It's owned by Scott Robinson an accomplished adventure traveller who has extensively travelled the world on two wheels. In fact, Scott is a Guinness World Record holder for the fastest crossing of Africa using human power. He accomplished this by cycling from the pyramids of Egypt to Cape Town in 120 days. Don't worry - your tour will be a little more laid-back.

We at Off Beat Roads look forward to offering you these and other unique rides for years to come. There's no shortage of off-the-beaten-path places waiting to explored on two wheels.

Through the ages Catania has been devastated by Mt. Etna's eruptions and lava flows but like the phoenix it always rises again better than ever. Consequently this city is younger than its Sicilian neighbors. Visitors to Catania discover a treasure trove of Baroque architecture and ancient ruins. But these monuments are not just historic site; they are still in use today. All are conveniently located in the compact city center so you can tour them through a leisurely daytrip.

The traditional heart of the city, the Piazza del Duomo at the intersection of Via Vittorio Emanuele II and Via Etnea, is the best place to begin your tour. Upon entering the piazza, the first thing you notice is the Fountain of the Elephant in front of the cathedral (duomo). The black lava rock elephant sits on top of a stone platform and trumpets in the direction of the duomo. This stalwart pachyderm has supported an ancient Egyptian obelisk on its back since 1735. The statue was adopted as the symbol of Catania because legend has it that pigmy elephants once lived in the area and protected the locals by warding off wild animal.

Your gaze invariably moves to the baroque architecture surrounding you. The baroque façade of the duomo, rebuilt after the 1693 earthquake, disguises a Norman apse and transept dating to 1092. The original structure was constructed on the site of the Roman baths known as the Terme Achilliane. A staircase to the right of the main entrance leads down to these ancient ruins. At this time of my visit, the baths were closed to the public however. Inside the duomo on the south side, the chapel of St. Agatha is dedicated to Catania's patron saint. Visitors find scenes from Agatha's life inside the choir stalls.

Exit the duomo and leave the piazza by way of the imposing Porta Uzeda on the south side. Follow your nose to the fish market (La Peschiera), approximately one block away. Here fish mongers hawk the catch-of-the-day as they have done for centuries. Colorful fish ranging in size from sardines to swordfish are neatly displaced upon trays loaded with crushed ice. Watch your step as the street may be slippery with discarded fish entrails.

Pass through the fish market to the Civic Museum (Museo Civico) inside the Castello Ursino at the Piazza Federico di Svevia, at the end of Via Auteri between Via Plebiscito and Via Garibaldi. The imposing 13th century castle was originally built near the seashore by Emperor Frederick II of Swabia. Upon arriving visitors soon realize that the shoreline is now much further away than it once was. In 1669 a lava flow from the erupting Mt. Etna altered this beachfront property forever.

Entering the austere grey lava rock fortress, you find Catania's historic past on display. Begin your visit with an outline of the castle's history, design and development. Other exhibits trace the history of Catania's Greek, Roman, Arab and Norman colonization over the ages. Black and orange Greek pottery, Roman mosaics, sarcophagi and a marble funerary altar are displayed on the main floor. The Parliamentary Chamber (Sala dei Parlamenti), on the upper floor, housed the Sicilian Parliament until 1693 when it was transferred to Palermo. A gallery of religious paintings now replaces the politicians.

Leave the castle for a short walk through a maze of narrow streets toward the Roman Theatre. This 2nd century CE structure, located at 266 Via Vittorio Emanuele II, is hidden from public view by a wall. Still in used for live performances, this theater accommodates as many as 6,000 people on carved lava rock seats. At the entrance I was greeted by a sinister-looking actress in costume and makeup. Public access was restricted because the cast was rehearsing for the evening performance but I was allowed to look around for a few minutes. Also on site is a smaller auditorium known as the Odeon. This 3rd century CE structure, seating 1300 people, is used for more intimate musical performances.

Re-enter the maze of streets and walk to the Benedictine Monastery of San Nicola L'Arena on Via Trinita at Piazza Dante. Upon arrival the first thing you notice is the crumbling wall fronting the street. I was later informed that there was little money available for repairs. Dating to the 1700s, this monastery was the second largest in Europe after Mafra in Portugal. Maintaining the monastic tradition of higher learning, this site is the literature department of the University of Catania.

To the right of the monastery, the Chiesa di San Nicolo has been emptied for renovation. Visitors can wander around the black and white marble interior of the largest church on the island in the company of a flock of birds above you. This is one time when you should not look toward heaven, just in case.

A ten minute walk from the church, the 2nd century CE lava and marble Roman amphitheater (Anfiteatro Romano) is below street level within the Piazza Stesicoro at Corso Sicilia and Via Manzoniand fenced off from the public. At most only about one-half of the original structure is visible. In its heyday, this arena seated 15,000 spectators and was second in size only to the Colosseum in Rome. Now the only gladiators on site are ferile cats which sometimes fight for scraps of food.

Speaking of food, you have likely worked up quite an appetite by now. You may wish to end your tour with some traditional Sicilian pizza baked in a wood-burning oven. "Eat Pizzeria Catania" at Via Coppola 42/44 features the "Norma" pizza which is named for hometown boy Vincenzo Bellini's opera by the same name.

After a delicious meal, opera buffs can top off the evening with a visit the nearby Teatro Massimo Bellini in the Piazza Bellini, at the end of Via Teatro Massimo. The Neo-Renaissance façade is particularly elegant in the evening when illuminated. At the same time, this illumination is also metaphorical; you realize that Catania and Mt. Etna are indissolubly united. They share the same destiny, evolution and eruption.

The hills around Safed are dotted with ancient tombs. To Jewish believers, these tombs of long-deceased tsaddikim, or holy men, are the meeting place between the living and the dead. People make pilgrimages to the burial places to ask for blessings, favors, surcease from suffering.

"They do not actually pray to the ancient rabbis; rather, they pray that the departed tsaddikim will intercede on their behalf with God," Nurit, my guide on this journey explained. "But because God looks favorably upon holy men and the merit of their lives, he is more likely to grant a request."

I wanted the hills surrounding Safed to be a spiritual place for me, but at the tomb of Rabbi Uziel, I was interested and amused, not inspired. My husband Paul came out of the men's side (men and women are separated in Orthodox Judaism) and when I asked him what had happened, he tersely responded, "Nothing."

Nevertheless, I decided to visit one other grave in the small, ancient village of Meron perched on the side of Mount Meron, with its abundant greenery, trees, and views of Safed and the Galilee. Meron village is the resting place of Shimon bar Yochai.

A Spiritual encounter at the grave of Shimon bar Yochai

One of the most famous of the tsaddikim, Shimon bar Yochai is credited with being the author of the central book of Kabbalah, called the Zohar, almost two thousand years ago. Believers go to his grave to pray for prosperity, peace in their souls, fertility, and healing. Paul and I climbed up the narrow main street of Meron to two stone archways with Hebrew inscriptions (one arch for men and one for women) that led to the whitewashed tsyun. Paul entered the men's section, looked around, shot a few photos, shrugged, and exited. "Don't ask. Nothing happened," he said pointedly. "Nothing."

But for me, things would be very different and unexpected. As soon as I entered the women's side of the tsyun, my body started to shake and I began to sob. I looked around, self-conscious. A few women sat on benches and others stood facing the walls or the tomb itself, praying. No one was paying any attention to me as I wept, drenching the front of my pale blue shirt.

I walked, no, I wove to the tomb, placed my head on the cool, white exterior, and prayed and cried for healing for my thinning bones. And I felt as though-- how can I describe this? I felt as though my words were heard. When I came out into the stark afternoon sun, Paul was waiting for me. I had been gone about twenty minutes. I told him what had happened, and he listened. He was surprised, but couldn't really connect to it.

For hours afterwards, tears welled up in my eyes. I knew that something had happened to me at the tomb of Shimon bar Yochai, but I didn't know what it was.

Later on we visited the tomb of Shimon bar Yochai on the holiday of Lag B'Omer.

The Lag B'Omer visit

As the sun disappeared in the west, a great bonfire was prepared near the tomb of Shimon bar Yochai. "When Rabbi Shimon revealed the Torah on his deathbed, there was a blazing light around him, and everyone saw it," explained a woman standing next to me. "To this day, he is associated with light, and fires are lit in his honor."

It was very difficult to see what was going on because of the thousands of people gathered near the sepulcher. Paul held his camera over his head, clicking away. A rabbi poured olive oil and the bonfire blazed, marking the formal beginning of the festivities. Immediately, there was an eruption of ecstasy. Men in black began to dance and sing. Everyone clapped and stomped and hooted with glee. Men wrapped their prayer shawls and fringed undergarments around each other. They danced, they bonded, they were transported with merriment.

Women danced in a circle. Everyone shared food, drinks, blessings.

By tradition, men bring their young sons to get their first haircuts on this night, so the actual tomb was mobbed. I was curious about whatthe faithful did inside the sepulcher, but women were not allowed entry. Paul decided to squeeze his way in so that he could get some photos. It took him about five minutes to work his way through the crowd, and I expected him to return in a minute or two, which is generally the limit of his tolerance for religious exposure.

Half an hour passed, and suddenly I saw Paul. His face was flushed.

"What happened?" I asked, afraid he'd had a negative experience.

"I got pulled into the dancing," he answered. "I was going to drop out, but I figured maybe I should just go with the experience. I had no idea what I was doing. I just followed what the others did. I put my hands around the shoulders of the men next to me, and I kicked up my heels. There were dozens and dozens of men in the dance."

"Did you enjoy it?"

"Enjoy?"

"Yes. Was it fun?"

Paul grew very quiet. "It took me by surprise," he said. "It wasn't really about fun. I found it oddly bonding and moving. It was meaningful."

EMOTIONAL RESONANCE

This was not the cerebral, institutionalized Judaism I had found so empty. It was an outpouring of joyful, crazy, irrational ecstasy. Whether I agreed with their brand of Orthodox Judaism or not, it was undeniable that these men in black and their families were moved and transported and had faith.

Faith. Yes. That was the key to it all. It was faith that made women looking for their soul mates leave behind scarves and underpants at the tomb of Rabbi Uziel. It was faith that I felt when I entered the sepulchral building that housed Shimon bar Yochai. Faith that I could be healed.

Over the years, millions of people had entered that same room, praying for favors and for healing; they had left behind a palpable energy that had emanated from their prayers and tears. It was faith that brought the Yemenite women to the tomb of Baba Sali, faith that he and everyone associated with him would help them to find well- being. And it was faith in the streets of Meron on Lag B'Omer. The belief that young couples could become fertile, that the spirit of Rabbi Shimon was hovering around, that humans could be blessed with prosperity and community and wholeness. That through the year-round study of torah and mysticism

Bajans, also known as Barbadians, are fiercely proud of Crop Over, which they say is "sweet fuh days," in local parlance, and of their island that they liken to a "little England," because of its well-oiled infrastructure (and, yes, the island is quite civilized, even a bit prim and proper). A celebration of music, masquerade, art and food, Crop Over is known across the world to revelers who hopscotch from Trinidad's Carnival, New Orleans' Mardi Gras or Rio de Janiero's Carnival. Bajans insist this festival means more than the others.

- Crop Over (literally "crop over") is a phrase that marks the end of the sugar cane harvest. The festival's roots date to the 1780s, when Barbados was the foremost producer of sugar and plantation slaves cut loose to celebrate a successful crop. Colonized by the English, who prospered with the crop, the slave trade was abolished in 1807; emancipation followed in 1834.

The modern festival was resurrected in 1974; today the merriment includes song and costume contests attended by locals, Caribbean citizens from nearby islands and returning Bajans, who often host family reunions during Crop Over.

Verdant, Prosperous Barbados

Barbados as an island has no high-rises or private beaches, and few large branded hotel chains, but instead a number of small, unique proprieties. Proud and prosperous, the year-round population of 270,000 is quiet affluent and includes a great many refugees from the U.K. The easternmost Caribbean island, part of the Lesser Antilles, Barbados is 21 miles long and 14 miles wide, a pear-shaped coral island with a tropical climate. The west and south coast beaches are palm-fringed with gentle waves; the Atlantic east coast possesses a rugged beauty with its limestone cliffs and wilder seas.

The democratic parliamentary government is stable and both tourists and residents enjoy golf, tennis, cricket, horse racing, diving, yachting, nightlife and the best windsurfing in the Caribbean.

The national dish is cou-cou and flying fish. Cou-cou is made of cornmeal and okra; the silvery blue flying fish are plentiful in the waters around Barbados, so named because they leap from the water and glide through the air. They are delectable when simply grilled with lemon, pepper and butter. The tap water is pure enough to drink when you aren't indulging in a "dark and stormy," ginger beer and Mount Gay dark rum, the rum made on the isle.

Riding in from the airport, I note that unlike many scrubby islands, Barbados is verdant, lush and blindingly green; sugar cane lines either side of the road (sometimes Crop Over is either a bit early or late for the festival). Passing a field, I see gorgeous dark skinned people clad in white playing cricket.

Lodging

A group of us is staying at Almond Beach Club, an all-inclusive resort with middling rooms, surprisingly good food, a kind staff and a small, disappointing patch of beach. If money is no object, Sandy Lane is the top address in town with a spectacular Sunday brunch. Cobblers Cove, an English country house hotel with tropical character and member of prestigious Relais & Chateaux, has a secluded setting on the Northwest coast, 40 suites and a French-trained chef. There are hundreds of lodging options in all price ranges.

Although I'd like to explore Bridgetown, the city center, I opt for an island tour on an open-back bus, which hurtles us pass the major sights, notably, Morgan Lewis windmill, the hamlet of Bathsheba and St. John's Parish Church. I'm really here for the festival, so the only other free time I have, I swim with sea turtles. Half submerged, peering through my mask, I count up to six beneath me at one time, threading under the flipper-clad feet of our group of ten. They are bigger than I expect in length, perhaps five feet long and width; back on the boat, someone says they look "Jurassic." It's a good description.

Crop Over is Party Time

One of the main ingredients in Crop Over is calypso. The Pic-0-de Crop finals are the culmination of several weeks of competition, showcasing singing artistry. Contestants are judged on lyrics, content, performance, melody and diction and it's a great honor to be crowned. There's a full moon tonight. As we enter the stadium, both the stands and field are packed with people of all ages dancing, waving their country flags and hoisting signs for their favorite calypso singer. There are ten contestants, two of whom are women; each will sing two songs. Many have messages.

MakeMyTrip India Ltd, India's largest online travel and hotel-booking firm, is looking to follow an off-beat path to fuel growth.

The company, which got listed on the Nasdaq last week, plans to woo the middle-class consumer with mid-priced holiday packages to uncommon destinations, co-founder and chief operating officer Keyur Joshi told DNA.

The company's primary focus will thus be on opening up unexplored destinations to Indian travellers. It will start charter flights in collaboration with low-cost carriers at mid-priced packages. It is tying up with hotels in bulk to bring down the cost of the packages.

"We are very focused for holidays within India and what we call as 'Greater India', which is destinations at 4-5 hours from India. That remains our primary focus, because the potential is just unimaginable. Not that we will not do Europe and Americas and Africa, but that will be secondary," Joshi said.

MakeMyTrip is looking to make the Maldives, a premium destination, more affordable. It has lined up charter flights twice a week from Mumbai to Gan in the southern part of the islands-nation. The flights will commence October, in collaboration with Kingfisher Airlines. It also plans to add flights from Delhi to Male, capital of the Maldives.

Also from October, the company will do a weekly charter flights to from Bangalore to Port Blair in the Andaman & Nicobar Islands. "Anything at 4-5 hours distance from India, we want to capture. We are looking at newer destinations and various options within Asian and Saarc countries," Joshi said.

In May this year, MakeMyTrip had started charter flights with Kingfisher to Leh, which Joshi said had received an "overwhelming" response. The company is looking at making Bhutan and Phuket similarly accessible. Joshi said compared to foreign travellers, Indians spent the most while on holiday, but still missed out on most exotic destinations. For example, the Maldives, which is an hour-and-a-half away from Bangalore by flight, receives only 3% of Indian tourists. Those from Europe, meanwhile, make up almost 80% of visitors.

The company is looking at offering packages along with the Maldivian Tourism Board starting Rs30, 000 per person for three nights.

6

READING CULTURE BY INHABITANTS DRESSING SENSE

Many people visit museums when they travel to new places. These museums mostly are visited for people, who are looking for cultural information about the place they are visiting. Also, they go to museums to have fun and sometimes people are interested on meet museums which show unusual subjects.

When people travel to a new location, habitually, they are interested about the culture of this place. A museum is a wonderful place to start a cultural research. Commonly, cities have History Museums, Art Museums and a lot more. Those museums offer a very good variety of cultural information to people. Actually, this is a great start to meet a new culture!

Nowadays, in many countries, people could find something call "Interactive Museums". There are museums where they can interact with everything. A case of point is; the museums located on Disney World (Florida, USA). Where people can learn about the American History while they interact with "animatronics" and other objects placed there. That is pretty funny and educative at the same time.

Normally, people are always interested on unusual subjects, trying to break their monotony. There are a lot of museums around the world that shows these unusual subjects. For example, in my hometown we have a museum about paper and the different unusual things that are possible to make with paper. Is possible to find from a simple letter up to a entirely functional boat made in paper. Everybody should try to visit this kind of museums there are incredible.

Summing up, people visit museums because they want to know something else about a culture, have an exceptional funny moment and watch out amazing unusual subjects. Visit a new place means, that you have a duty, visiting as many museums as you can!

A person's wardrobe is perhaps the best way to find out about their personality. You can quickly tell if a person is shy and quiet or loud and attention seeking just by looking at what they are wearing. Generally speaking, an individual who wants to blend into the crowd will not don a hot, sexy, and super-short dress. Furthermore, a loud and outgoing person will generally not wear a simple ho-hum sweater set. Before you choose your outfit for the day, think about how you want other people to see you and interpret your personality.

Clothing that is wild, scandalous, or super trendy may tell others that you are a hip woman fixated on the here and now. Similarly, individuals may look at these rather unique outfit choices in an unpleasant manner, thinking you have less than honorable intentions regarding a variety of issues. This is critical when seeking to dress to impress. Look at the given situation and strive to create a wardrobe that best conveys your particular point. However, do not think you are compromising your personality or individuality by worrying about what your clothing says about you. Work to incorporate unique pieces into your wardrobe that will best reflect your individuality or interests.

For the most part, we want our clothes to portray us in the most positive light possible. Your clothes say far more than you think. Additionally, your accessories or other items you wear can portray you in a variety of lights. Consider for example a woman dripping in diamonds and jewels. What do the specific accessories that she is wearing say about her and her status? Even the smallest-or largest-item in your wardrobe can speak volumes, so be sure your clothing is saying the right thing!

Perhaps the most important time to ensure your clothing is putting you in the best light is during a first meeting. Imagine the difference between meeting with a potential employer wearing a smart suit and carrying a demure bag as opposed to wearing an unsightly get up that includes an outrageously short skirt and a top with an astonishingly plunging neckline. Regardless if you are meeting a potential date, the family of your significant other, or applying for a job in person, what your wardrobe says about you is critical. Wear clothing that bests shows your interests, personality, and individuality instead of wearing clothing that may promote unnecessary misconceptions.

What do your clothes say about you? When you walk down the street or are out in public, what kind of attention are you attracting? Do people smile, stare, point at you and laugh, look away, or simply ignore you altogether? Like it or not, people judge a book by its cover. While it may not seem fair that people develop an immediate impression of who you are simply by the clothes you wear, it's still true that your clothes tell a story about your personality and how you are likely to be perceived by others.

With current fashion trends as they are, it seems that modesty and dressing appropriately has gone right out the window, replaced by the shortest, tightest, most revealing clothes women and tween-teen girls can find. Astonishingly plunging necklines, crop tops, mini or micro mini-skirts, short-shorts (or daisy dukes), and other provocative clothing styles that leave little to the imagination. The clothes you choose to wear on a daily basis provides important information about you as a person, your approximate education level, your income or social status, and even your level of self-esteem. What story is your clothes telling about you? (Men, What do your clothes say about you too?)

A recent telephone conversation with my 23 year-old daughter really drove home the point about girls and young women thinking they are being fashion conscious, but are really missing the mark. It seems my daughter has been trying to help a friend of hers understand why men have been treating the friend disrespectfully, from catcalls to sexual propositions, and how her provocative style of dress just might have something to do with it. This friend also seems to be surprised by the negative reaction she gets from female peers, and struggles to understand why she has lost friendships since "becoming fashionable".

When women dress in a skimpy, seductive style of dress akin to a street corner hooker, they shouldn't be too surprised when men treat them with less respect and dignity than a woman dressed more modestly. You teach people how to treat you. "Is what you wear who you are?" While it may be true that what you wear doesn't define you as a person, what you wear is a reflection of who you are, so choose wisely. Before you choose your outfit for the day, it's important to think carefully about how you want other people to view you and interpret your personality and intentions.

There are many clothing personality styles out there to choose from, from sloppy dressers ("I don't care about my appearance") to expensive designer styles, but the skimpy dressers who opt to wear the most inappropriate, skanky looking outfits that exude a poor self-image is truly alarming. Individuals may look at these wild, scandalous, "fashionable" outfits as a sign that you may have less than honorable intentions, rather than thinking you have a great sense of style.

Whatever bait you use determines the type of fish you'll catch. Having your ass-sets hanging out, your padded-bra enhanced "cleavage" falling out of your revealing top, boys and men are not going to be thinking about what a nice personality you might have. They are much more likely to have thoughts of wanting to "hit that" at the first opportunity possible. Is that really what you want? What you wear is a reflection of who you are as a person. Wear clothes that show your individuality, interests and real personality instead of wearing clothes that may illicit obscene and unnecessary misconceptions about you.

Even very young girls are being targeted to dress seductively and inappropriately, believed by many to be fueled by pop music stars, television and movies, teen magazines and clothing manufacturers. Personally, I blame the parents for buying these clothes for their young children and teens, or allowing them to be accepted as gifts from others.

The sexualizing of children, both girls and boys, has been going on for many years now. As soon as children's television became deregulated in 1984, marketers have been treating children as fair game for the almighty dollar. This new group of consumers are being targeted with lines of toys, clothing and other products with sexual content, imagery and violence. Children and parents are falling for these marketing tactics hook, line and sinker. I'll have more to say on the sexualization of children in an upcoming article.

Research shows that 65% of communication is non-verbal and based not on what you say but in a large part on how you look. The way you communicate yourself conveys positive or negative impressions and can determine whether you are 'seen' as suited for a job, as partner potential or as a match for a sorority. "Every item you are wearing is a word that says something about you," explains

Sarah Whittaker, The Wardrobe Shrink. "Together, your outfit makes up a statement that tells others how you see yourself and what you want them to think about you. You create your own "wardrobe language" from your life experiences and by those that influence you."

Using five tools - clothing type, form & texture, finishing & detailing, color psychology, and accessories - Whittaker profiles and counsels her clientele on how to dress according to their psychology. "Without realizing, people can inadvertently dress what they least want you to know about them or what they most want to hide. What you want to disguise, you only emphasize! This is why reinventing yourself can often lead to a new image...but the same signals."

Culture shock isn't a clinical term or medical condition. It's simply a common way to describe the confusing and nervous feelings a person may have after leaving a familiar culture to live in a new and different culture. When you move to a new place, you're bound to face a lot of changes. That can be exciting and stimulating, but it can also be overwhelming. You may feel sad, anxious, frustrated, and want to go home.

It's natural to have difficulty adjusting to a new culture. People from other cultures (whom you'll be hanging out with and going to school with) may have grown up with values and beliefs that differ from yours. Because of these differences, the things they talk about, the ways they express themselves, and the importance of various ideas may be very different from what you are used to. But the good news is that culture shock is temporary.

WHAT CAUSES CULTURE SHOCK?

To understand culture shock, it helps to understand what culture is. You may know that genes determine a big part of how you look and act. What you might not know is that your environment - your surroundings - has a big effect on your appearance and behavior as well.

Your environment isn't just the air you breathe and the food you eat, though; a big part of your environment is culture. Culture is made up of the common things that members of a community learn from family, friends, media, literature, and even strangers. These are the things that influence how they look, act, and communicate. Often, you don't even know you're learning these things because they become second-nature to you - for instance, the way you shake hands with someone when meeting them, when you eat your meals each day, the kind of things you find funny, or how you view religion.

When you go to a new place, such as a new country or even a new city, you often enter a culture that is different from the one you left. Sometimes your culture and the new culture are similar. Other times, they can be very different, and even contradictory. What might be perfectly normal in one culture - for instance, spending hours eating a meal with your family - might be unusual in a culture that values a more fast-paced lifestyle.

The differences between cultures can make it very difficult to adjust to the new surroundings. You may encounter unfamiliar clothes, weather, and food as well as different people, schools, and values. You may find yourself struggling to do things in your new surroundings that were easy back home. Dealing with the differences can be very unsettling; those feelings are part adjusting to a new culture.

One person's adjustment to a new culture is not necessarily like another's. In some situations, people are excited about their move. Though they may feel a little sad about leaving important people and places behind, they think of the move as a new adventure, or they've heard great things about the place that will become their new home. Some people stay this way. But difficulties adjusting often don't show up right away. In some people, the excitement gives way to frustration as time goes on and they still have trouble understanding their new surroundings.

On the other hand, there are people who never wanted to move in the first place. Their frustration starts the day they realize that they have to move to a new place, when they're perfectly happy where they are. It continues as they find out just how unfamiliar their new home is.

Though people experience culture shock in different ways, these feelings are common:

not wanting to be around people who are different from you

sadness

loneliness

anxiety

trouble concentrating

feeling left out or misunderstood

developing negative and simplistic views of the new culture

frustration

extreme homesickness

These difficult feelings may tempt you to isolate yourself from your new surroundings and dismiss the new culture. It's best not to withdraw like this. If you stay calm, observe and learn, and keep things in perspective, you'll probably find that your difficulties will pass. But if you're feeling depressed and you aren't able to function normally even after the first few months in your new environment, you should talk to a parent or trusted adult about whether to seek help from a physician or mental health professional.

So how do you deal with the frustration and fears you may be having? How can you begin to feel comfortable in your new surroundings?

Depending on where you come from and where you are now, you may or may not have trouble with the native language. It's a good idea to become comfortable with the language as soon as you can. Not being able to understand what people are saying is almost as frustrating as not knowing how to make people understand what you are saying.

Lots of good resources are around to help you practice. Many schools with a good number of students new to the country have language classes. If your school doesn't offer one, check out some of the community centers and libraries in your area. In addition, books make good resources too, and even some websites.

Whatever method you choose, practice is really important. A lot of people are worried about speaking a language they aren't completely comfortable with and think that people who speak the language well will tease them when they stumble over words. This might tempt you to practice the language with someone who is at the same comfort level as you, but it's also important to practice with people who have mastered the language, so that you know when you make a mistake and learn from it.

It might make you uncomfortable when it takes you twice as long to say the same thing as a native speaker, or use the wrong word, but remember that you have nothing to be ashamed of.

Even if you're familiar with the new language spoken around you, chances are you don't know a lot of the slang - casual speech that doesn't make it into translation dictionaries (or most dictionaries, for that matter). This is one of the many reasons why it's a good idea to do some studying on the culture you are immersed in.

A lot of the anxiety that comes with moving to a new place has to do with not knowing what to expect in your new environment. Learning things about your new environment will help you become more comfortable.

School is a great place to do this. Watch and learn from the people around you - see how the students interact with teachers and each other. Find out what your classmates do for fun and what kinds of things are important to them.

You can also get some insight from television and movies, but be careful - not everything you see on the screen is meant to be realistic. But these media do help if you're still trying to learn the language or catch up on some slang, and at the very least, give you something to talk about when you're trying to make a new friend.

You don't have to love everything you find out about the culture, or start acting the way that others do, but when you gain knowledge of what people mean when they say certain phrases or why they dress a certain way, you do begin to feel better.

COPING WITH TEASING

Your accent might be different from everybody else's. Your clothes may also be very different from those around you. Sometimes it can be really difficult being different, especially when compared to the other kids at school. But some people at your school will want to get to know you because your differences seem really cool. Other people, though, might try to give you a hard time.

Some of the people who may try to tease you might do so because of stereotypes. Stereotypes are simplified ideas, often exaggerated or distorted in a negative way, that one group of people holds about another. An example of a stereotype would be everyone with curly hair is lazy. Like this example, stereotypes are often wrong, and they can be hurtful.

If someone harasses you, walk away - don't give the person the satisfaction of seeing that his or her comments bother you. If you can't shake off the comments, talk about it with good friends, siblings, or parents. The people who love you and know that you're a great person can often help you understand that the bully has no idea what he or she is talking about. It also helps to find people at school to hang out with who are cool enough not to care what the bully says.

As much as you would hate to be boxed into a certain type, try and get away from doing the same to others. These characterizations are just as unfair as the ones people might use to describe you. And beliefs in these can get in the way of making some good friends.

It's important to realize that some people have an easier time adjusting to a new culture than others. Sometimes, if members in your family are having an easy transition, they'll be a great source of support - a group of people who are going through something very much like what you're going through. In addition, your family can be a big part of keeping ties to home.

But sometimes, members of your family might want to keep your ties to home too tight. Your parents might not expect the changes that may happen as you begin to learn more about your new culture. Or, they might need your help as they try and learn the new culture, especially if you have a better grasp on the language. Be patient with them; chances are they're trying to manage their culture shock - just like you.

Help If You Need It

You can do a lot to help yourself adjust to a new culture. But don't forget that you aren't alone - there are people you can go to who can help:

Family and friends. Find someone who has experience with culture shock - maybe an older relative who moved to the area before you did. Find out how they handled the newness of their surroundings.

Counselors. If you don't know someone who has been through what you're going through, try talking to counselors and teachers at your new school. They've been trained to help all students deal with a wide variety of concerns. Although they may not have personal experience with culture shock, they do have experience with helping people deal with rough times.

New friends. Making friends who aren't new to the culture may help you understand the culture better and have someone to talk to when you're feeling down.

Rather than giving up your culture so you can fit in, keep your mind open to new ways of doing and thinking about things. Notice things that are the same and things that are different. Appreciating that variety is what makes people so interesting.

Everyone feels the pressure to fit in at one time or another - whether they've lived in the area for days or years. But don't feel like you need to change everything about yourself so you can stand out less. All of your experiences before you came to your new home are part of you, and what makes you special.

Here are a few tips for making sure your new culture doesn't overpower the old:

Educate people about your culture. Just because you're the one entering the new culture doesn't mean you should be the one doing all the learning. Take the opportunity to teach classmates and new friends about your culture; they may know little about it. It will also help them to learn more about you in the process. Invite them over for traditional dishes from your culture, or show them how you celebrate your holidays.

Find a support group. Find kids in your class or neighborhood who recently moved, too. You can share experiences, cheer each other up when things get rough, and introduce each other to the new friends you've made.

Keep in touch with home. You probably left behind good friends and family when you moved. If it's going to be a long time until your next visit, keep in touch. Write letters, emails, and - if your parents are OK with it - make an occasional phone call so you can stay up-to-date on the things happening there, and talk about your new experiences. You've not only left behind people, but also other things - like your favorite spot to hang out. Keep pictures around to remind you of home.

Remember, the key to getting over your culture shock is understanding the new culture and finding a way to live comfortably within it while keeping true to the parts of your culture that you value.

It's important to be yourself. Try not to force yourself to change too fast or to change too many things all at once. You will have your own pace of adjusting. Everyone goes through changes in their life, and it may seem that you are going through more changes than the average person - but as long as you hold on to what's important to you and find a good combination between old and new, you'll be fine.

7

HAUTE COUTURE

Haute couture (French for "high sewing" or "high dressmaking"; pronounced [ot kuty?] OHT-koo-TOOR) refers to the creation of exclusive custom-fitted clothing. Haute couture is made to order for a specific customer, and it is usually made from high-quality, expensive fabric and sewn with extreme attention to detail and finish by the most experienced and capable seamstresses, often using time-consuming, hand-executed techniques. Couture is a common abbreviation of Haute Couture, which refers to the same thing in spirit.

It originally referred to Englishman Charles Frederick Worth's work, produced in Paris in the mid-nineteenth century. In modern France, haute couture is a "protected name" that can be used only by firms that meet certain well-defined standards. However, the term is also used loosely to describe all high-fashion custom-fitted clothing, whether it is produced in Paris or in other fashion capitals such as Milan, London, New York, Tokyo and Madrid.

The term can refer to:

(a) the fashion houses or fashion designers that create exclusive and often trend-setting fashions

(b) the fashions created

LEGAL STATUS

In France, the term haute couture is protected by law and is defined by the Chambre de commerce et d'industrie de Paris based in Paris, France. Their rules state that only "those companies mentioned on the list drawn up each year by a commission domiciled at the Ministry for Industry are entitled to avail themselves" of the label haute couture. The criteria for haute couture were established in 1945 and updated in 1992.

To earn the right to call itself a couture house and to use the term haute couture in its advertising and any other way, members of the Chambre syndicale de la haute couture must follow these rules:

(a) Design made-to-order for private clients, with one or more fittings.

(b) Have a workshop (atelier) in Paris that employs at least fifteen people full-time.

(c) Each season (i.e., twice a year), present a collection to the Paris press, comprising at least thirty-five runs/exits with outfits for both daytime wear and evening wear.

However, the term haute couture may have been misused by ready-to-wear brands since the late 1980s, so that its true meaning may have become blurred with that of prêt-à-porter (the French term for ready-to-wear fashion) in the public perception. Every haute couture house also markets prêt-à-porter collections, which typically deliver a higher return on investment than their custom clothing. Falling revenues have forced a few couture houses to abandon their less profitable couture division and concentrate solely on the less prestigious prêt-à-porter. These houses, such as Italian designer Roberto Capucci, all of whom have their workshops in Italy, are no longer considered haute couture.

Many top designer fashion houses, such as Chanel, use the word for some of their special collections. These collections are often not for sale or they are very difficult to purchase. Sometimes, "haute couture" is inappropriately used to label non-dressmaking activities, such as fine art, music and more.

Members of the Chambre Syndicale de la Haute Couture

The fashion houses listed on the definitive schedule for Haute-Couture Spring/Summer 2010 are:

Official members

Adeline André

Anne Valérie Hash

Chanel

Christian Dior

Dominique Sirop

Franck Sorbier

Givenchy

Jean Paul Gaultier

Maurizio Galante

Stéphane Rolland

Correspondent members (foreign)

Elie Saab

Giorgio Armani

Maison Martin Margiela

Valentino

Guest members

Adam Jones

Alexandre Matthieu

Alexis Mabille

Atelier Gustavo Lins

Christophe Josse

Felipe Oliveira Baptista

Jean-Paul Knott

Josep Font

Josephus Thimister

Lefranc.Ferrant

Maison Rabih Kayrouz

Marc Le Bihan

Jewelry

Boucheron

Cartier

Chanel Joaillerie

Chaumet

Dior Joaillerie

Mellerio Dits Meller

Van Cleef & Arpels

Accessories

Loulou de la Falaise

Maison Michel

Massaro

On Aura Tout Vu

Recent Guest members have included the fashion houses of Boudicca, Cathy Pill, Richard René and Udo Edling, as well as Eymeric François, Gérald Watelet, Nicolas Le Cauchois and WU YONG. In the 2008/2009 Fall/Winter Haute Couture week, Emanuel Ungaro showed as an Official Member.

Former members

Donatella Versace

Elsa Schiaparelli

Emilio Pucci

Chado Ralph Rucci

Christian Lacroix
Erica Spitulski
Erik Tenorio
Fred Sathal
Guy Laroche
Hanae Mori
Jean Patou
Jean-Louis Scherrer
Lanvin
Lecoanet Hemant
Loris Azzaro
Louis Feraud
Mainbocher
Marcel Rochas
Nina Ricci
Paco Rabanne
Pierre Balmain
Pierre Cardin
Ralph Rucci
Torrente
Yves Saint Laurent
Gai Mattiolo
Anna May

HISTORY

French leadership in European fashion may date from the 18th century, when the art, architecture, music, and fashions of the French court at Versailles were imitated across Europe. Visitors to Paris brought back clothing that was then copied by local dressmakers. Stylish women also ordered fashion dolls dressed in the latest Parisian fashion to serve as models.

As railroads and steamships made European travel easier, it was increasingly common for wealthy women to travel to Paris to shop for clothing and accessories. French fitters and dressmakers were commonly thought to be the best in Europe, and real Parisian garments were considered better than local imitations.

The couturier Charles Frederick Worth (October 13, 1826-March 10, 1895), is widely considered the father of haute couture as it is known today. Although born in Bourne, Lincolnshire, England, Worth made his mark in the French fashion industry. Revolutionizing how dressmaking had been previously perceived, Worth made it so the dressmaker became the artist of garnishment: a fashion designer. While he created one-of-a-kind designs to please some of his titled or wealthy customers, he is best known for preparing a portfolio of designs that were shown on live models at the House of Worth. Clients selected one model, specified colors and fabrics, and had a duplicate garment tailor-made in Worth's workshop. Worth combined individual tailoring with a standardization more characteristic of the ready-to-wear clothing industry, which was also developing during this period.

Following in Worth's footsteps were Callot Soeurs, Patou, Poiret, Vionnet, Fortuny, Lanvin, Chanel, Mainbocher, Schiaparelli, Balenciaga, and Dior. Some of these fashion houses still exist today, under the leadership of modern designers.

In the 1960s a group of young designers who had trained under men like Dior and Balenciaga left these established couture houses and opened their own establishments. The most successful of these young designers were Yves Saint Laurent, Pierre Cardin, André Courrèges, and Emanuel Ungaro. Japanese native and Paris-based Hanae Mori was also successful in establishing her own line.

Lacroix is perhaps the most successful of the fashion houses to have been started in the late 20th century. Other new houses have included Jean-Paul Gaultier and Thierry Mugler.

For all these fashion houses, custom clothing is no longer the main source of income, often costing much more than it earns through direct sales; it only adds the aura of fashion to their ventures in ready-to-wear clothing and related luxury products such as shoes and perfumes, and licensing ventures that earn greater returns for the company. Excessive commercialization and profit-making can be damaging, however. Cardin, for example, licensed with abandon in the 1980s and his name lost most of its fashionable cachet when anyone could buy Cardin luggage at a discount store. It is their ready-to-wear collections that are available to a wider audience, adding a splash of glamour and the feel of haute couture to more wardrobes.

The 1960s also featured a revolt against established fashion standards by mods, rockers, and hippies, as well as an increasing internationalization of the fashion scene. Jet travel had spawned a jet set that partied-and shopped-just as happily in New York as in Paris. Rich women no longer felt that a Paris dress was necessarily better than one sewn elsewhere. While Paris is still pre-eminent in the fashion world, it is no longer the sole arbiter of fashion.

Fashion design is the art of the application of design and aesthetics to clothing and accessories. Fashion design is influenced by cultural and social attitudes, and has varied over time and place. Fashion designers work in a number of ways in designing clothing and accessories. Some work alone or as part of a team. They attempt to satisfy consumer desire for aesthetically designed clothing; and, because of the time required to bring a garment onto the market, must at times anticipate changing consumer tastes. Some designers in fact have a reputation which enables them to set fashion trends.

Fashion designers attempt to design clothes which are functional as well as aesthetically pleasing. They must consider who is likely to wear a garment and the situations in which it will be worn. They have a wide range and combinations of materials to work with and a wide range of colors, patterns and styles to choose from. Though most clothing worn for everyday wear fall within a narrow range of conventional styles, unusual garments are usually sought for special occasions, such as evening wear or party dresses.

Some clothes are made specifically for an individual, as in the case of haute couture, or off-the-rack. Today, most clothing is designed for the mass market, especially casual and every-day wear.

Fashion designers can work in a number of ways. Fashion designers may work full-time for one fashion company, known as 'in-house designers' which owns the designs. They may work alone or as part of a team. Freelance designers work for themselves, selling their designs to fashion houses, directly to shops, or to clothing manufacturers. The garments bear the buyer's label. Some fashion designers set up their own labels, under which their designs are marketed. Some fashion designers are self-employed and design for individual clients. Other high-fashion designers cater to specialty stores or high-fashion department stores. These designers create original garments, as well as those that follow established fashion trends. Most fashion designers, however, work for apparel manufacturers, creating designs of men's, women's, and children's fashions for the mass market. Large designer brands which have a 'name' as their brand such as Calvin Klein, Gucci, or Chanel are likely to be designed by a team of individual designers under the direction of a designer director.

Designing a Collection

A fashion collection is something that designers put together each season to show their idea of new trends in both their high end couture range as well as their mass market range. It is considered to have a planned obsolescence usually of one to two seasons. A season is defined as either autumn/winter or spring/summer.

Designing a Garment

Fashion designers work in different ways. Some sketch their ideas on paper, while others drape fabric on a dress form. When a designer is completely satisfied with the fit of the toile (or muslin), he or she will consult a professional pattern maker who then makes the finished, working version of the pattern out of card. The pattern maker's job is very precise and painstaking. The fit of the finished garment depends on their accuracy. Finally, a sample garment is made up and tested on a model.

HISTORY

Fashion design is generally considered to have started in the 19th century with Charles Frederick Worth who was the first designer to have his label sewn into the garments that he created. Before the former draper set up his maison couture (fashion house) in Paris, clothing design and creation was handled by largely anonymous seamstresses, and high fashion descended from that worn at royal courts. Worth's success was such that he was able to dictate to his customers what they should wear, instead of following their lead as earlier dressmakers had done. The term couturier was in fact first created in order to describe him. While all articles of clothing from any time period are studied by academics as costume design, only clothing created after 1858 could be considered as fashion design.

It was during this period that many design houses began to hire artists to sketch or paint designs for garments. The images were shown to clients, which was much cheaper than producing an actual sample garment in the workroom. If the client liked their design, they ordered it and the resulting garment made money for the house. Thus, the tradition of designers sketching out garment designs instead of presenting completed garments on models to customers began as an economy.

Types of Fashion

The garments produced by clothing manufacturers fall into three main categories, although these may be split up into additional, more specific categories:

Haute Couture

Until the 1950s, fashion clothing was predominately designed and manufactured on a made-to-measure or haute couture basis (French for high-fashion), with each garment being created for a specific client. A couture garment is made to order for an individual customer, and is usually made from high-quality, expensive fabric, sewn with extreme attention to detail and finish, often using time-consuming, hand-executed techniques. Look and fit take priority over the cost of materials and the time it takes to make.

Ready-to-wear

Ready-to-wear clothes are a cross between haute couture and mass market. They are not made for individual customers, but great care is taken in the choice and cut of the fabric. Clothes are made in small quantities to guarantee exclusivity, so they are rather expensive. Ready-to-wear collections are usually presented by fashion houses each season during a period known as Fashion Week. This takes place on a city-wide basis and occurs twice a year.

Mass Market

Currently the fashion industry relies more on mass market sales. The mass market caters for a wide range of customers, producing ready-to-wear clothes in large quantities and standard sizes. Cheap materials, creatively used, produce affordable fashion. Mass market designers generally adapt the trends set by the famous names in fashion. They often wait around a season to make sure a style is going to catch on before producing their own versions of the original look. In order to save money and time, they use cheaper fabrics and simpler production techniques which can easily be done by machine. The end product can therefore be sold much more cheaply.

There is a type of design called "kitsch" design. . . originated from the German word "kitschen" meaning ugly or not aesthetically pleasing. Another way to describe the term "kitsch" is "wearing or displaying something that has passed its fashion date and is therefore no longer in fashion. so if you are seen wearing a pair of pants that was once worn in the 80's it is seen to be known as a "kitsch" fashion statement.

Income

The examples and perspective in this article may not represent a worldwide view of the subject. Please improve this article and discuss the issue on the talk page.

Median annual wages for salaried fashion designers were $61,160 in May 2008. The middle 50 percent earned between $42,150 and $87,120. The lowest 10 percent earned less than $32,150, and the highest 10 percent earned more than $124,780.. Median annual earnings were $52,860

(£28,340) in apparel, piece goods, and notions - the industry employing the largest numbers of fashion designers.

Fashion EducatiOn

A classroom filled with sewing machines and mannequins.

A student fashion show, 2007

There are a number of well known art schools and design schools world wide that offer degrees in fashion design. The most notable of design schools include Fashion Institute of Design & Merchandising, Fashion Institute of Technology, Istituto Marangoni, Central Saint Martins College of Art and Design, The Fashion Federation PARIS European Fashion Accreditation, Savannah College of Art and Design, Pratt Institute, London College of Fashion, and University of Westminster in London, Parsons The New School for Design in New York City, Politecnico of Milan, Columbia College Chicago, and National College of Arts (NCA) in Pakistan, and Shih Chien University, RMIT University in Melbourne, and Fu Jen Catholic University in Taiwan and Raffles Design in most parts of Asia.

Areas of Fashion Design

Many professional fashion designers start off by specializing in a particular area of fashion. The smaller and the more specific the market, the more likely a company is to get the right look and feel to their clothes. It is also easier to establish oneself in the fashion industry if a company is known for one type of product, rather than several products. Once a fashion company becomes established (that is, has regular buyers and is well-known by both the trade and the public), it may decide to expand into a new area. If the firm has made a name for the clothes it already produces, this helps to sell the new line. It is usually safest for a company to expand into an area similar to the one it already knows. For example, a designer of women's sportswear might expand into men's sportswear. The chart below shows the areas in which many designers choose to specialize.

Area	Brief	Market
Women's Day wear	Practical, comfortable, fashionable	Haute couture, ready-to-wear, mass market
Women's Evening wear	Glamorous, sophisticated, apt for the occasion	Haute couture, ready-to-wear, mass market
Women's Lingerie	Glamorous, comfortable, washable	Haute Couture, ready-to-wear, mass market
Men's Day wear	Casual, practical, comfortable	Tailoring, ready-to-wear, mass market
Men's Evening wear	Smart, elegant, formal, apt for the occasion	Tailoring, ready-to-wear, mass market
Kidswear	Trendy or Classy, practical, washable, functional	Ready-to-wear, mass market
Girls' Wear	Pretty, colorful, practical, washable, inexpensive	Ready-to-wear, mass market
Teenager Girl Wear	Colorful, comfortable, glamorous,pretty,	Ready-to-wear, mass market
Sportswear	Comfortable, practical, well-ventilated, washable, functional	Ready-to-wear, mass market
Knitwear	Right weight and color for the season	Ready-to-wear, mass market

Area	Brief	Market
Outerwear	Stylish, warm, right weight and color for the season	Ready-to-wear, mass market
Bridal wear	Sumptuous, glamorous, classic	Haute couture, ready-to-wear, mass market
Accessories	Striking, fashionable	Haute couture, ready-to-wear, mass market

Latoya Walker for 'Lost in Translation' collection 2008

Star System

Designers work within a hierarchical system.

"The designers are most stratified in the French system of fashion [...] Fashion ensures the functioning of a system of dominant and subordinate positions within a social order. Fashion is ideological in that it is also part of the process in which particular social groups, in this case elite designers, establish, sustain and reproduce positions of power and relations of dominance and subordination. The positions of dominance and subordination appear natural and legitimate, not only to those in positions of dominance, but also to those in subordinate positions. Fashion and the medium of fashion, that is clothing, offer means to make inequalities of socioeconomic status appear legitimate, and, therefore, acceptable."

A "mythical conception of a designer as a 'creative genius' disconnected from social conditions" is central for the working of the fashion system and for the reproduction of fashion as ideology. Creativity is socially constructed and not an innate given, i.e. many may be gifted but no one can become a famous designer without being legitimized by the fashion system and its gatekeepers.

The star system is as essential for the fashion industry as for any Culture industry. "Genre and the star system are attempts to produce something analogous to brand names in cultural industries. [...] Stars are indispensable because it is part of the ideology of creativity that creative works must have an identifiable author."

World Fashion Industry

Fashion today is a global industry, and most major countries have a fashion industry. Some countries are major manufacturing centres, notably China, South Korea, Spain, Germany, Brazil, and India. Five countries have established an international reputation in fashion design. These countries are France, Italy, the United Kingdom, the United States of America, and Japan.

American Fashion Design

The majority of American fashion houses are based in New York, although there are also a significant number in Los Angeles, where a substantial percentage of clothing manufactured in the US is actually made. There are also burgeoning industries in Miami and Chicago, which were once centers of American fashion. American fashion design is dominated by a clean-cut, casual style, reflecting the athletic, health-conscious lifestyles of some American city-dwellers. A designer who helped to set the trend in the United States for sport-influenced day wear throughout the 1940s and 50's was Claire McCardell. Many of her designs have been revived in recent decades. More modern influences on the American look have been Calvin Klein, Ralph Lauren, Anna Sui, Donna Karan, Tom Ford, Kenneth Cole, Marc Jacobs, Tory Burch, Elie Tahari, Michael Kors, Vera Wang, Betsey Johnson and Tommy Hilfiger.

British Fashion Design

London has long been the capital of the UK fashion industry and has a wide range of foreign designs which have integrated with modern British styles. Typical British design is smart but innovative yet recently has become more and more unconventional, fusing traditional styles with modern techniques. Among the most notable UK fashion designers are Burberry, Paul Smith, Vivienne Westwood, Stella McCartney, John Galliano, Jasper Conran and Alexander McQueen The last British Haute Couture House is said to be Saint-Hill & Von Basedow.

French Fashion Design

Most French fashion houses are in Paris, which is the capital of French fashion. Traditionally, French fashion is chic and stylish, defined by its sophistication, cut, and smart accessories. Among the many Parisian couture houses are Balmain, Hermès, Louis Vuitton, Chanel, Yves Saint Laurent, Christian Dior, Givenchy, Balenciaga and Chloé, who display their work at the designer collections that are held twice a year. Although the Global Language Monitor placed it 3rd in the Media, after Milan and New York, French fashion is internationally acclaimed and Paris remains the symbolic home of fashion.

Italian Fashion Design

Milan is Italy's capital of fashion. Most of the older Italian couturiers are in Rome. However, Milan and Florence are the Italian fashion capitals, and it is the exhibition venue for their collections. Italian fashion features casual elegance and luxurious fabrics. The first Italian luxury brand was the florentine Salvatore Ferragamo (who has exported exquisite hand-made shoes to the U.S. since the 1920s); among the best-known, exclusive fashion names, another florentine Gucci is the greatest-selling Italian fashion brand, and third greatest in the world, with worldwide sales of $7.158 billion dollars. Other well-known Italian fashion designers Valentino Garavani, Dolce & Gabbana, Bottega Veneta, Etro, Emilio Pucci, Roberto Cavalli, Versace,

Giorgio Armani, Fendi, Borbonese, Prada, Loro Piana, Byblos, Alberta Ferretti, Moschino, Ermenegildo Zegna, La Perla, Agnona, Laura Biagiotti, Lancetti, Iceberg, Carlo Pignatelli, MIla Schön, Roberta di Camerino, Solidea, Krizia, S.Nick Barua, Trussardi and Missoni. Even though Milan is the national and worldwide capital of fashion, Rome, Florence, Turin, Naples and Venice also contain many high-end fashion boutiques and are international capitals. But there are However, many designers that are not very famous... or not "equal" to the nominated before. some of this stilist are Armando Sauzullo, Arianna Morelli or Carmentea Tsparopulos.

Swiss Fashion Design

Most of the Swiss fashion houses are in Zürich. The Swiss look is casual elegant and luxurious. The fabrics manufactured in St. Gallen are exported to the most important fashion Houses all over the World (Paris / New York / London / Milan/ Tokyo). The first Swiss luxury brand is Alvoni from the italo/Swiss designer Marianne Alvoni.

Japanese Fashion Design

Most Japanese fashion houses are in Tokyo. The Japanese look is loose and unstructured (often resulting from complicated cutting), colours tend to the sombre and subtle, and richly textured fabrics. Famous Japanese designers are Yohji Yamamoto, Kenzo, Issey Miyake (masterful drape and cut), and Comme des Garçons 's Rei Kawakubo, who developed a new way of cutting (comparable to Madeleine Vionnet's innovation in the 1930s).

Fashion Design Terms

" A fashion designer conceives garment combinations of line, proportion, color, and texture. While sewing and pattern-making skills are beneficial, they are not a prerequisite of successful fashion design. Most fashion designers are formally trained or apprenticed.

" A pattern maker (or pattern cutter) drafts the shapes and sizes of a garment's pieces. This may be done manually with paper and measuring tools or by using an AutoCAD computer software program. Another method is to drape fabric directly onto a dress form. The resulting pattern pieces can be constructed to produce the intended design of the garment and required size. Formal training is usually required for working as a pattern marker.

" A tailor makes custom designed garments made to the client's measure; especially suits (coat and trousers, jacket and skirt, et cetera). Tailors usually undergo an apprenticeship or other formal training.

" A textile designer designs fabric weaves and prints for clothes and furnishings. Most textile designers are formally trained as apprentices and in school.

" A stylist co-ordinates the clothes, jewelry, and accessories used in fashion photography and catwalk presentations. A stylist may also work with an individual client to design a coordinated wardrobe of garments. Many stylists are trained in fashion design, the history of fashion and historical costume, and have a high level of expertise in the current fashion market and future market trends. However, some simply have a strong aesthetic sense for pulling great looks together.

" A buyer selects and buys the mix of clothing available in retail shops, department stores and chain stores. Most fashion buyers are trained in business and/or fashion studies.

" A seamstress sews ready to wear or mass produced clothing by hand or with a sewing machine, either in a garment shop or as a sewing machine operator in a factory. She (or he) may not have the skills to make (design and cut) the garments, or to fit them on a model.

" A teacher of fashion design teaches the art and craft of fashion design in art or fashion school.

" A custom clothier makes custom-made garments to order, for a given customer.

" A dressmaker specializes in custom-made women's clothes: day, cocktail, and evening dresses, business clothes and suits, trousseaus, sports clothes, and lingerie.

" An illustrator draws and paints clothing designs for commercial use.

" A fashion forecaster predicts what colours, styles and shapes will be popular ("on-trend") before the garments are on sale in stores.

" A model wears and displays clothes at fashion shows and in photographs.

" A fit model aids the fashion designer by wearing and commenting on the fit of clothes during their design and pre-manufacture. Fit models need to be a particular size for this purpose.

" A fashion journalist writes fashion articles describing the garments presented or fashion trends, for magazines or newspapers.

" An alterations specialist (alterationist) adjusts the fit of completed garments, usually ready-to-wear, and sometimes re-styles them. NOTE: despite tailors altering garments to fit the client, not all alterationists are tailors.

" An Image Consultant, wardrobe consultant or fashion advisor recommends styles and colors that are flattering to the client.

A fashion week is a fashion industry event, lasting approximately one week, which allows fashion designers, brands or "houses" to display their latest collections in runway shows and buyers to take a look at the latest trends. Most importantly, it lets the industry know what's "in" and what's "out" for the season. The most prominent fashion weeks are held in the four fashion capitals of the world - New York City, London, Milan and Paris.

In the major fashion capitals, fashion weeks are semiannual events. January through April designers showcase their autumn and winter collections and September through November the spring/summer collections are shown. Fashion weeks must be held several months in advance of the season to allow the press and buyers a chance to preview fashion designs for the following season. This is also to allow time for retailers to arrange to purchase or incorporate the designers into their retail marketing.

SCHEDULE

New York, London, Milan and Paris each host a fashion week twice a year with New York kicking off each season and the other cities following in the aforementioned order.

There are two major seasons per year - Autumn/ Winter and Spring/Summer. For Womenswear, the Autumn/Winter shows always start in New York in February. Spring/Summer shows start in September in New York. Menswear Autumn/Winter shows start in January in Milan for typically less than a week followed by another short week in Paris. Menswear Spring/ Summer shows are done in June. Womenswear Haute Couture shows typically happen in Paris a week after the Menswear Paris shows.

Over the past few years, more and more designers have shown inter-seasonal collections between the traditional Autumn/Winter and Spring/Summer seasons. These collections are usually more commercial than the main season collections and help shorten the customer's wait for new season clothes. The inter-seasonal collections are Resort/Cruise (before Spring/Summer) and Pre-Fall (before Autumn/Winter). There is no fixed schedule for these shows in any of the major fashion capitals but they typically happen three months after the main season shows. Some designers show their inter-seasonal collections outside their home city. For example, Karl Lagerfeld has shown his Resort and Pre-Fall collections for Chanel in cities such as Moscow, Los Angeles and Monte Carlo instead of Paris. Many designers also put on presentations as opposed to traditional shows during Resort and Pre-Fall either to cut down costs or because they feel the clothes can be better understood in this medium.

Some fashion weeks can be genre-specific, such as a Miami Fashion Week (swimwear), Rio Summer (swimwear), Prêt-a-Porter (ready-to-wear) Fashion Week, Couture (one-of-a-kind designer original) Fashion Week and Bridal Fashion Week, while Portland (Oregon, USA) Fashion Week shows some eco-friendly designers.

HISTORY

In 1943, the first New York Fashion Week was held, with one main purpose: to distract attention from French fashion during WWII, when workers in the fashion industry were unable to travel to Paris. This was an opportune moment - as for centuries designers in America were thought to be reliant on the French for inspiration. The fashion publicist Eleanor Lambert organized an event she called 'Press Week' to showcase American designers for fashion journalists, who had previously ignored their works. The Press Week was a success, and, as a result, magazines like Vogue (which were normally filled with French designs) began to feature more and more American innovations. Until 1994, shows were held in different locations, such as hotels, or lofts. Eventually, after a structural accident at a

Michael Kors show, the event moved to Bryant Park, behind the New York Public Library, where it still is today, held inside a number of large white tents.

However, long before Lambert, there were fashion shows throughout America. In 1903, an NYC shop, called Ehrich Brothers, put on what is thought to have been the country's first fashion show, to lure middle-class females into the store. By 1910, many big department stores were holding shows of their own. It is likely that American retailers saw that they were called 'fashion parades' in Paris couture salons and decided to use the idea. These parades were an effective way to promote stores, and improved their status. By the 1920s, the fashion show had been used by retailers up and down the country. They were staged, and often held in the shop's restaurant during lunch or teatime. These shows were usually more theatrical than those of today, heavily based upon a single theme, and accompanied with a narrative commentary. The shows were hugely popular, enticing crowds in their thousands - crowds so large, that stores in New York in the fifties had to obtain a license to have live models. Nowadays, access to NYFW (New York Fashion Week) is by invitation only, and only fashion magazine editors, fashion magazine journalists, models (and ex-models) and celebrities are invited. Other buyers are restricted to the showrooms/stores and the articles in the magazines.

Controversy

The dominance of the big four benefits industry participants. For example, buyers, journalists, models and celebrities can limit their travel and simply move from one to the other over the four week period. However the arrangement is criticized for stifling manufacturing employment in the UK and design talent in emerging fashion hubs such as Los Angeles.

Cities With fFashion Weeks

City	Name	Date established
Amsterdam	Amsterdam International Fashion Weeks (AIFW)	2004
Asunción	Asunción Fashion Week	2003
Austin	Austin Fashion Week	2009
Athens	Hellenic Fashion Week	2000
Atlanta	Haute.lanta Fashion Week	2006
	Atlanta International Fashion Week	2007
Auckland	New Zealand Fashion Week	2001
Baltimore	Baltimore's Fashion Week	2008
Bangalore	Bangalore Fashion Week (BFW)	2009
Bangkok	Bangkok Fashion Week	2005
Barcelona	080 Barcelona Fashion Week	1981 (Known as Pasarela Gaudí until 2001)
Beirut	Beirut Fashion Week	2008
Belgrade	Belgrade Fashion Week	1996
Bellevue, Washington	Bellvue Fashion Week	2007
Berlin	Mercedes-Benz Fashion Week Berlin	2007
Bogotá	Bogotá Fashion Week	2007
Boston	Boston Fashion Week	1995
Brooklyn	Brooklyn Fashion Week	2003-05 Brooklyn Designers 2008 its new form
Brisbane	Mercedes-Benz Fashion Festival Brisbane	2006
Buenos Aires	Buenos Aires Fashion Week	2008
Colombia	Colombiamoda Celebrate On Medellin city	2005

City	Name	Date established
Cork	Cork Fashion Week	2009
Cape Town	Cape Town Fashion Week	2003
Charleston	Charleston Fashion Week	2007
Casablanca	Casablanca fashion week	2005
Chennai	Chennai International Fashion Week (CIFW)	2009
Chennai	Chennai Fashion Week	2010
Chicago	Chicago Fashion Week	Marshall Field's Glamorama
Cleveland	Fashion Week Cleveland	2002
Columbus, Ohio	Columbus Fashion Week	2007
Copenhagen	Copenhagen Fashion Week	1964 (Unknown in its current form)
Cyprus	Cyprus Fashion Week	2008
Dhaka	Dhaka Fashion Week	2008
Dhaka	Bangladesh Fashion Week	2009
Dallas	Couture Fashion Week Dallas	2009 to present in its current form
Dallas	Dallas Fashion Week	2008
Dar es Salaam	Swahili Fashion Week	2008
Dubai	Dubai Fashion Week	2006
Dublin	Dublin Fashion Week	
Düsseldorf	Düsseldorf Fashion Week	1963
Gainesville	Gainesville Fashion Week	2009
Hong Kong	HKTDC Hong Kong Fashion Week for Fall/Winter	1968
Istanbul	Istanbul Fashion Week for Spring/Summer 2011	2007

City	Name	Date established
Jakarta	Jakarta Fashion Week	2008
Johannesburg	Joburg Fashion Week	2007
Kansas City	Glance Fashion Week KC	2009
Karachi	Fashion Pakistan Week	2009
Karachi	Karachi Fashion Week	2009
Kenya	Kenya Fashion Week	2005
Kiev	Ukrainian Fashion Week	1997
Kingston	Caribbean Fashion Week	Started November 2001 (Now held in June)
Kobe	Kobe Fashion Week	Started from 2006 A/W collection
Kuala Lumpur	Malaysia Fashion Week	2007-2008
Lahore	Lahore Fashion Week	2010
Lagos	Nigerian Fashion Week	2007
Las Vegas	Las Vegas Fashion Week	2009
Lisbon	Moda Lisboa/Lisbon Fashion Week	1994
Liverpool	Liverpool Fashion Week	2008
London	London Fashion Week	1961 (1993 in its current form)
Los Angeles	Los Angeles Fashion Week	2003
Luanda	Moda Luanda / Luanda Fashion: annually, on January/February	1997
	Angola Fashion Week: annually, on June/July	1999
ModAngola -	Mens Fashion Week Angola: annually, on November	2009
Lviv	Lviv Fashion Week	2008
Madrid	Cibeles Madrid Fashion Week	1963
Mallorca	Mallorca Fashion Week	2009

City	Name	Date established
Manila	Philippine Fashion Week	1997
Melbourne	L'Oreal Melbourne Fashion Festival	
	Melbourne Spring Fashion Week	
Mexico City	Fashion Week Mexico	1998
Miami	Funkshion: Fashion Week	
	Miami Beach	1998
	Miami Fashion Week	1998
	Mercedes-Benz Fashion Week Miami	1998
Midwestern United States	Midwest Fashion Week (MFW)	2004 (2008 current location)
Milan	Milan Fashion Week	1958
Montréal	Montréal Fashion Week	2001
Morocco	Morocco fashion week (caftan)	1996
Moscow	Fashion Week in Moscow	1994 (2003 in its current form)
Moscow	Russian Fashion Week	2001
Mumbai	Mumbai Fashion Week	2001
Nashville	Music City Fashion Week	2008
New Delhi	Delhi Fashion Week	2008
	India Fashion Week	2000
New York City	New York Fashion Week	1943 (1993 in its current form)
New York City	Africa Fashion Week New York	2008
New York City	Couture Fashion Week New York	2003 to present in its current form.
	Couture Fashion Week	
Omaha	Omaha Fashion Week	2007
Oslo	Oslo Fashion Week	2004
Ottawa	Ottawa Fashion Week	2008 in its current form

City	Name	Date established
Oxford	Oxford Fashion Week	2009 in its current form
Panama City	Panama Fashion Week	2008 in its current form
Paris	Paris Fashion Week	1973 in its current form
Plovdiv	Plovdiv Fashion Week	2000
Plovdiv	MEN`s Fashion Week	2010
Plovdiv	BRIDAL Fashion Week	2009
Philadelphia	Philadelphia Fashion Week	2009
Phoenix	Phoenix Fashion Week - separated from Scottsdale Fashion Week	2004
Portland	Portland Fashion Week	2003
Prague	Prague Fashion Week	2002
Raleigh	Raleigh Fashion Week	2009
Reykjavík	Iceland Fashion Week	2000
Riga	Riga Fashion Week	2004
Rio de Janeiro	Fashion Rio	
Rome	Rome Fashion Week	
Sacramento	Sacramento Fashion Week (SACFW)	2008
San Antonio	San Antonio Fashion Week	2010
San Francisco	San Francisco Fashion Week	2004
San Juan	Puerto Rico High Fashion Week	
Santiago	Santiago Fashion Week	2006
São Paulo	São Paulo Fashion Week	1995
Sarajevo	Sarajevo Fashion Weeks - two rival events	
Scottsdale	Scottsdale Fashion Week	2005
Skopje	Skopje Fashion Week	2005
Singapore	Singapore Fashion Week.	1987
Seattle	Seattle Fashion Week	2003
Seoul	Seoul Fashion Week	

City	Name	Date established
Shanghai	Shanghai Fashion Week	
Sydney	Australian Fashion Week	1995
	Sydney Fashion Festival	
	Sydney Fashion Weekend	
Sofia	SOFIA Fashion Week	2004
St. Louis	St. Louis Fashion Week	
Stockholm	Stockholm Fashion Week	1995
Tashkent	Tashkent Fashion Week	2006
Tbilisi	Georgian Fashion Week	2010
Tbilisi	Tbilisi Fashion Week	2010
Tehran		2006
Tirana	Albania Fashion Week	2007
Toronto	LG Fashion Week	1999 (2009 in its current form)
Trinidad and Tobago	Fashion Week Trinidad and Tobago	2008
Ulan Bator	Goyol	1988
Valencia	Valencia Fashion Week	2001
Vienna	MQ Vienna Fashion Week	2009
Warsaw	Warsaw Fashion Street	1996
Zagreb	Zagreb Fashion Week	2003

From bold themes to saluting patriotism - that's what the Delhi Fashion Week, which starts today, is all about; here's a peek into what two of the country's well-known designers - Ritu Beri and JJ Valaya - will dish out on Day 1.

Ritu Beri Salutes the Indian Army

Through her Autumn/Winter collection, designer Ritu Beri pays a tribute to the Indian Army for their constant and dedicated work towards making the nation a safe place to live in. She is dedicating her show at the Delhi Fashion Week to her father Balbir Singh Bedi who was in the Indian Army.

"I will be presenting a line that has been inspired by the colours of the Indian Army. It's my way of paying tribute to them and also to my father through my collection. My line is sharp and consists of structured silhouettes with a bright colour palette. I have jackets, coats and drapey dresses. The collection is not outlandish and has lots of reds, blacks, animal prints, etc. My dad's regiment had red, gold and black colours and I have tried to play around those. It has been a nostalgic journey for me," Ritu says.

So, why is she rooting for the military in the fashion extravaganza that is bigger and better this time with around 130 designers taking part?

She says, "I feel not much is done in our country to respect the army men who lay down their lives so that we can live safely. We should pay more gratitude. I have been disturbed with constant reports about army men being killed by militants, taken hostage or murdered and other such ghastly news."

She adds, "The Indian Army is very special for me because I was raised in an army background. That's another reason I decided that I should do something special for the army. Being in the army is also fun as a lot of fanfare happens with the band and the style of dressing. I have tried to integrate all these elements into my collection while saluting their heroics."

JJ Valaya Narrates a Courtesan's Tale

Fashion designer JJ Valaya's line narrates the story of a fictitious courtesan, Alika, who dreams of falling in love. The show promises to be a spectacle for the eyes with lots of drama on the ramp. Valaya will divide his show into acts and scenes that will take the narrative forward. Theme wise, Valaya is definitely going bold in his Autumn/Winter line.

He says, "The collection's inspiration is a dream. It has the story of a courtesan who will take everyone on a journey - from despair to hope and happiness. Her quest for love will have a lot of passion. She desires to fall in love and have a great life. The ensembles will have a running connection through the narrative of the tale as it will reflect the mood of the courtesan. The garments, hair and make-up - everything will be inspired by the emotions that the girl is going through. That way there will be lot of drama."

In two decades Valaya has left his mark on the national and international markets with his signature designs. This time he will play with a monochromatic colour palette with a dash of red thrown in. Valaya has also custom-made the music for the show to add to the drama when he rolls out his line.

"The story is beautiful and I have divided the entire show into acts. The colour will thus start with black and ivory and then red will set in to echo the passion that the courtesan has towards life and love. From thereon metallic hues will dominate. I don't think anyone will raise eyebrows because I am telling the story of a courtesan. I am trying to tell people to feel what this girl feels and how she is yearning for love even after living in an atmosphere that doesn't really give her freedom to live life according to her own terms. People need to see the beauty of the thought," Valaya ends.

India Fashion Week

The India Fashion Week (IFW), is an event organized and promoted by the Fashion Design Council of India and sponsored by Wills Lifestyle.

It is a fashion week and held in the national capital of India, New Delhi annually.

Wills Lifestyle India Fashion Week Autumn Winter 2010 had collections from 130 designers on the runway and the exhibition areas.

Since it is a national body for fashion industry, FDCI has built credibility over years by associating with the Indian government and various ministries. Recently FDCI was commissioned by the Ministry of External Affairs and the Indian Council for Cultural Relations to organize a SAARC fashion show.

8

FASHION INDUSTRY AND TINSEL TOWN

Bollywood fashion sets the tone for all South East Asian and much Middle Eastern fashion. In last two decades, the designers that are part of the largest film industry in the world have been shaping the fashion of Indian and Pakistani clothing. Interestingly Bollywood fashion has transcended that part of the world and is making a major impact on Western style as well. Here's a little history on the cultural phenomenon that is Bollywood and its impact on style and clothing.

Up until the late 1980s, fashions in Hindi films showed a limited sense of style. Even though Indian inspired silks and embroidery were unrivaled - the film industry did not showcase superior workmanship and fashion forward style. Costuming in film was either very ordinary street style clothing or extremely garish and gaudy.

During the 1990's and beyond, Indian designers became a force all their own. When Sushmita Sen appeared in flowing silk saris in a hit movie, this traditional dress was catapulted into the urban fashion scene. Shamita Shetty made the sharara (a Muslim inspired lehenga choli that is actually flared pants giving the illusion of a skirt) a hit and Priyanka Chopra made the red silk dupatta (drape) synonymous with Bollywood fashion.

Hindi films have inspired Indian style over the last two decades, but the fascinating phenomenon is the carry over of Indian fashion to the West. The recent tunic top craze is one example. It's a style that looks flattering on everyone - from teenagers to grandmothers. Then, of course, there's Boho Chic - bohemian or ethnic clothing driven by Indian, and Bollywood fashion. This trend has been around since the hippies of the 1960's and there seems to be no end in sight. TIME, MSN, and even Bella Online have all praised this hot ethnic trend.

The comfort, elegance, beauty and especially the versatility of Indian clothing are not lost to the western public. For example, a silk embroidered kurta or tunic top can be worn to the beach as a cover, a cocktail party, out clubbing, or even a formal event.

Where should you look for hip Bollywood fashion? A local Indian boutique is not a bad start. Another good place is the web. Plenty of sites such as Kaneesha.com (who offers free shipping and 10% off) and Benzer offer good choices. Kaneesha offers high quality silk embroidered fashions that appeal to western sensibilities while still being totally unique and easy on the budget.

"Bollywood" is the casual term widely used for the Mumbai based Hindi movie industry in India. Based on the decadent, opulent, yet trendy look and feel of these films, "Bollywood" or "Bollywood inspired" is also a phrase used to describe a wonderful rising trend in fashion.

Rich, vibrant, bright colors are combined with decadent fabrics such as silk, brocade, jacquard, chiffon, amazing beadwork, and meticulous embroidery. The result is elegant, theatrical and extremely wearable. Cues from some of the most beautiful Bollywood superstars like Aishwarya Rai, and Freida Pinto (Slumdog Millionaire), give this example of a movie inspired, yet beautifully wearable work of art. The colors and detailing on this saree (sari) are very traditional handworked designs reminiscent of Rajasthani and Kutchi colors, patterns and embroidery.

Also shown in the skirt is a tie die pattern know as "bandhni", or to bind with thread to achieve a pattern. A peacock green and gold saree.

Micro, Mini or Maxi 1970s Skirt Lengths

By 1970 women chose who they wanted to be and if they felt like wearing a short mini skirt one day and a maxi dress, midi skirt or hot pants the next day - that's what they did.

For eveningwear women often wore full length maxi dresses, evening trousers or glamorous halter neck catsuits. Some of the dresses oozed Motown glamour, others less so.

Left - Two young women in their early twenties on holiday in the Canary Islands c1972. The short check flared skirt was very popular, as was the empire style of the diamond check pattern mini dress. Right - Halter neck catsuit pattern of 1971. Exotic and tropical prints were a reflection of designers gaining inspiration from foreign travel destinations.

For evening in the early seventies, either straight or flared Empire line dresses with a sequined fabric bodice and exotic sleeves were the style for a dressy occasion.

One frequently worn style was the Granny dress with a high neck. Sometimes the stand neck was pie-crust frilled, or lace trimmed. Often they were made from a floral print design in a warm brushed fabric or viscose rayon crepe which draped and gathered well into empire line styles.

Right - Typical short and mini dresses worn at an office party in 1972/3. At the front a young girl wears a long floral granny dress that covers her knees.

Another hugely successful evening style of the 1970s was the halter neck dress, either maxi or above knee.

Left - Black halter neck dress pattern of 1971.

At a disco, girls might don hot pants. In contrast to the reveal all mini, a woman would suddenly confound men by completely covering her legs and retort that mini dresses were an exploitation, rather than a liberation of women.

Easier Travel Broadens the Fashion Mind

The influence of the self styled hippy clothes and the mish-mash of 1970s fashion from every corner of the global village crept into mainstream fashion. Easier travel meant that people brought ideas and accessories from abroad. Others looked for designers to provide styles that fitted the mood of an era, that had returned to nature and was anti-Vietnam-war in outlook.

Cars and Central Heating Bring Lighter Weight Clothes

If travel broadens the mind, enclosed eco systems alter the fabric options. By the late 1970s women travelling in enclosed heated cars could choose to wear lighter weight clothes and abandon full length coats. Homes and stores in the temperate climate of the United Kingdom almost universally became centrally heated and most women could tolerate a chill mad dash between car and front door knowing that warmth awaited them.

Long coats gradually began to decline as an essential winter buy and a series of garments from velvet jackets, quilted padded duvet coats, hip length wool velour jackets and shaded ombre dyed raincoats, were all a more usual sight as a quick cover up from the elements.

Caftan or Kaftan

The Hippies of the sixties had brought with them clothes from other ethnic groupings which had often never even been seen before in the west. Nehru jackets and loose flowing robes from hot countries made their way to world cities and permeated down to mainstream fashion, helped of course by designers like Yves St Laurent.

From the mid to late 70s, caftans, kaftans, kimonos, muumuus, djellaba (a Moroccan robe with a pointed hood) or jalabiya (a loose eastern robe) and other styles from every part of the Indian sub continent and Africa, were translated into at home style robes and comfort wear. They were worked in every fabric imaginable, but were especially suited as glamour dressing when sewn in exotic fabrics and edged in silver, gold or other metallic embroidered trims.

1970s fashion, which began with a continuation of the mini skirts, bell-bottoms and the androgynous hippie look from the late 1960s, was soon sharply characterized by several distinct fashion trends that have left an indelible image of the decade commemorated in popular culture. These include platform shoes which appeared on the fashion scene in 1971 and often had soles 2-4 inches thick. These were worn by both men and women. Wide-legged, flared jeans and trousers were another fashion mainstay for both sexes throughout most of the decade, and this style has been immortalised in the 1977 film Saturday Night Fever which starred John Travolta. The "disco look", complete with three-piece suits for men and wrap-around rayon or jersey dresses for women, which the film launched, lasted until it was gradually replaced by punk fashion and straight, cigarette-legged jeans. Platform shoes gave way to mules and ankle-strapped shoes, both reminiscent of the 1940s, at the very end of the decade.

The decade began with a continuation of the hippie look from the 1960s. Jeans remained frayed, and the Tie dye shirts and Mexican peasant blouses were still popular. In addition to the mini skirt, mid-calf length dresses called "midis" and ankle-length dresses called "maxis" were also worn in 1970 and 1971, thus offering women three different skirt lengths.

In 1971, extremely brief, tight-fitting shorts, called hot pants, were a fashion craze for girls and young women.

In Britain and the urban United States, from 1972-1974, fashions were inspired by extravagantly-dressed glam rock stars such as David Bowie, Roxy Music, and Marc Bolan. Glitter was in vogue. Women wore high-waisted, flared satin trousers or denims, the latter usually decorated with rhinestones, tight lurex halter tops, metallic-coloured lamé and antique velvet dresses, satin hot pants, sequined bra tops, and occasionally they wore ostrich- feather boas draped over their shoulders or turbans on their heads. The 1930s and 1940s look was also popular, and many women bought their clothes at second-hand shops. The short, imitaion rabbit-fur jacket was a hot fashion item during this period. Make-up was garish and glittery, with eyebrows thinly plucked. Bianca Jagger, who often used an ebony walking stick, wore peacock-feathers in her cloche hats, green sequined shoes, transparent blouses, and carried an ivory cigarette- holder, was a fashion icon. The men often wore lamé suits, silver astronaut-style outfits, satin quilted jackets, wide-legged denims or velvet trousers, and rhinestone-studded shirts. Their hair was long and softly layered, or spiky, multi-coloured mullets. Clothing shops which became associated with glam rock-inspired fashion were Biba, in London's Kensington High Street, and Granny Takes a Trip in Kings Road, which also had a branch in West Hollywood, California. Both shops had opened in the 1960s.

Platform shoes with soles 2-4 inches thick became the style for both men and women. Men's ties broadened and became more colourful, as did dress shirt collars and suit jacket lapels.

Another trend for both sexes was the fitted blazer, which flared slightly at the hip. It came in a variety of fabrics, including wool, velvet, suede, and leather. The buttons were covered and the lapels wide.

For teenage girls and young women the crop top was often worn, sometimes with a halter neck or else tied in a knot above the midriff.

By the mid-1970s hip-huggers were gone, replaced by the high-waisted jeans and trousers with wide, flared legs. In Britain, they were often referred to as "Loon pants". These lasted until the end of the decade when the straight, cigarette-leg jeans came into vogue.

The dancer's leotard became an important feminine fashion accessory in 1974. It remained in style throughout the decade.

In Britain and Ireland, in the early to mid-1970s, there was the bootboy subculture which influenced youthful male attire with the "parallel jeans", which were flared jeans that stopped at mid-calf. These were worn with heavy workman's "bovver" boots, braces, (US suspenders), and denim jackets. Their hair was usually worn longish by the middle of the decade.

The wrinkled look for women enjoyed a brief vogue in 1975, as did flared denim skirts which ended just below the knee. Trendy colours were dusty rose, Prussian blue, bottle green, rust, and brown.

Fashion influences were peasant clothing, such as blouses with laces or off-the-shoulder necklines, inspired by those worn in the 17th century. Yves St Laurent introduced the peasant look in 1976, and it became very influential. Skirts were gathered into tiers and shoulder lines dropped. Camisoles were worn. Clothing became very unstructured and fluid at this point. Embroidered clothing, either self-made or imported from Mexico or India also enjoyed favour. Floral-patterned prints were in fashion. Fake-flower chokers and hair combs were often worn with the peasant skirts. In 1977, the ruffled sundress coupled with a tight t-shirt worn underneath enjoyed a brief popularity.

Late 1970s

With the popularization of disco and the increasing availability and diversity man-made fabrics, a drastic change occurred in mainstream fashion, the likes of which had not been seen since the 1920s. All styles of clothing were affected by the disco style, especially those of men. Men began to wear stylish three-piece suits (which became available in a bewildering variety of colours) which were characterized by wide lapels, wide legged or flared trousers, and high-rise waistcoats (US vests). Neckties became wider and bolder, and shirt collars became long and pointed in a style reminiscent of the "Barrymore" collar that had been popular in the 1920s. The zippered jumpsuit was popular with both men and women, and clothing inspired by modern dance (wrap-around skirts and dresses of rayon or jersey) also became common. Neck-scarves were also used. Skin-tight Spandex trousers, tube tops, and slit skirts were popular for a while at the very end of the decade. In 1978, there was a brief craze for transparent plastic trousers worn with leotards underneath. Silk blouses, spaghetti-strapped tank tops and shirt-waist dresses were also worn. Women's shoes began to echo the 1940s, with high-heeled lower-platform mules--"Candies" made of molded plastic with a single leather strap over the ball of the foot or "BareTraps" made of wood becoming very popular. With the brief decline of disco late in 1979, these styles (which were by then being criticized as flamboyant) quickly went out of fashion. Designer jeans with straight, cigarette-legs, and painters' pants then started to come into style.

The top fashion models of the 1970s were Lauren Hutton, Margaux Hemingway, Cheryl Tiegs, and Jerry Hall

Custom T-Shirts / Baseball Jerseys

Short-sleeved t-shirts of various colors personalized with iron-on decal illustrations or appliquéd letters spelling a name or message were very popular among teen and pre-teen boys in the U.S. during the late 70s. It was also the trend for teenagers and young men to carry a pack of cigarettes under the sleeve. Also popular were baseball jerseys or "baseball sleeves" (white shirts with colored sleeves worn under baseball uniform shirts). These were worn plain or with appliquéd pictures or words, as described above.

One-Piece Swimsuits

American actress Farrah Fawcett, who starred in the 1970s programme Charlie's Angels, was a sex symbol for that time period. Her poster which was released in 1976 and sold 12 million copies, featured the actress with her long mane of streaked-blonde hair, perfect white teeth, and wearing a one-piece swimsuit that launched the trend for the maillot. This was, when it resurged in the 1970s, a sexy, tight swimsuit, with deep neckline and high-cut legs, worn by young women and girls in lieu of the bikini, although it did not entirely replace the latter.

Three-Piece Suits

The 1970s saw a return to three-piece suits (suits with matching vests), worn with the wide-collar shirts carried over from the 1960s. Sometimes these were worn without ties as dance-club wear, or even in just a vest and jacket combination as depicted in the film Saturday Night Fever. As formal wear, however, the three-piece slowly died out in the early 1980s, by which time the outfit had come to be associated with lawyers.

In the 1970s, women's hair was usually worn long with a centre parting

Hairstyles

Throughout much of the decade, women and teenage girls wore their hair long, with a centre or side parting, which was a style carried over from the late 1960s. Other hairstyles of the early to mid 1970s included the wavy "gypsy" cut, the layered shag, and the "flicked" style in which the hair was flicked into resembling small wings at the temples. This look was popularised by the stars of the television series Charlie's Angels. Blonde-streaked or "frosted" hair was also popular. In 1977, punk singer Debbie Harry of Blondie sparked a new trend with her shoulder-length, dyed platinum blonde hair worn with a long fringe (bangs). Young men's hair was worn long until well past the mid-1970s. Unlike the unkempt 1960s, it was often worn styled in soft layers. In California, the tousled blond, surfer hair was fashionable for teenage boys and young men. In the early part of the decade sideburns were popular. For Blacks in the United States and elsewhere, the afro was worn by both sexes throughout the decade. It was occasionally sported by whites as an alternative to the uniform long, straight hair which was a fashion mainstay until the arrival of punk and the "disco look" when hair became shorter and centre partings were no longer the mode.

Nostalgia

Dev Anand was very fair and remarkably handsome. He looked marvellous in black dresses. Who can forget the evergreen song picturised on him "tu kahan yeh batah ish nasili raat mein, mane na mera dil diwana" wooing innocent beauty Nutan in the streets of Shimla. I actually remember a lot of outfits/costumes from films, not all of them strange or peculiar. One particular type of dress that I grew up coveting immensely was the full circle skirt worn in many 50s films. I remember watching "Jaane kahan mera jigar" on TV and really wanting a dress with a full skirt like the actress (whose name I don't know) was wearing.

Mostly in the films from that era it would be the character of the Anglo-Indian or East Indian secretary in the movie who would be wearing a very westernized outfit, either dress with full skirt, or a blouse with a tight pencil skirt, matched with pumps and a short bob. Very chic.

Film-goers Still

I remember the skin-hugging sari that sexy and sultry Mumtaz wore in fast song "Jai Jai Shiv Shankar" in film Aap ki Kasam because for the life of me I couldn't figure out how she wrapped it around herself to get such a perfect hourglass figure. And then there were the tighter than tight salwar churidar sets that Asha Parekh, Mumtaz and Babita used to wear, which were miracles of garment technology. Or perhaps they had multiple sets of the same outfit to change into when they kept getting ripped apart.

One costume that was absolutely divine was the red angarakha-churidar set that Rekha wore for for "Dil cheez kya hai" in Umaro Jaan. It was the most perfect colour for her, and I honestly think she looked perfect feminine in that dress.

Sharmila Tagore looked elegant yet sensuous in Indian outfit. Who can forget extremely sharp featured Saira Banu who was chand ka tukda for her ardent male fans. Hmmm....and then there were the atrocious outfits that actresses wore in the 80s, which just in my opinion was a terrible decade, fashion wise (I'm not a big fan of shoulder plates or puffy sleeves). Biggest culprits include Jaya Prada, who was fine in sarees but looked awful in everything else.

Rekha in film Silsila : Her fishbone earrings - I longed and longed for a pair of those - but by the time they made their appearance in bangalore, they were outdated.

And Rekha in classical film Umrao Jaan.

Shabana's Azmi's bengal handlooms in film Swami and her mercerized cottons in film Ankur - I managed to get those in time!

Jaya Baduri's black-frame glasses and pallu draped over her jooda in film kora kagaz - I did that too.

Dimple's tie-up polka dotted choli in block-buster Bobby - I was too old by then.

Zeenat Aman's short haircut in super-duper hit film Don - went to the salon all prepared to shear off my rapunzel tresses - chickened out at the nth moment.

Parveen Babi was curvaceous, long, and fair skinned who looked western from every angle. She used to smoke openly, and was not afraid of criticism. Who can forget her flouncy skirt in super hit song"angrezi mein kehte hain ke I love you" opposite Amitabh Bachchan.

Neetu Singh looked attractive and sexy in trousers and side-slit shirt in film Deewar. In the coming years, she popularised these western outfits in the public and many college-going girls of that time used to imitate Neetu's dress sense.

9

SEA SURFING AND FASHION IN BEACH

Sea surfing is one of the most popular modes of recreation for the people who do not hold themselves back in undertaking perilous tasks just for the sake of fun and enjoyment. Primarily because of its geographic location, India is a dream destination for the lovers of adventure sports and adventure tourism. With more than 3000 kilometer-long coastline, the most part of which is accessible, adventure-loving individuals can plunge into a number of water adventure sports such as sea surfing, ocean surfing, scuba diving, white water rafting, wind surfing, etc.

The district of Ramanathapuram in Tamil Nadu is a sacred place of pilgrimage. Known as the holy domicile of the Hindu God Rama, this place is the Garden of Eden for any piously religious person. A number of myths and folklores are attached to this place to fill the tourists with awe and bewilderment. Lying in the extreme south of Ramanathapuram, Dhanushkodi offers you the chance to get yourself engaged in some adventure sports such as sea surfing and ocean surfing. Go and make your adrenaline rush!

Sea surfing in India has generated a tremendous amount of interest among the daring and adventure-loving people. Adventure tourism has scaled dizzying heights in the tourism sector in India. Sea surfing, diving and swimming, deep sea fishing, snorkeling, skin diving, wind surfing, white water rafting, scuba diving, etc. set the adventurous pulse of India when it comes to water adventure sports in India. The word adventure encompasses a broad spectrum of mental as well as physical attributes - inherent for some and acquired for others. Attributes like endurance, spirit to take calculated risks, mental frame to work as a team, vitality and readiness and so on are normally associated to enthusiastic youths of a nation. They tend to defy the orthodox and venture into some untrodden territories. This website hosted by the Ministry of Youth Affairs and Sports, the Government of India portrays the department's proposed scheme to promote adventure facility programs among young students. Check out the following link to learn in detail about the objectives of the program and a lot more.

Explore the thrill and intriguing experience of sea surfing and ocean surfing. Cleartrip.com brings you the profile of Aruba-California Lighthouse, one of the most popular sea surfing and dune surfing destinations in the world. The uninterrupted stretches of soothing coastline and blue water can be intoxicating for an ardent adventure seeker. Explore the thrill and intriguing experience of sea surfing and ocean surfing. Cleartrip.com brings you the profile of Aruba-California Lighthouse, one of the most popular sea surfing and dune surfing destinations in the world. The uninterrupted stretches of soothing coastline and blue water can be intoxicating for an ardent adventure seeker.

Welcome to a real natural setting adorned with sea, sun, sky and mountains. Yes, KwaZulu Natal is one of the top seaside destinations in the world with a perfect blend of modernity and primitive pampering. Beaches such as Ramsgate, Marina Beach, Margate and Hibberdene are just about ideal in case you want to go for scuba diving or sea surfing. It will be an enrapturing experience for adventure-loving person.

This website is going to provide you with detailed information on adventure sports in India. Places like the Andaman and Nicobar Islands, Goa, Kerala, Lakshadweep Islands, Orissa and Tamil Nadu offer an umpteen number of beach holiday options for ardent nature lovers. You can just laze around the beach or venture into some really serious water sports such as sea surfing, scuba diving, etc. Check out the following link to find your definitive online resources for adventure sports and beach holidays in India.

For many tourists, Orissa is not always on top of the list of chosen holiday destinations in India. But those who cherish adventurous escapades on the tip of topsy-turvy waves on the sea, Gopalpur-on-sea might be a dream destination indeed. 180 kilometers from the state capital Bhubaneswar, this place exercises a calming influence on your weary mind and soul. The Bay of Bengal has a lot in the offing when it comes to sea surfing and sailing. Take a look at the following link to explore more.

Experience the sheer pleasure of adventure sports like sea surfing, wind surfing and snorkeling in the islands of the Andaman and Nicobar. The serene tranquility of the beaches here attracts the tourists from all over the globe. The picturesque landscape surrounded by emerald seawater under the blue sky is just about the ideal tourist destination.

The sub-continent of India has 7,000 kilometers[4,349 miles] of coastline. The greater portion of thatis still unexplored in terms of locating surf spots. But with that much exposure to the Arabian Sea, the Indian Ocean and the Bay of Bengal and with nothing off the southern tip of India for thousands, and thousands of kilometers except Antarctica- with that much ocean out there, you know there are going to be some great waves when the conditions are favorable.You're right, there are!

There are waves in India all year round averaging 3 to 5 feet but the season for big waves [8feet plus] is May through September. This is the pre-monsoon and monsoon season. At this time the surf will range from 8 to 15 feet and bigger - often blown out and messy but sometimes the conditions are fantastic - super glassy and offshore winds, at which time you can expect some world class waves.

But before continuing about surfing in India there is one little bit of information that you might find interesting - the word 'SURF' came from India.

If there is any one word that surfers use the most it is probably 'SURF'. After all, where would surfing and surfers be without surf? Surf is everything. But did you ever stop to wonder where the word 'surf' came from? I did and what I found out from an Etymology Dictionary was that the word 'surf' came into use in 1685. The word 'surf' was derived from the Indian word 'suffe' meaning the coastline. This word was picked up by Portuguese sailer's in the 1600's and 'suffe' soon became 'surf'.

Is that far out or what? India, one of the last countries in the world to take up surfing actually gave surfing its name! India may be the last to get into surfing but the surf potential in India is already proving to be amazing! Mother India does it again.

A swimsuit, bathing suit, or swimming costume is an item of clothing designed to be worn while participating in water sports and activities such as swimming, water polo, diving, surfing, water skiing, or for any activity in the sun, such as sun bathing. It is also used as an undergarment in sports that require a wetsuit such as waterskiing, scuba diving, surfing, and wakeboarding. In New Zealand English and some areas of Australian English, swimsuits are usually called togs or bathers. They are less commonly called "cossies". The term "togs" is less common in other parts of the Commonwealth, where it can also refer to clothes in general.

Current Swimsuit Styles

In western culture, men's swimsuit styles include boardshorts, jammers, swim trunks, briefs or "speedos", thongs, and g-strings, in order of decreasing lower body coverage.

Women's swimsuits are generally one-piece, bikinis, or thongs. The most recent innovation is the burqini, a more modest garment designed for Muslim women, which covers the whole body and head (but not face) in a manner similar to a diver's wetsuit. These are an updated version of full-body swimwear, which has been available for centuries, but complies with Islam's traditional emphasis on modest dress. In Egypt, hi term "Sharia swimsuit" is used to describe full-body swimwear.

Special swimsuits for competitive swimming, designed to reduce skin drag, can resemble unitards. For some kinds of swimming and diving, special bodysuits called diveskins are worn. These suits are made from spandex and provide little thermal protection, but they do protect the skin from stings and abrasion. Most competitive swimmers also wear special swimsuits including partial and full bodysuits, racerback styles, jammers and racing briefs to assist their glide through the water thus gaining a speed advantage (see competitive swimwear).

Swimsuits are also worn for the purpose of body display in beauty pageants. Magazines like Sports Illustrated's annual "swimsuit issue" feature models and sports personalities in swimsuits.

Body Coverage

Swimsuits range from garments designed to almost completely cover the body to garments designed to expose as much of the body as possible within personal and community standards of modesty, the choice of garment also depending on factors such as how much or how little sun protection desired, and prevailing fashions.

Swimsuits can be skin-tight or loose-fitting. They are often lined with another layer of fabric if the outer fabric becomes transparent when wet. Almost all swimsuits cover the genitals and pubic hair, while most except thongs cover much or all of the buttocks. Most swimsuits in western culture leave at least the head, shoulders, arms, and lower part of the leg (below the knee) exposed. Women's swimsuits generally cover at least the aereola and bottom half of the breasts, but some are designed for the top part of the swimsuit to be removed . In many countries, young girls and sometimes women choose not to wear a swimsuit top, and this can vary with the occasion, location, age, etc. Men's swimsuits which cover the upper body are relatively rare in western culture.

Both men and women may sometimes wear swimsuits covering more of the body for cold water swimming (see also wetsuit and dry suit), or for swimming competitions where they may be constructed of a special low resistance fabric.

Unlike regular swimsuits, which are designed mainly for the physical appearances, competitive swimwear is manufactured for the purpose of aiding athletes in swim competitions. They reduce friction and drag in the water, increasing the efficiency of the swimmer's forward motion. The tight fits allow for easy movement and are said to reduce muscle vibration, thus reducing drag. Starting around 2000, in an effort to improve the effectiveness of the swimsuits, engineers have taken to designing them to replicate the skin of sea based animals, sharks in particular.

In July 2009, FINA voted to ban non-textile (non-woven) swimsuits in competitive events from 2010. The new policy was implemented to combat the issues associated with performance enhancing costumes, hindering the ability to accurately measure the performance of swimmers. Subsequently, the new ruling states that men's swimsuits may maximally cover the area from the navel to the knee, and women's' counterparts from the shoulder to the knee.

1858 Woman's bathing suit.

Cartoon by George du Maurier in Punch, 1877. Shows men's and children's bathing suits.

Some swimmers use a specialized training suit called drag suits to artificially increase drag during practice. Drag suits are swimwear with an outer layer of looser fabric - often mesh or nylon - to increase resistance against the water and build up the swimmer's endurance. They come in a variety of styles, but most resemble a looser fitting square-cut or swim brief.

SwimWear and Hygiene

Germs, bacteria and mold can grow very quickly on wet bathing suits. Medical professionals warn that wearing damp swimwear for long periods of time can cause a number of infections and rashes in children and adults, and warn against sharing bathing suits with others. They suggest changing out of a wet bathing suit right away can help prevent vaginal infections and itching in females and Tinea Cruris "Jock Itch" in males

In Classical antiquity swimming and bathing was done nude. There are Roman murals which show women playing sports and exercising wearing two-piece suits covering the areas around their breasts and hips in a fashion remarkably similar to a bikini of ca. 1960. However, there is no evidence that this was used for swimming. All classical pictures of swimming show nude swimmers.

In various cultural traditions one swims, if not in the nude, in a version in suitable material of a garment or undergarment commonly worn on land, e.g. a loincloth such as the Japanese man's fundoshi.

The invention of the railway, and the proliferation of rail travel in the mid 1800s made it possible for large numbers of people to visit coastal regions. In the 18th century women wore "bathing gowns" in the water; these were long dresses of fabrics that would not become transparent when wet, with weights sewn into the hems so that they would not rise up in the water. The men's swim suit, a rather form-fitting wool garment with long sleeves and legs similar to long underwear, was developed and would change little for a century.

In the 19th century, the woman's two piece suit became common-the two pieces being a gown from shoulder to knees plus a set of trousers with leggings going down to the ankles.

In the Victorian era, popular beach resorts were commonly equipped with bathing machines designed to avoid the exposure of people in swimsuits, especially to people of the opposite sex.

In 1907 the swimmer Annette Kellerman from Australia visited the United States as an "underwater ballerina", a version of synchronized swimming involving diving into glass tanks. She was arrested for indecent exposure because her swimsuit showed arms, legs and the neck. Kellerman changed the suit to have long arms and legs and a collar, still keeping the close fit that revealed the shapes underneath. She later starred in several movies, including one about her life.

After this, bathing wear started to shrink, first uncovering the arms and then the legs up to mid-thigh. Collars receded from around the neck down to around the top of the bosom. The development of new fabrics allowed for new varieties of more comfortable and practical swim wear.

Due to the figure-hugging nature of these garments, glamour photography since the 1940s and 1950s has often featured people wearing swimsuits. This subset of glamour photography eventually evolved into swimsuit photography exemplified by the Sports Illustrated annual swimsuit issues.

The first bikinis were introduced just after World War II. Early examples were not very different from the women's two pieces common since the 1920s, except that they had a gap below the breast line allowing for a section of bare midriff. They were named after Bikini Atoll, the site of several nuclear weapons tests, for their supposed explosive effect on the viewer.

Through the 1950s, it was thought proper for the lower part of the bikini to come up high enough to cover the navel. From the 1960s on, the bikini shrank in all directions until it sometimes covered little more than the nipples and genitalia, although less revealing models giving more support to the breasts remained popular. At the same time, fashion designer Rudi Gernreich introduced the monokini, a topless suit for women consisting of a modest bottom supported by two thin straps. Although not a commercial success, the suit opened eyes to new design possibilities. In the 1980s the thong or "tanga" came out of Brazil, said to have been inspired by traditional garments of native tribes in the Amazon. However, the one-piece suit continued to be popular for its more modest approach.

Men's swimsuits developed roughly in parallel to women's during this period, with the shorts covering progressively less. Eventually racing-style "speedo" suits became popular-and not just for their speed advantages. Thongs, G-strings, and bikini style suits are also worn, typically these are more popular in more tropical regions; however, they may also be worn at public swimming pools and inland lakes. But in the 1990s, longer and baggier shorts became popular, with the hems often reaching to the knees. These were often worn lower on the hips than regular shorts.

ALTERNATIVES TO SWIMSUITS

Swimming without a swimsuit is a form of social nudity. Nude beaches may be reserved for nude sun bathing and swimming. For women, swimming or sun bathing with the upper half of the body uncovered is often known as "toplessness" or "topfreedom".

As an alternative to a swimsuit, some people wear trousers, underpants or a T-shirt either as a make-shift swimsuit or because they prefer regular clothes over swimsuits. In some countries, such as Korea or Thailand, swimming in regular clothes is the norm while swimsuits are rare. At beaches, this may be more accepted than at swimming pools, which tend not to permit the practice because underwear is unlined, may become translucent, and may be perceived as unclean.

The Goans are a bunch of happy-go-lucky people and their chilled-out attitude is reflected in the clothes they wear. Goa is the perennial party zone and regarding clothes casual wear is the order of the day. As such if one is embarking on a detour to Goa, efforts should be made blend oneself with the Goan life by wearing clothes that embody the carefree Goan spirit.

You don't need to fret over what to wear in Goa since the dressing style draws heavily on high street fashion characterized by bold and bright floral prints. Moreover as Goa is endowed with a balmy weather the need for specific clothing is done away with. The clothes to wear during the summer are cotton apparels while in winters you can put on some light woolens.

Beachwear and other accessories figure prominently in clothes to wear in Goa. Swimsuits and colorful sarongs are the favorite beachwear for the fairer sex. Those planning to bask in the sun should carry along sunscreen lotions and sunglasses. One can also opt for tees, shorts and jeans while loitering in the scenic beaches of Goa.

10

STEALING LIMELIGHT IN TOURIST SPOT

It can be quite a challenge to pack for a vacation when going to a destination with a climate that you are not relatively used to. If you are out for some fun in the sun, here are important items that you shouldn't forget to pack in your suitcase when jet-setting to a tropical paradise.

First and foremost, don't forget to bring the necessary IDs for identification purposes. As you all know, security at airport terminals has been stricter these days as a result from bombings and terrorist attacks. Be sure as well to bring identification for your children who will be accompanying you on your trip.

Bring appropriate clothing. It can be very hot in a tropical country but don't limit your clothes to summer outfits. A storm may often brew in a tropical paradise and having a light jacket with you can keep you warm on some cool nights. Bring along as well a good pair of extra shoes aside from what you will be wearing on the trip and some pants as well apart from the shorts.

It is better to pack light as you'll never know how far you will be walking and carrying your luggage especially if you are destined for a tropical island paradise.

It is important not to forget to bring along your sunscreen. The sun's scorching rays can be harmful for your skin and you need the necessary sun protection factor to avoid damage and possible development of skin cancer. Your sunscreen should have a minimum SPF of 30 otherwise you burn your skin.

Don't forget to bring any prescriptive medication which is very important for you to maintain your health. Bring as well aspirin and other pharmacy items. Bring along the medicine from their original packaging and bring along with you your prescription.

Bringing along a guide book to your vacation destination will not only provide you with a guide on the best attractions that you could visit but it could as well provide information with regards to important phone numbers in emergency cases.

Don't forget to bring your credit cards and traveler's checks. Bring as well some cash in case you will need some. This cash on hand will prove to be useful should tropical storms knock down power and you wouldn't get the chance to withdraw any money or use your credit card.

If you have plans of going snorkeling, you might as well bring you own. While you can rent them there, bringing your own assures you that you are utilizing clean and sterile equipment.

For the golf enthusiast, there are over 200 courses to challenge you and many of the PGA and LPGA tournaments are held in Phoenix. If speed is your thing, Phoenix International Raceway (PIR) hosts Indy Car and NASCAR.

Wine And Dine Napa Valley Style

While the passengers make themselves comfy on the lavish, swivel chairs, wineglasses will be handed to them as they gaze across the hillside that's tinged with tiny traces of mustard.

India's Tourism Set To Rise

Amazingly, these figures are only for the period during the Commonwealth Games period in October. The period leading up to the games is going to have an even bigger impact on the country but over a wider period of time.

Spice Island Of Grenada

For this very reason it is known as the Spice Island of the Caribbean and is known world-wide for its nutmeg, cloves, ginger, cinnamon and allspice. Visitors to the island will no doubt be enticed by the sweet smell of various spices lingering in the air.

Take A Joy Ride On The Napa Valley Wine Train

Keywords: Sacramento Limosines, Napa Valley Limos, Napa Valley Wine Train, Wine Tours, Napa Valley Wine Tour If you see more than 300 people waiting to get aboard one green, gold and burgundy train at 11:30 am or 6:30 pm on any day, do not wonder where they are going.

Touring Napa Valley

Here you can sample some of your favourite wines, while also discovering some new varieties. There are two ways to go about your Napa Valley tour; planned and unplanned.

Wines Of Napa Valley

Chenin Blanc The Chenin Blanc grape is a functional grape. It is used to make many wines like Vouvray, Anjou, Saumur and wines that vary from crisp, fruity, dry to rich, full and smooth.

Travel Destinations -- How You Too Can Get The Most From Your Travel Destination - Part 2

The hotel knew this but my friend and other hotel guests didn't until the accident. 8. Do you know anyone else who has been there and how did they find it?

Yachting World Boost For Menorca 2007 Tourism

Vintage yachts, which were launched before 1949, Claasic Yachts that were built before 1975, and at the organisers' discretion Spirit of Tradition Yachts. The timing of the weekend is good for Menorca.

Travel Destinations -- How You Too Can Get The Most From Your Travel Destination - Part 1 (10)·

You already know how much the weather affects our daily activities. Then you agree that the weather absolutely rules your vacation at your travel destination. Be prepared in terms of clothing but also in terms of the activities you plan and possibly pre-book.

DISCOUNTS FOR TRAVELELRS

2Things To Do In Cape Cod

By making a hotel booking online well in advance, you can ensure that you'll be able to secure rooms for your vacation with ease. Furthermore, many hotels offer discounts for travellers who book their hotel accommodation early and online, meaning that you could save a significant amount on your holiday if you plan ahead carefully.

African Safari Trips - 3 Ways To See Africa On Safari

How do you plan for African safari trips; where do you start; where do you go and what do you see? Beginning to see the picture. This article is not so much about how to prepare but what's available for those seeking to head to one of the world's most visited destinations.

Last Minute Cruise Deal - How To Find Them!

Cruise companies don't like sailing with empty staterooms as it means lost revenue and the off-peak season is a great time to find the best deals. If you are planning a trip to the Caribbean for example, the period from September to the end of the year can present excellent late opportunities.

How To Enjoy Your Italian Cooking School Tour To The Max

Some tour guides and chefs notice who is shy and hanging back in the kitchen and encourage them to "step up to the plate", but others don't. You have to be assertive and volunteer.

The Pacific Islands A South Sea Dream

Weddings can be arranged here in these locations with a little excitement. Things are different in French Polynesia; there marriages can only be performed for those who stay there for at least 30 days.

Majorca To Have Spain's Top Hotel

Menorca has a season that traditionally is at its peak early May to end September, but is now trying to extend that from mid April to mid October. As part of the Balearic Islands, Mallorca has welcomed many visitors back to live full time on the island.

The Hilton Hotel & Beach Club In Dubai

The staff at the beach club were friendly and we liked the fact that they brought food and drinks over to us. The suites were furnished very nicely and had an Arabian feel to them.

How To Realize A Discount Disney Vacation

You may wish to consider a discount Disney vacation package that offers a good deal. Souvenirs that you may be able to find discounted items in your own town so purchase souvenirs ahead of time because souvenirs can be very expensive inside the park.

A Merlot Lover's Wine Tour In Napa Valley

Duckhorn is also the place to be if you want to learn about their portfolio of wines, as you taste their exclusive limited-production wines along with some delectable food compliments.

Planning Walt Disney Vacations The Right Way

Keywords: disney vacation, disney vacations, walt disney vacations, disney world vacations Walt Disney vacations appeal not only to children but adults as well. There is always something for everyone and Disney vacations can become a memorable experience for everyone.

What To Wear To A Hot Spot: Women

What is the one thing I might wear that will keep me from getting into a hot bar or club?

If you were a hot girl, your chances of getting in a hot spot are pretty high as long as you know the right people. If you're a hot girl, that shouldn't be a problem. One of the things that would keep you out of a club is if maybe you were wearing something completely super baggy that makes you look a lot bigger than you normally would be. Generally, hot women do not have problems.

Is it better to overdress or underdress when going to a hot spot?

If you are a girl, I don't think there is such thing as overdressing. The great thing is you can put on jeans and a pair of heels and you are fine. You can wear a beautiful dress. Beautiful women can wear whatever they want. They'll look great in it.

Will dressing slutty get me into a hot night club?

Slutty could get you in a club. You might not get all the respect in the world, but if that is what you want, then go with it.

What kinds of clothes will help me fit in at a hot spot?

You can't go wrong with jeans. Any wealth that are designer jeans can compliment pretty much anybodys shape. So you really can't go wrong with jeans in heals if you're a girl, and a cute top. Also, there are a lot of flattering A-line dresses that you can get anywhere on Melrose, or any boutique store, or any mall that pretty much fits any body type extremely well. So that would be a great bet for a girl. And generally in New York, I would suggest dressing up more, just because New York is more formal and people tend to dress up more. Which is nice. And in Vegas, since people are just there to just have an amazing time, I would suggest dressing, I guess more fun. And I guess where you want to end up that night.

What kinds of clothes will make me look like a tourist at a hot spot?

Basically, you can tell a tourist from a mile away if they are wearing just completely dated clothes, like a florescent green t-shirt that says "I love L.A." with their fanny pack and their tube socks. They just stand out a mile away. Even in Europe you can tell who the Americans are because they are wearing the shorts, and the tube socks, and the hat, and the t-shirt. I can spot them in an instant. Also, a tip for women is if you've never been out in a big city before, don't come in your prom dress. You might see stars in the fashion magazines with their beautiful designer gowns, but that's because they are going to the Oscars or a big special event. If you are just going out on the town to a normal club or restaurant, yes you can dress up, but not like you're going to the Oscars or with pantyhose.

Should I wear a dress or pants to a hot spot?

You could wear a dress or a pants to a hot spot, depending on weather. Usually it's nice, sometimes it is windy at night, so you might want to wear pants. It just depends on your mood.

Is it OK to wear shorts to a hot spot?

Generally if you are a girl, yes, shorts are a very good, hip trend right now. The short shorts make your legs look long, especially with the right heels. Girls can pull that off.

What kind of shoes should I wear to a hot spot?

Generally, heels make any legs look very good. There's a reason why people wear heels on the catwalk and at special events all the time. Its because it makes your legs look longer and leaner, and just better all around. So you can't go wrong with heels.

What kind of bag should I bring to a hot spot?

It depends on the outfit you are wearing. Designer bags are usually good. If you are going to be dancing and moving around a lot, maybe a smaller purse is better, for instance one of those big, huge hall-ball bags.

Should I wear a coat to a hot spot?

Yeah, you can wear a coat to a hot spot if you have a great outfit underneath. You can definitely coat check. LA generally does not have coat checks, so you might want to leave the coat in the car.

Do I have to wear all black to fit in at a hot spot?

Well black is a very slimming color so if you are worried about your weight or how you are going to look in a certain outfit black is always a very safe choice to go because it just makes everyone look slimmer especially if you're on TV. I mean you can wear whatever color you like to as long as you look good in it. Especially summer dresses come in pretty much any hue. If you don't wear black you will not stick out like a tourist, you can basically wear what ever color of your choice, of your mood, whatever matches your eyes.

Have good hygiene. Take care of yourself by showering daily. If you are very active and sweat a lot you should consider showering twice a day. Brush and floss your teeth after every meal for a beautiful smile. Remember to use lotion for soft, smooth skin! Wash your clothes every weekend or whenever you have time, and wear a clean outfit daily. Comb your hair, spray on a good perfume, and blow your nose. Consider shaving. Shaving yourself these days is sometimes considered hygienic, but did you know that it helps you get rid off unwanted odors? It is important to shave your legs,bikini line, and armpit hair. Armpit hair holds odor longer than skin, and you don't want to smell bad. If shaving is too annoying you could try hair removal cream, but it can irritate the skin. Also, before going to the beach, make sure you have a good bikini line.

Take care of your hair. Wash your hair about 3-6 times a week - it varies how much you should wash your hair depending on your hair type. Wash it with shampoo that is appropriate for your hair.

Rinse the shampoo out with lukewarm water, or, if you are tough enough, you can rinse it with cold water (the cold water will give your hair an extra shine). After you wash your hair, you should condition it, but maybe not every time if your hair gets oily easily. Be sure to use a good shampoo and conditioner made for your hair type or use a different kind that makes your hair shine bright and smell good.

- Make sure to get a hair cut about every two months/3 months to avoid split ends. If you have frizzy hair, find a good anti-frizz spray at a local store.
- If you want, you can try extensions. Since going to a salon can burn a hole in your wallet, and damage your hair, why don't you try a clip on piece?

Get in shape. Exercise, and tone up your body. Find an exercise that works for you. You don't have to look anorexic to be in shape. Looking fit is more attractive than being too skinny. Remember, the people in magazines are not the real image of beauty. Do little things like integrate more fruits and vegetables into your diet. Eat all of the required amounts of fruit and/or vegetables for your age, and make sure to make an effort to work out at least a little bit. It gets old, but drink at least 8 glasses of water per day.

1. Take care of your face and skin. Taking care of your skin and face can be hard because everyone's skin is different. You can have oily skin, dry skin, sensitive skin, or acne. Which is why it is important to experiment with different face care products, or little things to do by yourself and find one that fits you.

For people with dry skin: if your skin is so dry to the point that its flaking off; in the shower, or with warm water in the sink, take a washcloth and rub the extremely dry areas on you face with a little soap on the washcloth. Dry, and then apply toner and lotion after-wards, to your whole face. If your skin isn't as dry, then just apply the toner, and a good moisturizing lotion. Sun lotions (for after tanning) are the most hydrating.

11

BUBBLES OF FASHION SAIL OVER PARIS

Paris and French fashion are world famous. French fashion is setting the trend with icon brands such as Chanel, Dior, Hermes, Jean-Paul Gaultier, Louis Vuitton and Yves Saint Laurent.Many lesser known French fashion designers turn Paris into the fashion city of the world. Look at our selection of French fashion brands. All of these fashion brands have stores in Paris. While in Paris, discover the best French fashion. French fashion is a tricky business. As in any country, the styles you see on the streets of Paris are not the same kinds you'd see in a student-friendly town like Montpellier, a small fishing town in Brittany, or in a cultural melting pot like Marseilles.

Paris, the city of light, has many of the world's most visited attractions,. Among them, the Eiffel tower, the Louvre palace, the Notre-Dame cathedral and the near-by Versailles palace are truly unique. The business district of La Défense with the Grande Arche from Danish architect Otto von Spreckelsen testifies to the economic and artistic vitality of Paris.

Can't decide how to spend your time in Paris City? Start with this list of Paris City's most popular attractions to get started planning your trip to France.

Most French fashion top brands have their main store on Avenue Montaigne or Rue du Faubourg Saint-Honore, both near Champs-Elysees avenue.

The Saint-Germain des Pres district on the left bank has many French fashion clothing stores. Look for them in streets around rue de Sevres with flagship Le Bon Marche luxury department store.

More recently, the rue des Rosiers in Le Marais emerged as one of Paris foremost fashion streets.

To match a dress, look for jewels on high-end rue de la Paix near Paris Garnier Opera House.

The French and world greatest jewellers are all there in a splendid 17th century setting.

Many French fashion brands have a corner at the Boulevard Haussman department stores.

Locate all these venues on Paris shopping map

The big shopping centers in and around Paris have many French fashion shops with affordable prices.

Going there, you will have the opportunity to meet French people doing their weekly shopping. A good way to discover the contemporary Paris way of life.

Paris fashion shows are restricted to professionals. You can see their schedule and some pictures. The Arts Decoratifs museum near Louvre museum regularly stages first class fashion exhibitions.

That being said, I believe I can help you look your best while traveling throughout France this summer. I'll give some general tips, and then break it down for you by category.

French Fashion Fact: There Is No Singular "French Look"

Sit outdoors at a café on any given day, and you'll see a veritable parade of styles walk by. But still, you can see a difference. What is it that makes the French seem just a cut above us mere mortals when it comes to fashion? Here are some hints.

Please note that this is not the final word; like snowflakes on a winter's day, everyone has their own unique style. You'll see exceptions to these hints at every turn. But after living in France for six years, I've seen a thing or two.

" First of all, they live there; you're not going to see French locals carting around backpacks and large bottles of water. That's a big difference that maybe can't be helped, but there it is.

" Their clothes fit them correctly. Pants are hemmed to the correct length. Shirts match the person's silhouette; no one is swimming in a baggy shirt.

" They have great haircuts.

" Their look matches. Sneakers are worn with workout gear, shoes with all other clothes. They have different jackets for all occasions, from wintertime to rainy days to a chilly summer night.

" Both men and women accessorize well - sunglasses, watches, purses in general are the best they can find (even if they bought it at a discount).

" They put their look together and then forget about it. They don't fuss and fidget with their clothing while out and about. It's simply a part of them.

Well. Now that the mystery's solved - ha! - let's get down to business: What do you pack for a trip to France this summer?

Here are some general tips for blending in during your next trip to France:

" Unsure what to wear to a restaurant? Try to walk past it during lunch or even dinner the night before, and see what others are wearing.

" No fanny packs. Seriously, you guys. There are a million ways to carry your stuff that look better than a fanny pack.

" Find a decent, attractive bag to carry your big hulking D-SLR camera in. That goes for you too, men. If not for fashion, then to avoid being mugged.

" Take the time and spend the money to find a comfortable pair of shoes that look nice. Leave the white sneakers at home. Please.

" Find a comfortable, nice outfit for traveling. Watching you guys come off a plane or train is like witnessing a 4AM fire drill at a college dorm.

" Shoulders and legs should ALWAYS be covered whenever visiting ANY house of worship in France for ANY reason. Do whatever it takes to respect this unspoken rule, no matter how hot it is.

>>Wondering what to do in France in the summer? Check out my France in July and my France in August posts.

Your Biggest Fashion Question Answered: Can I Wear Flip-Flops In France In The Summer?

The short answer? Yes. The French do. But here are some really, really important things to note before you throw those raggedy, cheap plastic atrocities into your suitcase.

" The flip-flops that French people wear, by and large, are not your standard-issue disposable Old Navy kind. They're very nice. Follow their lead, and you can wear them day and night.

" Women, opt for some bling, a heel, or more complicated straps for your flip-flops or sandals.

" Men, invest in a really nice pair of simple, brown or black leather flip-flops. I once saw a Frenchmen wearing these with linen pants and a crisp white t-shirt at a brasserie in Paris in 1997. That's how much of an impression he made on me.

" Get a pedicure. That goes for men, too, so no eye-rolling. And carry some tissues or wipes with you throughout the day to clean up your feet before heading in to eat somewhere.

Fashion Tips For Young Women Visiting France In The Summer

Here are some tips I've compiled from a list of fashion don'ts I've seen recently:

" You know that cute sundress you want to wear to dinner? Don't wear it with your cheapo flip-flops. Get a decent sandal or adorable flats.

" If you're going to pack those sexy heels, own them. Confidence is 90% of what make French women so fabulous.

" American girls have this habit of wearing a really beautiful/sexy/expensive top with some jeans they pulled out of the bottom of a backpack. Either wear pants or a skirt, or bring fitted jeans and wear them with heels. See my "everything matches" hint above.

" Heading to the beach? Cover up on your way there unless your hotel is across the street from the shoreline.

" Make your ponytail look nice, like you meant to wear your hair that way, not like you've just finished doing laundry.

" When in doubt, find a long, light cotton scarf and wear it all the time. French girls do this with practically any outfit, no matter how warm it is, and it just pulls the whole look together.

Fashion Tips For Older Women Visiting France In The Summer

" Older French women do not hide their attractiveness. They are the Helen Mirren to your Joy Behar.

" Less equals more. Don't wear every piece of jewelry you own in an attempt to dress up an outfit. French women do not over-accessorize with jewelry.

" The shoes thing goes double for you - invest in the most comfortable, most attractive shoes you can find. Nothing ruins your outfit more than your go-to sneakers.

" Go with light, natural fabrics - first of all, synthetics will overheat you in four seconds flat. Secondly, older French women tend to be of a generation that bought nice things and tended to them well. They have not bought into the disposable clothing trend of Americans.

" Otherwise, y'all look fine - have fun!

Fashion Tips For Young Men Visiting France In The Summer

Guys, you've got it rough. The differences are so great between you and your French counterparts, I don't even know where to begin. And, chances are you could give a rat's ass. But French girls will be watching you, so listen up if you want to make an impression.

" You know what I said above about looking like a 4AM college dorm fire drill? That's all you, hon. Leave the beer promotion t-shirts, frat wear and wrinkled cargo shorts at home.

" All your clothes are freaking enormous. Bring stuff that fits you correctly. You're competing with French boys in stovepipe jeans and skin-tight tees.

" Suck it up and bring a decent pair of shoes. Unless you plan on eating at McDonald's every day, those flip-flops aren't going to do you any favors at dinnertime.

" Flip-flops and sandals - guys, I feel you on this one. Your choices seem to be either Hippie Jesus sandals, reverse-engineered hybrid jobs or shower shoes. Please, take some time to find a decent summer shoe.

" When in doubt, go preppy. Well-fitting Bermuda shorts from the L.L. Bean catalog never killed anyone.

" No baseball cap. Bring a comb instead.

Fashion Tips For Older Men Visiting France In The Summer

Like your female companions, you're almost there. Here are a few hints to help you look suave during your stay.

" No white sneakers, Pops! You've got it easiest when it comes to footwear,.so take advantage of it. Find a comfortable pair of neutral-colored shoes that go with anything. Boom, you're done.

" Unless you're willing to get a pedicure, leave the open-toes sandals for going directly from your hotel room to the beach.

" I know you think those loud print shirts are your vacation fashion statement, but listen to your wife and leave them at home.

" I know you're a huge fan of your local sports team; again, leave the jerseys and paraphernalia at home.

" The safari hat is a good look - while on safari. Wear sunglasses instead.

" Purchase several pairs of ankle-length athletic socks for your shoes, if you're a sock wearer. Wear dress socks only when dressing in full-length pants for dinner.

" If you've got a neutral-color linen jacket, bring it and wear the hell out of it. You'll look like a million bucks.

What Kids Should Wear When Visiting France In The Summer

Mom and Dad, you do a pretty excellent job of making your tykes look adorable on vacation. Pretty much anything goes for the little ones; but there are some pretty bad-ass French toddlers around, so if you wanted an excuse for your tot to wear that baby-sized Ramones t-shirt, then go for it.

A fashion week is a fashion industry event, lasting approximately one week, which allows fashion designers, brands or "houses" to display their latest collections in runway shows and buyers to take a look at the latest trends. Most importantly, it lets the industry know what's "in" and what's "out" for the season. The most prominent fashion weeks are held in the four fashion capitals of the world - New York City, London, Milan and Paris.

In the major fashion capitals, fashion weeks are semiannual events. January through April designers showcase their autumn and winter collections and September through November the spring/summer collections are shown. Fashion weeks must be held several months in advance of the season to allow the press and buyers a chance to preview fashion designs for the following season. This is also to allow time for retailers to arrange to purchase or incorporate the designers into their retail marketing.

Fashion Week

New York, London, Milan and Paris each host a fashion week twice a year with New York kicking off each season and the other cities following in the aforementioned order.

There are two major seasons per year - Autumn/ Winter and Spring/Summer. For Womenswear, the Autumn/Winter shows always start in New York in February. Spring/Summer shows start in September in New York. Menswear Autumn/Winter shows start in January in Milan for typically less than a week followed by another short week in Paris. Menswear Spring/ Summer shows are done in June. Womenswear Haute Couture shows typically happen in Paris a week after the Menswear Paris shows.

Over the past few years, more and more designers have shown inter-seasonal collections between the traditional Autumn/Winter and Spring/Summer seasons. These collections are usually more commercial than the main season collections and help shorten the customer's wait for new season clothes. The inter-seasonal collections are Resort/Cruise (before Spring/Summer) and Pre-Fall (before Autumn/Winter). There is no fixed schedule for these shows in any of the major fashion capitals but they typically happen three months after the main season shows. Some designers show their inter-seasonal collections outside their home city. For example, Karl Lagerfeld has shown his Resort and Pre-Fall collections for Chanel in cities such as Moscow, Los Angeles and Monte Carlo instead of Paris. Many designers also put on presentations as opposed to traditional shows during Resort and Pre-Fall either to cut down costs or because they feel the clothes can be better understood in this medium.

Some fashion weeks can be genre-specific, such as a Miami Fashion Week (swimwear), Rio Summer (swimwear), Prêt-a-Porter (ready-to-wear) Fashion Week, Couture (one-of-a-kind designer original) Fashion Week and Bridal Fashion Week, while Portland (Oregon, USA) Fashion Week shows some eco-friendly designers.

In 1943, the first New York Fashion Week was held, with one main purpose: to distract attention from French fashion during WWII, when workers in the fashion industry were unable to travel to Paris. This was an opportune moment - as for centuries designers in America were thought to be reliant on the French for inspiration. The fashion publicist Eleanor Lambert organized an event she called 'Press Week' to showcase American designers for fashion journalists, who had previously ignored their works. The Press Week was a success, and, as a result, magazines like Vogue (which were normally filled with French designs) began to feature more and more American innovations.

Until 1994, shows were held in different locations, such as hotels, or lofts. Eventually, after a structural accident at a Michael Kors show, the event moved to Bryant Park, behind the New York Public Library, where it still is today, held inside a number of large white tents.

However, long before Lambert, there were fashion shows throughout America. In 1903, an NYC shop, called Ehrich Brothers, put on what is thought to have been the country's first fashion show, to lure middle-class females into the store. By 1910, many big department stores were holding shows of their own. It is likely that American retailers saw that they were called 'fashion parades' in Paris couture salons and decided to use the idea. These parades were an effective way to promote stores, and improved their status. By the 1920s, the fashion show had been used by retailers up and down the country. They were staged, and often held in the shop's restaurant during lunch or teatime. These shows were usually more theatrical than those of today, heavily based upon a single theme, and accompanied with a narrative commentary. The shows were hugely popular, enticing crowds in their thousands - crowds so large, that stores in New York in the fifties had to obtain a license to have live models. Nowadays, access to NYFW (New York Fashion Week) is by invitation only, and only fashion magazine editors, fashion magazine journalists, models (and ex-models) and celebrities are invited. Other buyers are restricted to the showrooms/stores and the articles in the magazines.

Controversy

The dominance of the big four benefits industry participants. For example, buyers, journalists, models and celebrities can limit their travel and simply move from one to the other over the four week period. However the arrangement is criticized for stifling manufacturing employment in the UK and design talent in emerging fashion hubs such as Los Angeles.

Where to go to take back home a little je ne sais quoi

For reasons that elude most of us, Parisians seem to make impeccable fashion sense look like a walk in the park. It's no surprise, then, that Paris remains the reigning center of all things haute couture. After museums and monuments, shopping is one of the main reasons Paris draws millions of visitors each year.

While the city is studded with great places to shop, these top Paris shopping districts are guaranteed to satiate discount-hunters, designer divas, window shoppers, and fashion victims alike.

1. Louvre-Tuileries and Faubourg Saint-Honoré

Best for: Crème de la crème designer fashion, chic home furnishings, and quality cosmetics

Getting there: Metro Concorde, Tuileries (Line 1), Pyramides (Line 7, 14)

Main streets: Rue du Faubourg Saint-Honoré, Rue Saint-Honoré, Rue de la Paix, Place Vendome.

The Faubourg Saint-Honoré district is the pulse of Paris design and fashion. Part of the Louvre-Tuileries neighborhood and just a few blocks from the Opera Garnier and the Paris department stores block on Boulevard Haussmann, the Saint-Honoré fashion district is occupied by classic designers like Versace, Hermes, and Yves Saint Laurent, but also houses resolutely trendy concept shops such as Colette.

" For after-shopping unwinding: Hotel Costes Bar and Lounge

" Paris Department Stores District - Boulevard Haussmann

" Best for: Getting lost in Paris' prestigious-- and dizzying-- department stores (grands magasins)

Getting there: Metro Havre-Caumartin, Opera, RER Auber.

Main streets: Boulevard Haussmann

" Paris department stores are famous for being worlds unto themselves. Galeries Lafayette and Printemps department stores dominate Boulevard Haussmann with real Belle Epoque grandeur, concentrating top designer collections for men and women, gourmet food shopping, home design, jewelry, and even hardware into a labyrinth of consumer delights.

The Marais

Best for: Eclectic fashion, unique jewelry, antiques and fine art.

Getting there: Metro Saint-Paul or Hotel de Ville.

Main streets: Rue des Francs-Bourgeois, Place des Vosges, Rue de Turenne, Rue des Rosiers

The historic Marais quarter is prime stomping ground for shoppers with an eye for the unique and finely-crafted, not to mention antique and art lovers. Try antiques or fine-arts shopping on the Place des Vosges, jewelry shopping at boutiques like Satellite on Rue des Francs-Bourgeois, or explore boutiques featuring up-and-coming designers on Rue des Rosiers.

Avenue Montaigne and Avenue des Champs-Elysées

Best for: Designer shopping, trendy chain stores, Sunday shopping

Getting there: Metro Alma Marceau (Line 9), Franklin D. Roosevelt (Lines 1 and 9), George V (Line 1), RER A (Charles de Gaulle-Etoile)

Avenue Montaigne and Avenue des Champs-Elysées form one of the city's hottest fashion junctures. Ave.

Montaigne is fast outstripping Saint Honoré in notoriety, with legendary designers like Chanel and Dior lining the street. The Champs-Elysées features luxury names (Louis Vuitton) while also being a major spot for shopping in trendy global chains like Zara.

Sweet tooth? Try a legendary macaroon at Laduree.

Saint-Ouen Flea Market

Best for: Antiques and oddball items, discounted and vintage clothes and shoes

Getting there: Metro Porte de Clingancourt or Garibaldi .

The Saint-Ouen flea market (or "puces"-- literally, "fleas") is the city's largest, and dates to the 19th century. Located at the very northern tip of Paris, les puces are an essential shopping stop. Come here for a few hours to browse the antique furniture, odd objects, or vintage clothes. You may not come away with a masterpiece painting (as once was the case), but a find you are likely to make. Weekdays are preferable to avoid the inevitable crowds, though.

Saint-Germain-des-Prés

Best for: Chic classic design, books, home furnishings

Getting there: Metro Saint-Germain-des-Prés, Sèvres-Babylone .

Main streets: Blvd. St.-Germain, Rue St. André-des-Arts, Rue de Sèvres

Once synonymous with the famous intellectuals who haunted local cafés, St.-Germain-des-Prés has acquired several shades of chic and is now a preferred spot of BCBG's (yuppies). Sonia Rykiel and Paco Rabanne have boutiques here, and the famous department store Le Bon Marché includes a gourmet market that all foodies should pay a visit to.

Try Rue Saint-Andre des Arts for rare books and vintage threads.

Les Halles and Rue de Rivoli

Best for: Major chains and trendy boutiques

Getting there: Metro Chatelet-Les Halles (Line 4, RER A,B)

Main streets: Rue de Rivoli, Rue Pierre-Lescot, Rue Etienne Marcel, Rue de Turbigo

Once the locus of "the guts of Paris"-- an enormous outdoor food market, the area around Châtelet-les Halles was transformed into a major shopping area in the 20th century. At metro Les Halles is a monstrous underground mall, where global chain stores reign. Rue de Rivoli is much the same. In the Rue Montorgueil area, quirky contemporary boutiques abound, including Barbara Bui and young cutting-edge designers.

BIBLIOGRAPHY

- Fashion Tourism by A Kumar, Publishers: Sonali Publications, English (Hardbound), Published in 2010, ISBN 9788184112665

- The Art of Fashion Draping, 3rd Edition by Connie Amaden - Crawford, Publisher: Fairchild Books, List Price: $101.50, ©2005, 464 pp., illustrated, softcover, 9 x 11.875 (1-56367-277-4)

- Timothy Brook: "The Confusions of Pleasure: Commerce and Culture in Ming China" (University of California Press 1999); this has a whole section on fashion.

- al-Hassani, Woodcok and Saoud (2004), 'Muslim Heritage in Our World', FSTC publisinhg, pp. 38-9

- Terrasse, H. (1958) 'Islam d'Espagne' une rencontre de l'Orient et de l'Occident", Librairie Plon, Paris, pp.52-53.

- Josef W. Meri & Jere L. Bacharach (2006). "Medieval Islamic Civilization: A-K". Taylor & Francis. p. 162.

- Alter, Stephen. Fantasies of a Bollywood Love-Thief: Inside the World of Indian Moviemaking. (ISBN 0-15-603084-5)

- Begum-Hossain, Momtaz. Bollywood Crafts: 20 Projects Inspired by Popular Indian Cinema, 2006. The Guild of Mastercraftsman Publications. (ISBN 1-86108-418-8)

- Bose, Mihir, Bollywood. A History, New Delhi, Roli Books, 2008. (ISBN 978-81-7436-653-5)

- Ganti, Tejaswini. Bollywood, Routledge, New York and London, 2004.
- Bernard 'Bollywood' Gibson. Passing the Envelope, 1994.
- Jones, Colin (2005) Paris: The Biography of a City (New York, NY: Penguin Viking), p. 334.
- Jones, Colin (2005) Paris: The Biography of a City (New York, NY: Penguin Viking), pp. 388-391
- Humphrys, Julian (June 2010). BBC History magazine. Bristol Magazines Ltd.
- Overy, Richard (2006). Why the Allies Won. Pimlico. pp. 215-216. ISBN 1845950658.
- Bell, Kelly. "Dietrich von Choltitz: Saved of Paris From Destruction During World War II". www. TheHistory Net.com. http://www.historynet.com/magazines/world_war_2/3031316.html.
- (French) Émilie Willaert, professor of History and Geography. "La région parisienne en chantier". http://www.cndp.fr/revueTDC/913-81441.htm.
- (French) Jérome Toulza, Université de Marne-la-Vallée. "La conception du RER" (PDF). http://www.univ-mlv.fr/mastergu/Docs_IMO/Memimo_0304/Toulza.PDF.
- (French) Thomas Sauvadet. "Les jeunes de la cité - Processus de ghettoïsation et mode de socialisation" (PDF). Université Paris 8. http://www.univ-paris8.fr/sociologie/fichiers/sauvadet-journalparis8.pdf.
- (French) Hervé Vieillard-Baron, professor at the Université Paris 8. "Les quartiers sensibles, entre disqualification visible et réseaux invisibles". http://fig-st-die.education.fr/actes/actes_2005/viellard-baron/article.htm.
- (French) "Roland de Laage (Devoteam) : "L'Ouest

parisien, ce sont des départements technologiques à haute valeur ajoutée"". Journal du net. 16 January 2006. http://www.journaldunet.com/solutions/0601/060116_prestas-hauts-de-seine-delaage.shtml.

- (French) Pierre Beckouche. "Une région parisienne à deux vitesses - L'accroissement des disparités spatiales dans l'Île-de-France des années 1980". Strates - Matériaux pour la recherche en sciences sociales. http://strates.revues.org/document1155.html.

- "Special Report: Riots in France". BBC News. 2005-11-09. http://news.bbc.co.uk/1/hi/in_depth/4417096.stm.

- The City of Antiquity, official history of Paris by The Paris Convention and Visitors Bureau

- Mitchell, Jonathan (2009) Value chain analysis and poverty reduction at scale London: Overseas Development Institute

- Wurzburger, Rebecca; et al (2009). Creative Tourism: A Global Conversation: How to Provide Unique Creative Experiences for Travelers Worldwide: As Presented at the 2008 Santa Fe & UNESCO International Conference on Creative Tourism in Santa Fe, New Mexico, USA. Santa Fe: Sunstone Press. ISBN 9780865347243. OCLC 370387178.

- Quinion, Michael (26 November 2005). "Dark Tourism". World Wide Words. http://www.worldwidewords.org/turnsofphrase/tp-dar2.htm. Retrieved 9 April 2010.

- Lennon, J. John; Foley, Malcolm (2000). Dark Tourism. London: Continuum. ISBN 0826450636. OCLC 44603703.

- Cooper, Chris; et al (2005). Tourism: Principles and Practice (3rd ed.). Harlow: Pearson Education. ISBN

027368406X. OCLC 466952897.

• "Long-term Prospects: Tourism 2020 Vision". World Tourism. 2004. http://www.world-tourism.org/market_research/facts/market_trends.htm.

• "airports & tourists". Global Culture. 2007. http://global-culture.org/blog/2007/01/27/airports-tourists/.

• World Tourism Organization (October 2008). "UNWTO World Tourism Barometer October 2008" (PDF). UNWTO. http://unwto.org/facts/eng/pdf/barometer/UNWTO_Barom08_3_en_Excerpt.pdf. Retrieved 2008-11-17. Volume 6, Issue 3

• Pancevski, Bojan (18 April 2010). "Get packing: Brussels decrees holidays are a human right". The Sunday Times. http://www.timesonline.co.uk/tol/news/world/europe/article7100943.ece.

• Laidlaw, Katherine (19 April 2010). "Vacationing a human right, EU chief says". National Post. http://www.nationalpost.com/news/story.html?id=2923469.

• "UK-born euromyths echoed by Wikipedia". EurActiv. 18 May 2010. http://www.euractiv.com/en/infosociety/uk-born-euromyths-echoed-wikipedia-news-494082. Retrieved 30 June 2010.

• Holder IV, Floyd William (2009). An Empirical Analysis of the State's Monopolization of the Legitimate Means of Movement: Evaluating the Effects of Required Passport use on International Travel. (M.P.A. thesis). Texas State University-San Marcos. OCLC 564144593. Docket Applied Research Projects. Paper 308.

• Wilkerson, Chad (2003). "Travel and Tourism: An Overlooked Industry in the U.S. and Tenth District". Economic Review 88 (Third Quarter): 45-72. ISSN 0161-2387. OCLC 295437935. http://www.kc.frb.org/publicat/econrev/Pdf/3q03wilk.pdf.

- Jolly, Gurbir, Zenia Wadhwani, and Deborah Barretto, eds. Once Upon a Time in Bollywood: The Global Swing in Hindi Cinema, TSAR Publications. 2007. (ISBN 978-1-894770-40-8)
- Joshi, Lalit Mohan. Bollywood: Popular Indian Cinema. (ISBN 0-9537032-2-3)
- Kabir, Nasreen Munni. Bollywood, Channel 4 Books, 2001.
- Mehta, Suketu. Maximum City, Knopf, 2004.
- Mishra, Vijay. Bollywood Cinema: Temples of Desire. (ISBN 0-415-93015-4)
- Pendakur, Manjunath. Indian Popular Cinema: Industry, Ideology, and Consciousness. (ISBN 1-57273-500-5)
- Prasad, Madhava. Ideology of the Hindi Film: A Historical Construction, Oxford University Press, 2000. (ISBN 0-19-565295-9)
- Raheja, Dinesh and Kothari, Jitendra. Indian Cinema: The Bollywood Saga. (ISBN 81-7436-285-1)
- Raj, Aditya (2007) "Bollywood Cinema and Indian Diaspora" in Media Literacy: A Reader edited by Donaldo Macedo and Shirley Steinberg New York: Peter Lang
- Rajadhyaksa, Ashish (1996), "India: Filming the Nation", The Oxford History of World Cinema, Oxford University Press, ISBN 0-19-811257-2.
- Rajadhyaksha, Ashish and Willemen, Paul. Encyclopedia of Indian Cinema, Oxford University Press, revised and expanded, 1999.
- Laver, James: The Concise History of Costume and Fashion, Abrams, 1979, p. 62

INDEX